Festschrift in Honor of
V. Rev. Dr. Paul Nadim Tarazi

Festschrift in Honor of V. Rev. Dr. Paul Nadim Tarazi

Edited by

Andrea Bakas

OCABS PRESS
ST PAUL, MINNESOTA 55124
2020

FESTSCHRIFT IN HONOR OF
V. REV. DR. PAUL NADIM TARAZI

Copyright © 2020 by
OCABS Press

ISBN 1-60191-050-9

All rights reserved.

PRINTED IN THE UNITED STATES OF AMERICA

Festschrift in Honor of V. Rev. Dr. Paul Nadim Tarazi

Copyright © 2020 by OCABS Press
All rights reserved.

ISBN 1-60191-050-9

Published by OCABS Press, St. Paul, Minnesota.
Printed in the United States of America.

Books are available through OCABS Press at special discounts for bulk purchases in the United States by academic institutions, churches, and other organizations. For more information please email OCABS Press at press@ocabs.org.

Contents

Foreword	11
Biography	13
Bibliography	15
The Man of Fortunate Steps *Rev. Dr. Herman R. Acker*	17
There are No Curse Words in Church Slavonic: Musings about Missionary Morphology *Rev. Fr. Michael Arbanas*	29
Nomads of the Word: Reading the Book of Acts from a Semitic Perspective *Dr. Daniel Ayuch*	37
Acts 18:3 – "Tentmakers": A Discussion *Andrea Bakas*	55
Hebrew as Literary Language *Dr. Richard Benton*	63
Jonah: Do What He Says, Not What He Does *V. Rev. Fr. Marc Boulos*	81
Hard, Fat and Dull Hearts: The Function of Divinely Induced Obduracy in Exodus 4-14, Isaiah 6 and Matthew 13 *V. Rev. Dr. J. Sergius Halvorsen*	91
Stones Rolled and Rolled Away: Kerygmatic Structures in Mark 15:40-16:8 *Rev. Fr. Duane M. Johnson*	107

The Last Discourse – John 13-17   129
    V. Rev. Fr. Timothy Lowe

Becoming Enlightened: The Healing of the Blind Man at Bethsaida   145
    Rev. Fr. Dustin M. Lyon

Biblical Interpretation In Between Science and Worship 161
    Dr. Merja Merras

The Desert as Image of God   177
    Dr. Robert D. Miller II, OFS

The Parable of the Wicked Servant (Matthew 18:21:-35) and its Implications for the Understanding of Salvation   197
    Rev. Fr. Ron Poworoznik

The Seleucid Period in Light of *The Rise of Scripture*   205
    Dr. Nicolae Roddy

The Bible in Miniature: The Blasphemer and the Law in Leviticus 24:10–23   219
    Harrison Russin

The Mary and Martha Paradigm (Luke 10:38-42): A Call to Training for Mission and Contemplation of the Word of God. A Roumanian Orthodox Point of View   227
    Rev. Fr. Cătălin Varga

Introduction to Philippians: *A Commentary*   251
    V. Rev. Dr. Paul Nadim Tarazi

Foreword

We live in a time when professional titles are dismissed in favor of egalitarianism, even as egalitarians clamor for professional acknowledgment. No one wants to say Mr., Ms. or Dr. when addressing a teacher, and parishioners delight in pastors who go by their first name. Equally offensive are those who benefit from their title for self-serving reasons, without shouldering the burden of their station for the sake of the common good. The problem with all these attitudes is that each are based on a false reference: the individual.

Titles do not matter for their own sake and certainly not for the building up of those who bear them. Likewise, the dismissal of titles for the sake of informality is at best morally neutral and more often harmful to those who champion informality. Knowledge and its acquisition are exceedingly formal, and knowledge held is objective and quantifiable. You either have knowledge or you do not. In this regard, we are not all equal, let alone students and teachers. The value of each person pertains to their knowledge in a specific field. It is knowledge that is the measure of one's title and objective knowledge that entitles the untitled to speak with authority. What matters, Fr. Paul has taught us, is not our title, but the body of knowledge we serve and our duty to share it with anyone who is willing to learn. This is what it means to be a Biblical scholar.

You do not need a university to study Hebrew, but you do need knowledge of Hebrew to study Scripture. It is a fact that most clergy today do not study Hebrew. It is also true that an individual who is not a Ph.D. can acquire the same knowledge as any scholar through faithful study. In the end, the purpose of both roles—priest and scholar—is to bring the light of Scriptural knowledge to the faithful. It is *access* to this knowledge that must be egalitarian, whether the parishioner has been to college or not, let alone completed a Ph.D. This is the high calling of the priesthood and the grave duty of the laity. It is also the mission of the Orthodox Center for the Advancement of Biblical Studies: to make the scholarly study of the Bible accessible to everyone.

Nowhere is this mission more beautifully and fully expressed than in the variety of students—people from all walks of life and professions—whom Fr. Paul has inspired to study Scripture with the same discipline and zeal as those who do it professionally. This Festschrift in his honor bears papers written by laity with no title, scholars eminent in their field, and clergy. This is the true Eucharistic fellowship in which all of us share, as we gather in thanksgiving at the Lord's table, where only his Biblical scroll is elevated to the seat of honor. The rest of us, no matter our station, are but little children, eagerly seeking a word—a scrap of bread—from our heavenly Father's table. To him alone be the glory.

Fr. Marc Boulos

V. Rev. Dr. Paul Nadim Tarazi Biography

The V. Rev. Dr. Paul Nadim Tarazi has been teaching Scripture for fifty years. His teaching ministry has included a full-time professorship at St Vladimir's Orthodox Theological Seminary in Crestwood, New York, as well as adjunct positions at Holy Cross Greek Orthodox School of Theology in Brookline, Massachusetts, and the St. John of Damascus Institute of Theology in Balamand, Lebanon. His work covers the full range of scriptural studies in Old and New Testaments, Biblical Hebrew and Greek, Academic Arabic, and Homiletics. He has been a guest lecturer at numerous universities and institutions in the United States and Canada, as well as Australia, Chile, Estonia, Finland, Greece, Israel, Jordan, Palestine, Romania, Serbia, and Syria, and has represented the Antiochian Orthodox Church at various ecumenical gatherings.

Fr. Paul is the author of a three volume Introduction to the Old Testament, a four volume Introduction to the New Testament, Galatians: A Commentary, I Thessalonians: A Commentary, and Land and Covenant. His work in the Chrysostom Bible series includes Genesis: A Commentary, Philippians: A Commentary, Romans: A Commentary, Colossians & Philemon: A Commentary, 1 Corinthians: A Commentary, 2 Corinthians: A Commentary, Ezekiel: A Commentary, Joshua: A Commentary, Isaiah: A Commentary, Jeremiah: A Commentary, Hebrews: A Commentary, The Pastorals: A Commentary, Ephesians & 2 Thessalonians: A Commentary, and The Rise of Scripture. His Audio Bible Commentaries on the books of the Old and New Testament are available online through the Orthodox Center for the Advancement of Biblical Studies (OCABS).

Fr. Paul was born in Jaffa, Palestine, moved to Cairo, Egypt and then to Beirut, Lebanon, where he studied at the Christian Brothers French School prior to attending the Jesuit University School of Medicine in Beirut. He pursued theological studies at the Orthodox Theological Institute in Bucharest, Romania where he received his Th.D. degree in New Testament in 1975. He was ordained to the holy priesthood in the United States in 1976 and served as pastor of parishes in Connecticut and New York. He currently lives in St. Paul, Minnesota.

V. Rev. Dr. Paul Nadim Tarazi Bibliography

I Thessalonians: A Commentary
Galatians: A Commentary

The Old Testament: An Introduction
Volume 1: Historical Traditions, revised edition
Volume 2: Prophetic Traditions
Volume 3: Psalms and Wisdom

The New Testament: An Introduction
Volume 1: Paul and Mark
Volume 2: Luke and Acts
Volume 3: Johannine Writings
Volume 4: Matthew and the Canon

The Chrysostom Bible
Genesis: A Commentary
Philippians: A Commentary
Romans: A Commentary
Colossians & Philemon: A Commentary
1 Corinthians: A Commentary
Ezekiel: A Commentary
Joshua: A Commentary
2 Corinthians: A Commentary
Isaiah: A Commentary
Jeremiah: A Commentary
Hebrews: A Commentary
The Pastorals: A Commentary
Ephesians & 2 Thessalonians: A Commentary

Land and Covenant
The Rise of Scripture

The Man of Fortunate Steps

Rev. Dr. Herman R. Acker

This article will offer some reflections on certain aspects of Psalm 1 with the conviction that this Psalm orients one to the function of not only the Torah, which it reflects,[1] but that of all of Scripture as well. The Scriptures are the counsel of God, which ought to determine a believer's thinking and manner of living. How we think about God, the world, and ourselves will determine how we live. The first Psalm will provide a window, a view, which shows the function of Scripture as a whole, wherein lies the "blessedness" of which this Psalm speaks. This short Psalm of only 6 verses provides us with a sound foundation for thinking about Scripture in general and how it is intended to function in the life of a believer--or better yet, in keeping with the Psalm itself, how to live a life that is "blessed." The Scripture functions as *the* source of God's counsel to his people.

Here is Psalm 1 (RSV):

> Blessed is the man who walks not in the counsel of the wicked, nor stands in the way of sinners, nor sits in the seat of scoffers; but his delight is in the law of the LORD, and on his law he meditates day and night. He is like a tree planted by streams of water, that yields its fruit in its season, and its leaf does not wither. In all that he does, he prospers. The wicked are not so, but are like chaff which the wind drives away. Therefore the wicked will not stand in the judgment, nor sinners in the congregation of the righteous; for the LORD knows the way of the righteous, but the way of the wicked will perish.

---

1. The very structure of the Psalter is reminiscent of the Pentateuch or Law, in that it too is divided into five books (Book I: Pss 1- 41. Book II: Pss 42-72. Book III: Pss 73-89. Book IV: Pss 90-106. Book V: 107-150), thereby underscoring the preeminence and centrality of the Torah or Law of God given through Moses.

In this Psalm, the individual who is called "blessed" is introduced in the first part by how he does *not* live his life (Ps 1:1): He lives his life without any reference to the "wicked," the "sinners," or the "scoffers." Then there is a shift to a positive description (Ps 1:2): Here we are given *the* reference point for this man's walk or life: the "Law of the Lord. " This man is said to "delight" in and "meditate" on this Law at all times. The text then presents two similes to describe the "blessed" man on the one hand and the "wicked" ones on the other (Ps 1:3-4): This blessed man is "like a tree," whereas the wicked ones are like "chaff." Finally, the text ends with reference to God's judgment (Ps 1:5-6): We are told the wicked will not "stand" (i.e., be vindicated) at God's judgment; indeed, they will ultimately "perish." In contrast to those who perish, the "righteous" ones are "known" by God. Because they "delight," "meditate" and "walk" in God's law.

This word, "blessed" (*ashre*), is translated in the LXX by the Greek word *makarios,* which appears in the New Testament Beatitudes: "*Blessed* are the poor in spirit... " (Matt 5:3-11). The Sermon on the Mount is the Teaching/Law of the kingdom of God, which characterizes how a believer should walk, live, conduct one's life in the kingdom.

The words "blessed, " "walk" (*halak*) and "way" (*derek*) are words which have reference to living or conducting one's life. There is reference here to the good fortune (blessedness) of one whose feet travel on a straight path and who walks on a way which is blameless. The word "blessed" is based on a root which means to "go straight, go on, advance, "[2] and is connected to the notion of movement on a path--indeed to the very "steps" of one's feet on secure ground:

---

2. Francis Brown, S. R. Driver, and Charles Briggs, *A Hebrew and English Lexicon of the Old Testament* (Oxford: Clarendon Press, 1957), 80.

My steps (*ashuray*) have held fast to thy paths, my feet have not slipped. (Ps 17:5)

He drew me up from the desolate pit, out of the miry bog, and set my feet upon a rock, making my steps (*ashuray*) secure. (Ps 40:2)

But as for me, my feet had almost stumbled, my steps (*ashuray*) had well nigh slipped. (Ps 73:2)

One could understand the words "*Blessed is the man who...*" (*ashre haish asher...*) to mean something like "O the fortunate steps of the man who..." "Blessed are those whose way (*derek*) is blameless, who walk (*halak*) in the law of the LORD!" (Psalm 119:1). In order to follow a blameless path, one must exclude as a source of inspiration for action and conduct in life the influence of the "wicked" (*rasha*), the "sinners" (*khata*), and the "scoffers" *(lits)*. It is interesting to note that although three groups are mentioned (wicked, sinners, scoffers), the first appears in the Psalm four times (Ps 1:1, 4, 5, 6), the second two times (Ps 1:1, 5), and the third only once (Ps 1:1). It seems that the first in the triptych is the dominant category and the others are expressions of it. Indeed, biblically speaking, there are only two possible paths, one that leads to blessings and the other that leads to curses.

> Behold, I set before you this day a blessing and a curse: the blessing, if you obey the commandments of the LORD your God, which I command you this day, and the curse, if you do not obey the commandments of the LORD your God, but turn aside from the way which I command you this day, to go after other gods which you have not known. (Deut 11:26-28)

Even the text of the Didache recognizes, "There are two ways, one of life and one of death, and there is a great difference between these two ways."[3] Those who follow the way of death are the

---

3. Didache 1:1. Holmes, Michael W., ed. and trans., *The Apostolic Fathers: Greek Texts and English Translations*, 3rd ed., (Grand Rapids: Baker Academic, 2007), 344.

wicked of whom the Psalmist writes: "He loved to curse; let curses come on him! He did not like (*khafets*, i.e., delight in) blessing; may it be far from him!" (Ps 109:17). What one delights in determines what one meditates on and consequently what one does.

The "wicked" are those who disobey the commandments of God and follow the path that leads to the curse. The righteous one will not follow the advice of the one whose end is cursed, for as it says in verse 6, "the way of the wicked will perish. " This man will not walk "*in the counsel of the wicked.*" The word "counsel" (*etsah*) is the noun form of the verb meaning "to advise, counsel"[4] someone to take or not take a certain course of action. The counsel in this case, in which this man will not walk, is that of the "wicked" because they are, by definition, guilty. The root for "wicked" and "guilty" is the same:

> Be not silent, O God of my praise! For wicked (*rasha*) and deceitful mouths are opened against me, speaking against me with lying tongues. ... Appoint a wicked (*rasha*) man against him; let an accuser bring him to trial. When he is tried, let him come forth guilty (*rasha*); let his prayer be counted as sin! May his days be few; may another seize his goods! (Ps 109:2-8)

This man does not simply turn his back to negative influences but turns his face toward God's counsel, in which he delights. It is not enough to be empty; one must be filled with something.[5] Turning away from the influence of the "wicked" is not sufficient

---

4. Brown, et al., *A Hebrew and English*, 419-420.

5. Matthew 12:43-45: "When the unclean spirit has gone out of a man, he passes through waterless places seeking rest, but he finds none. Then he says, "I will return to my house from which I came." And when he comes he finds it empty, swept, and put in order. Then he goes and brings with him seven other spirits more evil than himself, and they enter and dwell there; and the last state of that man becomes worse than the first. So shall it be also with this evil generation."

for life. One must be influenced by someone or something. This man of fortunate steps finds his "delight" in a specific source of inspiration for action and conduct. He does not follow the path of the wicked, which ultimately leads to God's curse. Instead he desires always to seek God's counsel, which is found in God's teaching, which alone provides the preparation necessary for walking on the path which leads to blessings. This "delight" leads to an action.

This activity of "meditation" *(hagah)* refers to an audible sound and is used in parallel with words such as "tongue," "speaks," "lips," "mouth." Notice the following references:

> My lips will not speak falsehood, and my tongue will not utter (*hagah*) deceit. (Job 27:4)

> The mouth of the righteous utters (*hagah*) wisdom, and his tongue speaks justice. (Ps 37:30)

> For my mouth will utter (*hagah*) truth; wickedness is an abomination to my lip. (Prov 8:7)

> The mind of the righteous ponders (*hagah*) how to answer, but the mouth of the wicked pours out evil things. (Prov 15:28)

> For their minds (*levav*) devise (*hagah*) violence, and their lips talk of mischief. (Prov 24:2)

In Proverbs 24:2 above, this meditation is connected to the "mind" which, when cultivated, brings forth fruit, good or bad. The word *levav* refers to the "inner man, mind, will, heart."[6] The LXX uses *kardia*. Jesus said, "For out of the abundance of the heart (*kardia*) the mouth speaks" (Matt 12:34). Counsel feeds the heart; the heart produces words and actions.

---

6. Brown, et al., *A Hebrew and English*, 523.

"Meditation" comes before doing or speaking. Before taking action, one takes counsel. The question is, who is one's counselor? The wicked or God? Whose counsel will determine this man's path or way of walking? God, who speaks in his word.

This individual who "meditates" takes pleasure in "tasting" and taking "refuge" in God through his teaching: "O taste and see that the LORD is good! Happy is the man who takes refuge in him!" (Ps 34:8)

He is involved in this activity "day and night; " that is, continually, or all the time. Of course, one need not imagine that this man never eats or sleeps and only utters God's teaching every moment. It does, however, emphasize the seriousness of his commitment to seek God's will.

The "inner" person is what is influenced by seeking counsel, or deliberation. One does not seek counsel unless one has questions to be answered, a dilemma to be solved. The question to be answered is of course what is God's will for the human being? Yet there is more to it than that. Genesis 6:5 says: "The LORD saw that the wickedness of man was great in the earth, and that *every imagination of the thoughts of his heart was only evil continually*". The remedy is to seek God's counsel *continually*. Though *hagah* is connected to sound, the words spoken need only be loud enough to be heard by those gathered. One seeks counsel for the purpose of learning how one should act or speak in a given situation. One speaks and acts only after receiving proper counsel. In the context of seeking counsel one ponders what one is to do. Even a lion, before it lunges on its prey, growls as if in preparation, ignoring everything except its intended goal.

---

7 Emphasis is mine.

For thus the LORD said to me, As a lion or a young lion growls (hagah) over his prey, and when a band of shepherds is called forth against him is not terrified by their shouting or daunted at their noise, so the LORD of hosts will come down to fight upon Mount Zion and upon its hill. (Isa 31:4)

The one who follows this path "is like a tree[8] planted by streams of water, that yields its fruit in its season, and its leaf does not wither. In all that he does, he prospers (*tsalakh*)." Trees bear fruit in keeping with the kind of tree they are. In Biblical terms, a tree is either a "good" tree or a "bad" tree.[9] The good tree yielding good fruit is sustained by God and prospers, in that its produce is in keeping with its character. It prospers in that it bears God's will, so to say. The blessed one prospers in all that he does because all that he does is according to God's word. Jesus said:

Truly, truly, I say to you, he who believes in me will also do the works that I do; and greater works than these will he do, because I go to the Father. Whatever you ask in my name, I will do it, that the Father may be glorified in the Son; if you ask anything in my name, I will do it. (John 14:12-14)

The phrase "in my name" is equivalent to saying, "according to God's will." Asking God for something is not a blank check but a commitment to conform to the will of God as contained in his teaching. The good tree rooted in God bears "good" fruit according to God's definition, not ours. The word of God never fails. This prosperity has nothing to do with human success. From

---

8. cf. Jer 17:7-10: "Blessed is the man who trusts in the LORD, whose trust is the LORD. He is like a tree planted by water, that sends out its roots by the stream, and does not fear when heat comes, for its leaves remain green, and is not anxious in the year of drought, for it does not cease to bear fruit. The heart is deceitful above all things, and desperately corrupt; who can understand it? I the LORD search the mind and try the heart, to give to every man according to his ways, according to the fruit of his doings."

9. Matt 3:10; 7:17ff; 12:33; Lk 3:9; 6:43.

a human vantage point, the suffering servant of Isaiah was nothing if not a failure, and yet of him Isaiah writes:

> Yet it was the will of the LORD to bruise him; he has put him to grief; when he makes himself an offering for sin, he shall see his offspring, he shall prolong his days; *the will of the LORD shall prosper (tsalakh) in his hand.*[10] (Isa 53:10)

> So shall my word be that goes forth from my mouth; it shall not return to me empty, but it shall accomplish that which I purpose, and prosper (*tsalakh*) in the thing for which I sent it. (Isa 55:11)

The parallel between Psalm 1 and Joshua 1 cannot be missed. This is God's word to Joshua before his campaign into Canaan.

> Only be strong and very courageous, being careful to do according to all the law which Moses my servant commanded you; turn not from it to the right hand or to the left, that you may have good success wherever you go (*halak*). This book of the law shall not depart out of your mouth, but you shall meditate *(hagah)* on it day and night (*yomam valaylah*), that you may be careful to do according to all that is written in it; for then you shall make your way (*derek*) prosperous (*tsalakh*), and then you shall have good success. Have I not commanded you? Be strong and of good courage; be not frightened, neither be dismayed; for the LORD your God is with you wherever you go (*halak*). (Josh 1:7-9)

In order for Joshua to be successful in *God's* will, he must make God's way his way and must have the book of the law in his mouth to meditate on it day and night (v. 8) and walk in it (vv. 7, 9).

> The wicked are not so, but are like chaff which the wind drives away. Therefore the wicked will not stand in the judgment, nor sinners in the congregation of the righteous; for the LORD knows

---

10 Emphasis is mine.

the way of the righteous, but the way of the wicked will perish. (Ps 1:4-6)

The wicked are insubstantial, blown away by the wind. Therefore, they will not be vindicated at the time of judgment or be numbered among the righteous who have delighted, meditated, and lived according to God's will. They have not made God's will their will and therefore he does not recognize them.

One is known by one's deeds. This is true of God and of human beings. Neither Pharaoh nor the Israelites could know God apart from his acting. Notice in the contest between God and Pharaoh what Pharaoh said to Moses: "Who is the LORD, that I should heed his voice and let Israel go? *I do not know the LORD* [emphasis mine], and moreover I will not let Israel go" (Exod 5:2). The Lord had no temple, no image for him to appeal to. From Pharaoh's point of view the LORD had no past history. The Israelites, too, did not know the Lord and would have no chance of knowing him apart from his actions.

> Say therefore to the people of Israel, "I am the LORD, and I will bring you out from under the burdens of the Egyptians, and I will deliver you from their bondage, and I will redeem you with an outstretched arm and with great acts of judgment, and I will take you for my people, and I will be your God; and *you shall know that I am the LORD your God*[11], who has brought you out from under the burdens of the Egyptians." (Exod 6:6-7)

There are many references that clearly show that our knowledge of God follows his actions and indeed cannot precede it. That is to say, he cannot be known until after he acts.[12]

---

11 Emphasis is mine.
12. Exod 7:5 And the Egyptians shall know that I am the LORD, when I stretch forth my hand upon Egypt and bring out the people of Israel from among them."

It is in and from the Scriptures that we learn of God's actions. What he has done and the lessons we draw from it are found there. "For whatever was written in former days was written for our instruction, that by steadfastness and by the encouragement of the scriptures we might have hope" (Rom 15:4). We "know" him by meditating on his works as recorded in the Bible and living according to its teaching.

According to Scripture, God too knows us based upon our actions. God said to Abraham, "Do not lay your hand on the lad or do anything to him; *for now I know that you fear God*[13], seeing you have not withheld your son, your only son, from me" (Gen 22:12). Only after Abraham was in the process of sacrificing his son does God know or recognize him as having trust in his word. If we know God, he knows us. Only when we act in faith as Abraham did will we be known by God. We know God by what he does as recorded in Scripture and he knows us by our obedience to its teaching. Jesus said:

> Not every one who says to me, "Lord, Lord," shall enter the kingdom of heaven, but he who *does* the will of my Father who is in heaven. On that day many will say to me, "Lord, Lord, did we not prophesy in your name, and cast out demons in your name, and do many mighty works in your name?" And then will I declare to them, "*I never knew you*, depart from me, you evildoers." Every

---

Exod 7:17 Thus says the LORD, "By this you shall know that I am the LORD: behold, I will strike the water that is in the Nile with the rod that is in my hand, and it shall be turned to blood."

Exod 8:10 And he said, "Tomorrow." Moses said, "Be it as you say, that you may know that there is no one like the LORD our God."

Exod 8:22 But on that day I will set apart the land of Goshen, where my people dwell, so that no swarms of flies shall be there; that you may know that I am the LORD in the midst of the earth.

Exod 9:14 For this time I will send all my plagues upon your heart, and upon your servants and your people, that you may know that there is none like me in all the earth.

13 Emphasis is mine.

one then who hears these words of mine and does them will be like a wise man who built his house upon the rock; and the rain fell, and the floods came, and the winds blew and beat upon that house, but it did not fall, because it had been founded on the rock. And every one who hears these words of mine and does not do them will be like a foolish man who built his house upon the sand; and the rain fell, and the floods came, and the winds blew and beat against that house, and it fell; and great was the fall of it. (Matt 7:21-27[14])

The teaching is clear: One knows God through his deeds by means of his Law and he knows us by our deeds which are in conformity with the same Law. In order for one to know another it is necessary to spend time with that person; knowing God entails spending time with him, listening to him speak. By meditating on the Law of God, one gets to know God's will and thus know God. God and his will are coextensive. One must listen to God in order to get to know him. When one gets to know God then one is known by God. In Psalm 1, however, the accent is on God knowing us. "The Lord knows the way of the righteous," which means they will not perish.

To "know the way of the righteous" is a way of saying that the righteous man is known by his path, that is, his manner of life or conduct. In other words, the only one God knows or pays attention to is the one who walks in or conforms his life to the Teaching or Torah of God.

> Beware of false prophets, who come to you in sheep's clothing but inwardly are ravenous wolves. You will *know* them by their fruits. Are grapes gathered from thorns, or figs from thistles? So, every sound tree bears good fruit, but the bad tree bears evil fruit. A sound tree cannot bear evil fruit, nor can a bad tree bear good fruit. Every

---

14 Emphasis is mine.

tree that does not bear good fruit is cut down and thrown into the fire. Thus you will *know* them by their fruits. (Matt 7:15-20[15])

The good tree is known by its good fruit. One's steps determine who one is.

The man of fortunate steps is such because his steps are directed by the Law of the Lord in which he delights. This Law is continually on his lips so that his ears may hear, so his heart, which is under its influence, will direct his feet in the way of God's commandments, causing his hands to be occupied by the deeds that please his Lord. He is successful in what he does because the seed of the Word he plants in his heart always produces the fruit corresponding with its nature, i.e. God's will. Because this man is in the presence of God when the word is on his lips and in his heart and in his actions, he is known and recognized by the God whose Word sustains his life. The Lord knows the one who looks like his will. This man begins and ends with the Law of the Lord and has the hope to stand in the judgment, unlike the wicked, who are dispersed like chaff, unable to stand at the time of judgment and who will ultimately perish, to be unknown, forgotten.

Bibliography

Brown, Francis, S. R. Driver, and Charles Briggs. *A Hebrew and English Lexicon of the Old Testament.* Oxford: Clarendon Press, 1957.

Holmes, Michael W., ed. and trans. *The Apostolic Fathers: Greek Texts and English Translations.* 3rd ed. Grand Rapids: Baker Academic, 2007.

---

15 Emphasis is mine.

There are No Curse Words in Church Slavonic: Musings about Missionary Morphology

Rev. Fr. Michael Arbanas

In *The Rise of Scripture*, Paul Nadim Tarazi asserts, based on his years of studying the Scriptures, that Biblical Hebrew is a "concocted" language – an artificial creation drawing from the several Semitic languages spoken in the Ancient Near East.[1]

While this contention may raise a few eyebrows and even draw criticism from those who have accepted without question the common narratives regarding authorship and composition of the Scriptures, the very notion should not be terribly challenging to Orthodox Christians – the majority of whom worship in a "literary" language of similar origin – Church Slavonic.

Created by the missionary brothers Cyril and Methodius in the 9th century with the express purpose of spreading Christianity among the Slavic-speaking peoples, Old Church Slavonic features word roots from the spoken Slavic dialects of the day with a grammatical structure that closely corresponds to the Koine Greek of the New Testament. More than a thousand years later, it remains exclusively a language of worship – and not daily conversation, which tends to spawn both commonplace phrases and curse words – for some 150 million Russian Orthodox Christians (not to mention millions more Serbians) out of 250 million Orthodox worldwide.[2]

---

[1] Paul Nadim Tarazi, *The Rise of Scripture* (St. Paul: OCABS Press, 2017), 68.

[2] Estimates of the actual number of practicing Orthodox Christians in any country, or throughout the world, are notoriously optimistic. The point is that more than half of the Orthodox Christians in the world hear Church Slavonic when they go to church.

This combination of Slavic words and Greek grammar proved incredibly effective for the missionary purposes of Cyril and Methodius. It allowed for the rapid translation of Scriptures and Church services from Koine Greek to the Church Slavonic. And while Cyril's creation of an alphabet in which to render their work (as the Slavs previously had none) receives most of the attention in their hagiographies, the ability to translate the Scriptures and services quickly and artfully through the close grammatical equivalence was every bit as important to the success of their endeavor.

"Naked are all nations without Scriptures, weaponless, unable to fight with the Adversary of our souls, ready for the prison of eternal torment," proclaims the Prologue – most commonly attributed to Cyril -- to the Church Slavonic translation of the Gospels. "But you nations that don't love the Enemy, and truly intend to fight against him, open diligently the doors of your minds, having received now the sturdy weapons forged by the Scriptures of the Lord."[3]

Cyril (then known by his baptismal name of Constantine; he took the name Cyril when he was tonsured as a monk toward the end of his life) and Methodius were brothers from Thessalonica, sons of a high-ranking provincial official. Methodius himself became a local governor before taking monastic vows. Cyril, the younger brother, was a leading intellectual figure of his day, becoming a teacher of philosophy and a favorite of the Emperor in Constantinople.[4]

---

3 Thomas Butler, *Monumenta Serbocroatica* (Ann Arbor: Michigan Slavic Publications, 1980), 13. For attribution to Cyril, see pp. 3-4.
4 Matthew Spinka, "Slavic Translations of the Scriptures," *The Journal of Religion* 13, no.4 (Oct. 1933): 417-418.

Thessalonica was a mixing place of Byzantine Greeks and Slavs, who had migrated into the Balkan peninsula in the past centuries, and the brothers were at least somewhat able to speak the Slavic language that surrounded them when they were young.[5] In 862, Emperor Michael III received a request from Prince Rastislav of Moravia (in present-day Slovakia) to send missionaries who could teach Rastislav's subjects in their native tongue, and Cyril and Methodius were the Emperor's natural choices.

Moravia had been the subject of attention from Frankish missionaries connected with Rome, but they insisted on the services being conducted in Latin, and Rastislav's people found it difficult to embrace their new faith fully. Both his request for missionaries willing to incorporate the Slavic language and Michael's agreement to send them satisfied political considerations of the day, but those lie outside the scope of these comments.[6] In any case, the mission was, at its heart, a religious effort.[7]

The first task was to devise a written alphabet for the Slavs, who had none. As the *Life of Constantine*, composed not long after Constantine-Cyril's death, recounts: "Thereupon the philosopher went and gave himself, in accordance his habit, to prayer, along with other helpers. Soon God, having the prayers of his servants, revealed Himself to him, and immediately composed the letters and began writing the prologue of the Gospel: "In the beginning

---

5 Spinka, "Slavic Translations", 417-418.
6 See, for example, A.P. Vlasto, *The Entry of the Slavs into Christendom* (Cambridge: Cambridge University Press, 1970), 28-29.
7 Vlasto, "Entry," 28-29.

was the Word, and the Word was with God, and the Word was God" (John 1:1).[8]

Those who are familiar with the Gospel lectionary in the Orthodox Church should not be at all surprised that the prologue to John's Gospel (read at the Paschal Divine Liturgy) was the first passage to be translated. In the Orthodox tradition, it is the very first reading in every Gospel book. Therefore, as the linguist Alexander Schenker notes, it not only "points up the linguistic and inspirational nature of Constantine's efforts," but it also reflects the intention of first translating those materials that would be immediately useful in the Slavic-language services that the brothers intended to offer the Moravians.[9]

From there, the work went quickly. Before the brothers left Constantinople for Moravia in 863, about a year after their initial commission, they had already translated not only the Gospel lectionary but also "the other books necessary for the Divine Liturgy – the Psalter, Acts and the Epistles."[10] In other words, their mission dictated that they first translate the Scriptural passages necessary to begin worshiping in the Slavic as soon as possible.

After they arrived in Moravia, the translation efforts continued at a rapid pace. Within 40 months, the brothers and their followers had translated the services of the daily cycle – Matins, the Hours, Vespers and Compline. Cyril, still in his mid-40s, died in 869, and Methodius was appointed bishop of the region in 870, but disputes with the Frankish clergy in the area slowed the

---

[8] Quoted in Spinka, 420. It should be noted that the alphabet that Cyril derived was almost certainly Glagolithic, a very ornate script that faded from use, to be replaced by Cyrillic script (named in honor of Cyril) still in use today.

[9] Alexander M. Schenker, *The Dawn of Slavic* (New Haven: Yale University Press, 1996), 31.

[10] Marvin Kantor, *Medieval Lives of Saints and Princes* (Ann Arbor: University of Michigan Dept. of Slavic Languages, 1983), 6.

translation work. Finally, between 882 and his death in 885, Methodius was responsible for the translation of every remaining book of the Scriptures except Maccabees.[11]

This speed in translation was possible because of the strong similarities between the Koine Greek of the Scriptures and the Old Church Slavonic. As Horace Lunt notes,

> The surface structures of O.C.S. and Greek coincide in nearly all major features. The form-classes are generally the same: verbs (conjugated for several tenses, with person-number desinences), substantives (nouns and adjectives, including participles, declined for case and number), pronouns (personal, demonstrative, interrogative, relative; declined for gender, case, and number), numerals (declined), prepositions, adverbs, a variety of conjugations and particles. Syntactical devices are closely comparable and even word formation follows the same general patterns.[12]

Working so efficiently was especially important to Cyril and Methodius because their main object was instruction, rather than conversion. Rastislav's appeal makes it clear that many of his subjects had already converted to Christianity. The brothers' main purpose was to educate and train the local clergy in the Church Slavonic translations of the Scriptures and services. Therefore, it makes sense that they would want to have the services and Scripture reading translated as quickly as possible.[13]

As Kantor notes, the Koine Greek provided not only grammatical structure, but also a broader vocabulary, making translation much more effective: "Adopting the Bulgaro-

---

11 Kantor, *Medieval*, 6.
12 Horace G. Lunt, "Limitations of Old Church Slavonic in Representing Greek," in Bruce M. Metzger, *The Early Versions of the New Testament* (Oxford: Clarendon Press, 1977), 431-432.
13 Francis Dvornik, *Byzantine Missions Among the Slavs* (New Brunswick: Rutgers University Press, 1970), 105.

Macedonian dialect [from the area around Thessalonica] for this purpose, [Cyril] modeled this literary language on Byzantine Greek syntax and word-formation, using it for the enrichment of vocabulary, and religious and legal terminology."[14]

There is, to my knowledge, no writing by Cyril, Methodius or their contemporaries that explicitly states that the brothers imposed Greek grammar on the Slavic dialect with which they were familiar. As Lunt notes, "We have not original O.C.S. writings to serve as a measure of 'normal' usage."[15] And the proto-Slavic language of the centuries before Cyril and Methodius is inaccessible, re-created by scholars using, at least in part, the Church Slavonic itself, so it is not a good source of information about the grammar of the mid-9th century.

Of course, the possibility remains that the brothers *didn't* change the Slavic grammar at all – that the Greek and the Slavic languages retained almost exactly the same grammatical structures over the thousands of years of their evolution from the Proto-Indo-European language that scholars have reconstructed as the common ancestor of both. Or perhaps the two grammars did evolve, but in nearly-exact parallel over those thousands of years, even though the vocabulary changed to the point that they had few, if any, words in common.

But neither of these possibilities seems as likely as the simpler, mission-driven theory: the brothers had to translate a large quantity of Scriptural writings, services, hymns and other writings quickly, and imposing the Greek grammatical structure (that of their source documents) upon the spoken Slavic word-roots allowed Cyril and Methodius to fulfill their missionary work rapidly and efficiently, devising a language their Slavic charges

---

14 Kantor, *Medieval*, 6.
15 Lunt, "Limitations," 431-432.

could understand, even if it was not exactly the Slavic they spoke at home.

So we return to the saying that provides the title for these musings. It usually comes into play as the final word in an argument against replacing Church Slavonic with the modern Russian, Serbian or whatever language is spoken in the country in question. Referring to the account of Cyril and Methodius receiving the Slavic letters as a revelation from God Himself, the speaker asks, somewhat incredulously, "Why should we abandon this gift from God, this holy language the Lord created to bring the Gospel to us Slavs? It's so holy, in fact, that *there are no curse words in Church Slavonic.*"

It's true; there are no curse words. And since Slavic-speakers can be as creative as any other language group in coming up with colorful language, the absence of curse words points us once again to the conclusion that Church Slavonic was never a spoken language. Rather, it abides to this day, more than a thousand years later, as it has been from the beginning – a literary language – created specifically for worship by two brilliant scholars and missionaries.

Bibliography

Butler, Thomas. *Monumenta Serbocroatica.* Ann Arbor, MI: Michigan Slavic Publications, 1980.

Dvornik, Francis. *Byzantine Missions Among the Slavs.* New Brunswick, NJ: Rutgers University Press, 1970.

Kantor, Marvin. *Medieval Slavic Lives of Saints and Princes.* Ann Arbor, MI: University of Michigan Dept. of Slavic Languages, 1983.

Lunt, Horace G. "Limitations of Old Church Slavonic in Representing Greek." Pages 431-442 in Metzger, Bruce M. *The*

Early Versions of the New Testament. Oxford: Clarendon Press, 1977.

Schenker, Alexander M. *The Dawn of Slavic.* New Haven: Yale University Press, 1996.

Spinka, Matthew. "Slavic Translations of Scripture." *The Journal of Religion* 13 (1933): 415-432.

Tarazi, Paul Nadim. *The Rise of Scripture.* St. Paul, MN: OCABS Press, 2017.

Vlasto, A.P. *The Entry of the Slavs into Christendom.* Cambridge: Cambridge University Press, 1970.

Nomads of the Word: Reading the Book of Acts from a Semitic Perspective

Dr. Daniel Ayuch

Introduction

Some books have the power to touch your mind and others, very few, can touch both your mind and soul. From an early age, the Bible has awakened my curiosity. It has amazed me with its stories, and it has touched me as a person who seeks for a meaning to life. As a young man I read several books about the Bible and later in my professional life, I read specialized studies of all kinds. But the day of October 2, 2017, had prepared a great surprise for me: the publication of *The Rise of Scripture*.[1] Of course, it is not the first time I read from among Father Paul Tarazi's extensive production. Several books in English and Arabic were scrutinized by my curiosity and desire to learn, particularly after having listened to him in regular courses at Balamand and in many other seminars in Lebanon in which he dazzled us with his methodical, critical and creative interpretation of the Bible in its two Testaments.

From this unique experience of reading and studying *The Rise of Scripture*, this article presents an application of its message and method in relation to one of the New Testament books that I have studied for several years, which is the Lucan story of Acts of the Apostles.

---

1 Paul Nadim Tarazi, *The Rise of Scripture* (St. Paul: OCABS Press, 2017).

This article proposes a narrative reading based on Father Tarazi's understanding of the Biblical *mashal* as an "edifying story"[2] and his approach to the figure of the shepherd in Biblical literature. Some selected texts from Acts will be interpreted in order to show how the Apostles adopted and put into practice this Old Testament model, offering an alternative to the hegemony and oppression of worldly powers represented in this case by the Roman Empire. The image of a shepherd of sheep wandering in the Syrian Desert as a witness of the One God proposes a model of life that will form the identity of those who believed in Jesus Christ as Lord and Savior. The apostles and preachers are nomads, travelers who carry the Word from one place to another in order to feed the people, to take care of those who were taught to live detached from this world and following the steps of their Master.

Shepherdism According to Tarazi

Father Paul knows the Hebrew Bible as the palm of his hand and moves in it with such a mastery and naturalness as a shepherd who, knowing the pastures of the land, leads his flock to the right place at the right time. And this is how Tarazi points out the importance of a fundamental Hebrew verb in the Old Testament narratives. This verb is *hithallek*, a word that denotes the most important action of the shepherds: "The habitual continuous movement of a shepherd and his flock in the wilderness whether it is over the area of grazing where they settle for a time or the relocation from one grazing spot to another within the boundaries of that same wilderness."[3]

In the Hebrew Bible, the verb *halak* in its stem *hithpael* occurs 64 times in a total of 60 verses and in 25 different forms. In

---

[2] Paul Nadim Tarazi, *The Old Testament: An Introduction*, vol. 1 *Historical Traditions*, new revised ed. (Crestwood: St. Vladimir's Seminary Press, 2003), 22.

[3] Tarazi, *Rise*, 144.

Semitic languages, the variation of verbal stems serves to grant certain features to the verb in its simple form, and *hithpael* is the one that gives the sense of both a reflexive and an intensive action, this is how *halak* simply means to walk while *hithallek* means rather to come and go, to wander, to travel from one place to another. For those who understand Arabic, it is like the root *tafa''ala* when it is applied to the simple stem *masha* (to walk) and takes the form of *tamasha* meaning to come and go or to wander. The same happens with *jâla* (to go around) and *tajawwala* (to patrol, to explore).

For Tarazi, the text that best demonstrates the peculiar semantic connotation of this verb is the whole chapter of Genesis 13. In this narrative, Abram returns from Egypt and walks through extensive lands where "ten" nations dwell.[4] His journey through the desert as a witness to the one God is an imitation of how the Lord walked in the garden of Eden looking for his lost sheep in the oasis[5] (Gen 3:8). In the Bible, God is the model of a shepherd who walks among his people: "Yet his bow remained taut, and his arms were made agile by the hands of the Mighty One of Jacob, by the name of the Shepherd, the Rock of Israel" (Gen 49:24 NRS). And again: "And I will walk among you (*we-hithallakhti be-tokhekhem*), and will be your God, and you shall be my people" (Lev 26:12 NRS).

From then on, of course, Tarazi refers to Ezekiel as the prophet who best develops the image of God as a shepherd, especially in Ezekiel 34, which is known as the chapter about "the shepherds of Israel."

---

4 Actually, the number 10 is not explicitly mentioned in Genesis 13, but it is implicitly present in the list of the ten nations of Genesis 15:18-21 giving a particular reading to the characteristics of the Syrian desert. See p. 146 and especially note 3 in which it is indicated that this numeral expresses the universality of Abram's mission.

5 Cf. Tarazi, *Rise*, 148.

Abram is not the only one to imitate God as a shepherd. In the first part of Genesis (chapters 1-11), Enoch stands out as the one who "walked with God" (Gen 5:22, 24) and in both verses, the verb is again *hithallek*. Father Paul points out that Enoch followed in the footsteps of the Lord as did Noah and Isaac (Gen 6:9; 17:1; 24:20; 48:15). And among them, Noah is the one that at the end of his life hesitated, abandoned shepherdism and chose to settle in a piece of land and planted a vineyard. He represents in his person the struggle between the ancestral brothers Cain and Abel and deals with the origins of conflicts between a sedentary lifestyle and nomadism (Gen 9:20; see Gen 4:3; *Rise*, p. 205-206):

> Noah reneges on that way of life in favor of urbanism, which introduces a curse on his progeny. Consequently, the scriptural story dismisses him in order to prepare the scene for the true 'heir' of Enoch, Shem whose progeny, as I shall show, is essentially one of shepherds.[6]

It should be noted here how the American historian and social critic Morris Berman presents evidence of deep rivalry between sedentary and nomadic life forms. In his book *Wandering God*, he points out that in the ancient world, sedentary people showed a strong obsession for making the nomads cease their human flow, while the latter saw the life of farmers as a form of slavery.[7] Particularly interesting for the Arab context are the statements of Ibn Khaldun (born 1332), who saw an implacable opposition between *badâwah* (desert life) and *hadârah* (urban life) and said in his *Muqaddimah*: "All the customary activity of the Bedouin

---

6 Tarazi, *Rise*, 253.
7 Morris Berman, *Wandering God: A Study in Nomadic Spirituality* (New York: SUNY Press, 2000), 164-165.

(nomads) lead to wandering and movement. This is the antithesis and negation of stationariness, which produces civilization."[8]

Tarazi understands that Biblical literature adopts this urbanism-nomadism opposition and defends the latter as the only plausible option in face of the oppressing foreign imperialist forces that afflict the weak and small community of authors and readers of the Bible. Shem, son of Noah, is the true heir of Enoch because he continues with the line of shepherds. Shem is a true *ro'eh tson* (shepherd of the flock) who takes care of her community. So, in Hebrew the same word can be used to say both tribe and staff, because the mere existence of a staff implies that the community is still there, and it is being taken care of. *Shebet*, which is the staff, is the proof that there is a flock.[9] Therefore, the sense of traveling and wandering in the desert is imitating God's providence and expresses the determined and caring attitude of those leaders, who do not travel for a personal benefit, but they rather serve others, the members of the people of God.

Apostles as Shepherds in Acts

The Book of Acts is the second volume of the Lucan diptych and it is well-known for narrating the so-called "missionary" trips of the Apostles with a vivid intensity. "Missionary" is written in quotation marks because it is a term that has been particularly manipulated by the great expansionist states of Christian culture throughout history. If we go to analyze the narrative stages of this book, we see that the essential plan of the apostolic work is to move from one place to another gaining amplitude from the very center of the great salvific acts of the Passion, the Resurrection, and Pentecost in Jerusalem. Already at the end of the Gospel of Luke we read "that repentance for forgiveness of sins should be

---

8 As quoted in: Thomas J. Barfield, *The Nomadic Alternative* (Englewood Cliffs: Prentice Hall, 1993), 210.
9 Tarazi, *Rise*, 50.

proclaimed in His name to all the nations, beginning from Jerusalem" (Luke 24:47 NAS) and at the beginning of Acts we find again: "You shall be my witnesses both in Jerusalem, and in all Judea and Samaria, and even to the remotest part of the earth" (Acts 1:8 NAS). This last saying summarizes the outspreading movement and indicates the three great narrative stages of Acts. The Risen Christ marks the guidelines of preaching in Acts. Therefore, the first stage is to be fulfilled in Jerusalem (Acts 1:1-8:4). Then, the second one takes place on the roads going down from Jerusalem, such as the roads to Samaria, Damascus, Caesarea Maritima and Antioch, being this latter, the chosen place as the new center of evangelization (Acts 8:5-12:25). Finally, the stage of traveling to the remotest parts of the earth will be achieved by the Apostle Paul who will leave the Asian continent and preach the Christian kerygma in Europe until he reaches the capital, Rome, even though he is in prison (13:1-28:31). Thus, the general lines of the structure of the book are based on these three stages: the preaching in Jerusalem, the preaching on the roads descending from Jerusalem and finally the preaching to the nations:

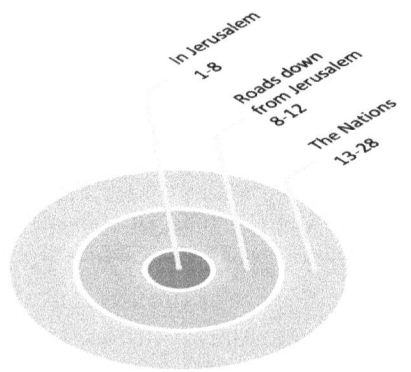

The Christian community in Jerusalem was neither an original community **from** this city nor did it belong to the ruling establishment. With some exceptions like Joseph of Arimathea, who according to Luke 23:50 was a member of the council, the community of Jerusalem was first formed by those Galileans who came along with Jesus, to whom a large number of Jewish pilgrims in Jerusalem joined up on the day of Pentecost, as the catalog of the nations in Acts 2:5, 9-11 states. Let's not forget that the members of the Galilee community used to meet with the Resurrected Christ on the Mount of Olives, outside of Jerusalem, and that their commonplace of prayer was the upper room and not the Temple, although they still used to frequent the Temple as members of Israel and not as leaders of a new movement. The first church in Jerusalem shows in its texture a strong inclusive power, as also indicated by the Cypriot origin of Barnabas (4:36) and the scene of "the Hellenists against the Hebrews" (6:1). It is the episode of Stephen's martyrdom that causes a decisive turning point in the narrative and the active Christian community in Jerusalem begins to leave the city. Above all, the narrator's approach to the roads leading to the four cardinal points is highlighted: Damascus representing the east, Samaria the north, Azotus the south, and the island of Cyprus the west. Acts 8:4 is part of the concluding paragraph to the Jerusalem cycle and is fundamental to understanding the Lucan vision of the nomadic vocation of the Church:

Therefore, those who had been scattered went about preaching the word. (Acts 8:4 NAS)
Οἱ μὲν οὖν διασπαρέντες διῆλθον εὐαγγελιζόμενοι τὸν λόγον. (Acts 8:4 BGT)

In this sentence, there are two verbs that stand out: "to scatter" (διασπείρω) and "to go about" (διέρχομαι). Usually, scholars understand the derived noun "dispersion" (διασπορά) as a loss of power because it implies separation, abandonment, and detachment, which are all concepts that describe a defeat. One can read in Greek Lexica that, in the background of the LXX and Early Judaism, this term has as its main meaning the "Jewish minority that lived among people of other beliefs and, in this case, in a Greek and pagan environment."[10] Yet, the author of Acts does not see it this way. To understand his approach, we need to go back to the original root of the verb διασπείρω (to scatter) which is σπείρω and means to sow. Moreover, σπείρω derives, in its turn from the Greek noun σπέρμα, which means seed. The prefix *dia-* serves to intensify the sense of dispersing the seed,[11] it could be translated as "to distribute seed widely."[12] Hence, this verb does not have in Acts the negative connotation of people being separated or going lost in a sea of Paganism and strange cultures, but rather it shows that the strong seed was sown in new lands to germinate and bear fruit. An attentive reader cannot fail to link this story with the parable of the sower "a man who sowed good seed in his field" (ἀνθρώπῳ σπείραντι καλὸν σπέρμα ἐν τῷ ἀγρῷ αὐτοῦ, Matt 13:24 RSV, BGT), in the sense that the Lord is sowing the good seed in all the earth, his earth, as the psalm says: "The earth is the Lord's and the fullness thereof" (Ps 24:1 RSV). Besides, the reader also remembers the parable of the mustard seed "smaller than all other seeds", which was sown by the Lord in his field and produced a great tree, larger than the garden plants, despite its weakness (Matt 13:31-32, NAS). So was the Jerusalem

---

10 Dieter Sänger, " διασπορά." Pages 940-943 in vol. 1 of *Diccionario Exegético del Nuevo Testamento*. Edited by: Horst Balz and Gerhard Schneider. 2 vols. Salamanca: Sígueme, 1996.

11 It means seed in the plant kingdom, and sperm in the animal kingdom. By metonymy it also means offspring. It is a colossal term in the theology of the Old Testament, which Tarazi analyzes in several books, particularly in *Rise*, 66-70, and *Galatians*, 138-143.

12 HELPS Word-Studies. "1290 diasporá."

church when the Lord took her out of his bag of seeds and sowed her in his field.

The first church is dispersed with a function,[13] which is to walk among the nations and preach the power of the Gospel. This is how the people, who were in constant preaching and witnessing in Jerusalem, now go out in search of new lands where their seed can germinate and give new life. The verb to scatter in Acts 8:4 serves to indicate this outreaching movement of preaching. This is a peculiarity of the author of the third Gospel, as Sänger says: "According to Luke, the scattered are an essential factor for the diffusion of early Christianity."[14]

Already aiming at the final expansion towards the nations, the verb "to disperse" reappears in a phrase parallel to 8:4 as Luke writes down the closing scenes for the preaching cycle on the roads going down from Jerusalem:

> So then those who were scattered because of the persecution that arose in connection with Stephen made their way to Phoenicia and Cyprus and Antioch, speaking the word to no one except to Jews alone.(Acts 11:19 NAS)
>
> Οἱ μὲν οὖν διασπαρέντες ἀπὸ τῆς θλίψεως τῆς γενομένης ἐπὶ Στεφάνῳ διῆλθον ἕως Φοινίκης καὶ Κύπρου καὶ Ἀντιοχείας μηδενὶ λαλοῦντες τὸν λόγον εἰ μὴ μόνον Ἰουδαίοις. (Acts 11:19 BGT)

This sentence offers a flashback to the scene of Stephen and tells how the work of sowing reached this time even farther lands; away from Judea and its surroundings. It was able to reach Phoenicia, Cyprus and Antioch.

---

13 To define the functionality of a text is an important step in Tarazi's exegetical method. See: Marc Boulos, "It's Functional!", The Ephesus School, https://ephesusschool.org/its-functional/.

14 Dieter Sänger, " διασπορά," DENT 1:940-943.

Both here and in 8:4, the verbs "to go about" and "to sow about" appear in the same sentence forming a semantic pair of great relevance for our topic. With the sowing of Christians in new fields, the verb διέρχομαι intensifies the sense of expansion thanks to the prefix *dia-* added to the simple stem "to go" (ἔρχομαι). No doubt, Luke uses this verb in Acts as an equivalent to *hithallek* in the Hebrew Bible. That is, the heralds travel as if they were shepherds taking care of their flock. No doubt, Luke knows the importance of the nomadic lifestyle and expresses this teaching narratively, through a *mashal* (an edifying story), to hand it over for future generations.[15] It is more than evident that when this verb is used in connection with the preachers of the word, it functions as an equivalent to *hithallek* in Hebrew. In combination with "sowing around," this verb indicates "walking around" and specifies the necessary nomadic nature of preachers. The apostles and the preachers must arrive at each point of the earth with the seed to sow. And they must return later to take care of the communities as shepherds tend their sheep. This verb highlights the passing by of the person in charge in the community. In the Greek Old Testament, διέρχομαι is one of the most used verbs to translate *hithallek*.[16] And Luke knows this feature in texts that in some way evoke the experience of a small congregation that goes out to preach the nations. For example, there is Psalm 105 which recalls the wonderful history of Israel and when mentioning its beginnings as a people it says: "When they were only a few men in number, very few, and strangers in it. And they wandered about (διῆλθον) from nation to nation, From one kingdom to another people" (Ps 105:12-13 NAS). And we also read the interesting

---

15 About the term mashal see Tarazi, *Rise*, 41 footnote 17 and *Historical*, 22-25.

16 The LXX has 16 variants to translate *hithallek*. The most frequent ones are περιπατέω with 12 times and διέρχομαι together with εὐαρεστέω which appear 9 times each. The verb διέρχομαι as a translation of *hithallek* occurs in: Josh 18:4; 1 Sam 2:30.35; 12:2; 30:31; 2 Sam 7:7; 1 Chr 17:6; 21:4; Ps 105:13.

connection between the Lord's shepherding of his people and the walking of the people in 2 Samuel 7:7:

> Wherever I have moved about (διῆλθον) among all the people of Israel, did I ever speak a word with any of the tribal leaders of Israel, whom I commanded to shepherd my people Israel, saying, "Why have you not built me a house of cedar?"

Luke the Evangelist uses διέρχομαι following this biblical scheme. Throughout the New Testament this verb is used a total of 41 times, 21 of which occur in Acts and 10 in the Gospel. Thus, it can be said that Luke is by far the author that uses διέρχομαι the most. The shepherds who received the announcement of the birth of the Messiah cross distances to reach Bethlehem as it is told in Luke 2:15. In 4:30 Jesus passes amidst his people, just like the Lord in the Old Testament did, symbolizing thus a shepherd's caregiving visitation. In this sense also, Zacchaeus waited for the shepherd to pass in 19: 4. In Acts of the Apostles, there are many quotes that highlight the importance of this verb apart from the two given above. One of them is, for example, 8:40 where Philip traveled "preaching the Gospel" to all the cities of the coast of Palestine, from Azotus to Caesarea. Peter also "went here and there among all the believers" in his work of evangelization in Judea (Acts 9:32). Paul "went through" the whole island of Cyprus preaching (Acts 13:6). Paul always "crosses" territories to preach and the interpreter cannot but remember the term *hithallek* in the Hebrew Scriptures (Acts 13:14; 14:24; 15:3, 41). In Acts 18:23 we read another example of a shepherd who moves from place to place taking care of his flock and "strengthening" them. The last time the term appears is in Acts 20:25 where Paul summarizes in his farewell speech his apostolic work as a "going about preaching the Kingdom" (διῆλθον κηρύσσων τὴν βασιλείαν).

Of course, the terms flock and sheep, as well as the verb for "to shepherd" are not absent in Acts and they allude to the pastoral care of God's people and the church. Nevertheless, the absence of the noun "shepherd" (ποιμήν) is striking. It only appears in the Gospel and in relation to the scene of the shepherds of Bethlehem (Luke 2:8, 15, 18, 20) and nowhere else. Curiously enough, Christ takes care of his people as a good shepherd in the Gospel and the apostles do so in Acts, as well. However, Luke narrates this ministry without resorting to the technical term shepherd (see Luke 15:4-6). On the other hand, the word flock (ποίμνιον) is present in Luke 12:32 in that exclusive saying of Luke's "do not fear small flock," as well as in Paul's farewell speech in Acts 20. Besides, the verb "to shepherd" (ποιμαίνω) appears not only in Acts 20:28 but also in Luke 17:7, although in the latter with the literal sense of tending or guiding sheep.

Among all these examples, the legacy of Paul in Acts 20:28-29 stands out because it includes several of the above-mentioned terms and reflects the attitude of the shepherd of people:

> Be on guard for yourselves and for all the flock, among which the Holy Spirit has made you overseers, to shepherd the church of God which He purchased with His own blood. I know that after my departure savage wolves will come in among you, not sparing the flock. (Acts 20:28-29 NAS)

> προσέχετε ἑαυτοῖς καὶ παντὶ τῷ ποιμνίῳ, ἐν ᾧ ὑμᾶς τὸ πνεῦμα τὸ ἅγιον ἔθετο ἐπισκόπους ποιμαίνειν τὴν ἐκκλησίαν τοῦ θεοῦ, ἣν περιεποιήσατο διὰ τοῦ αἵματος τοῦ ἰδίου. ἐγὼ οἶδα ὅτι εἰσελεύσονται μετὰ τὴν ἄφιξίν μου λύκοι βαρεῖς εἰς ὑμᾶς μὴ φειδόμενοι τοῦ ποιμνίου. (Acts 20:28-29 BGT)

In this similitude of the shepherd, it is understood that the heads of communities must be careful and alert so that the flock does not perish. There are not only wolves coming from outside, but also false shepherds trying to divert the flock (v. 30). Finally, Paul reminds his audience, the elders of Ephesus, that he performed his role as a shepherd without sparing efforts, with tears, with watchfulness and admonition so that no one would be lost. The dangers are many. They may come from outside or inside. They may threaten the whole community or some individuals. Each person must be taken care of if they are to imitate God as a good shepherd.

In Acts, Paul himself is an example of good shepherd too. This is what he affirms in his last discourse as a free man and this is what is shown in his trips and journeys to proclaim the kerygma and to visit those who already believed. Paul moves from one place to another following the old tradition of shepherds in the Old Testament, who like Enoch or Abraham walked before the Lord. The Apostle is a nomad of the Word, who goes from one place to another to gather both the lost sheep of Israel and all nations and to guide them. Just as Abraham traveled through the Syrian desert among the nations that resided there, Paul travels among the nations without belonging to any of them. He made the entire Roman Empire his desert through which he led the flock.

If we take as an example the foundation of the Corinthian church story in Acts 18:1-18, we see Paul as a traveler that came from Athens to Corinth and chooses to reside as a guest in the dwelling place of a Jewish-Christian couple. Then he changes his center of preaching from the synagogue to a gentile house in a very short time. Aquila and Priscilla were, as a matter of fact, like refugees forced to return to Pontus by order of Emperor Claudius. In this scene, the reader is informed about Paul's secular profession. He was a "tentmaker" (σκηνοποιός, 18:3), says Luke, a profession that is not mentioned anywhere else. Biblical scholars tend to discuss the exact activity of Paul's handwork, whether he did tents of leather or of a special kind of material. However, within the nomadic aspect of Paul's life and considering his permanent state of being on the way, the making of tents is a clear wink of eye between the author and his reader to affirm that Paul was neither a sedentary person nor a sedentary worker, since even his worldly profession proves his nomadic lifestyle.[17]

The shepherds of the Bible and the nomads of Acts are far away from those heroes coming forth in the Renaissance pastoral novel, whose main pattern is *Arcadia* by the Italian writer Jacopo Sannazaro (1504). Those idealized shepherds living in an idyllic nature are actually people of sedentary customs, like urban nobles who are delighted in producing poems of their passionate misadventures in such an egocentric and lazy attitude that the reader wonders where their sheep might be lost. It is enough to see the artistic representation of the Arcadia shepherds of the Italian painter Giovanni Benedetto Castiglione (1655), for instance, to understand that these are perfect antitypes to Biblical shepherds.[18] According to Castiglione, those romantic people have instruments of music, paintings, and writings. They look interested in everything except in working for the flock. They are rather court gentlemen disguised as shepherds who are enjoying a good life.

Speaking of Biblical antitypes, it is worth mentioning that when Father Paul refers to the Jewish historian of the first century of our era, Flavius Josephus, he does so to demonstrate how he betrayed the nature of Scriptures when he wrote his *Jewish Antiquities* outlining a glorious past of Jewish people and borrowing the style in which the oppressor nations wrote their own history.[19] On the other hand, notes Tarazi, Luke chose to follow the model of the Old Testament prophets. The Apostles, and especially Paul, are depicted as ordinary people, without a royal lineage or a glorious

---

17 About the power of those peoples that expanded in tents see Tarazi, *Rise*, 132 and especially note 7 where he refers to the Mongol civilization.
18 "Arcadian Shepherds," The J. Paul Getty Museum, http://www.getty.edu/art/collection/objects/622/giovanni-benedetto-castiglione-arcadian-shepherds-italian-genoese-about-1655/.
19 Tarazi, *Rise*, 398.

past. They dedicated and committed themselves to preaching the Gospel and nothing else. They are a people wandering within the Roman Empire to convey the divine message and pointing out all injustice and iniquity.

Just as Greeks and Romans came to conquer the Semitic Asian world, the extensive Syrian desert of Father Tarazi, which is much of the MENA-Region in contemporary geopolitics, so does Luke as he narrates the reconquest of Asia Minor and the expansion to Europe by these nomads who move along proclaiming the resurrection of a Nazarene and compelling the inhabitants of the Roman Empire to live an new lifestyle, one that liberates them and saves them from their yoke. In this context, it is worth highlighting the vision of the Macedonian standing and appealing to Paul: "Come over to Macedonia and help us," said he in Acts 16:9 (NAS). In his recent commentary on Acts 13-28, Daniel Marguerat rightly points out that "premonitory dreams and oracular visions" are a common leitmotif in the accounts of conquests of new lands.[20] So was it written about Alexander the Great before penetrating the Persian Empire and about Xerxes before invading Greece. Something similar it is to be found about Julius Caesar before crossing the Rubicon and about Hannibal before crossing the Ebro. Starting from these literary witnesses, Marguerat deduces that what Luke recounts in Acts 16:6-10, is the decision making to evangelize Europe. With this deduction I agree, Paul decides in Troy to make the leap to Europe and continue his way in a new continent. What I would add to Marguerat is that Luke also narrates the capitulation of the Greek-Western oppressive culture to the power of the Gospel and therefore one cannot help seeing in this vision that the nameless Macedonian man stands there representing the most famous

---

20 Marguerat, *Actes* 2, 122.

among them, i.e., Alexander the Great, who would be symbolically submitting to the Apostolic Word.[21]

Conclusions

In that delicate moment of the story in which Joseph must allow the passage of his brothers to Egypt and asks the Pharaoh permission for them to stay, Genesis 46:34 summarizes very well the conflict between nomads and sedentary people saying: "every shepherd is loathsome to the Egyptians." On this background, one can read between the lines in Acts that Luke is saying "Romans detest them too." And it could not be otherwise. These shepherds wandering in open areas and regions have been able to transmit a message of liberation and hope to people mainly oppressed with slavery.

With *The Rise of Scripture,* we have been able to rediscover the itinerant nature of the people of God through the desert. The Bible does not merely contain accounts of a remote past, but it rather conveys an intense call to live today following the footsteps of those who committed themselves to bear a testimony of faith among the nations. This article shows that the book of Acts works in the same way and that even if Luke writes in Greek and frequently uses a cultivated language and refined phrases common sometimes to Greek philosophical writings, his message is far from agreeing with Greek thought. On the contrary, his work conveys a Semitic vision of the world as it was revealed in the Old Testament Scriptures.

---

21 It is interesting how the text in manuscript D, which represents the long Western version of Acts, begins verse 10 saying, "So, when he woke up, he told us the vision and we realized that *he* had called us to preach the Gospel to the people of Macedonia." Here I understand the *he* pronoun as an ironic allusion to Alexander the Great rather than to the Lord calling Paul, who is usually named as in Acts 18:9.

Finally, and in the light of Fr. Tarazi's interpretation, the Lucan story outlines a challenging church that is very committed to the call of being a wandering witness of the word. It is a church that reckons herself small and weak and knows the challenges implied in trying to subsist in the immense sea of worldly powers. Nevertheless, they take courage and follow the call of the Lord, as the first Apostles did in Luke 5:11: "And when they had brought their boats to land, they left everything and followed Him."

Bibliography

"Arcadian Shepherds." The J. Paul Getty Museum, http://www.getty.edu/art/collection/ objects/622/giovanni-benedetto-castiglione-arcadian-shepherds-italian-genoese-about-1655/.

Barfield, Thomas J. *The Nomadic Alternative.* Englewood Cliffs, NJ: Prentice Hall.

Berman, Morris. *Wandering God: A Study in Nomadic Spirituality.* New York: SUNY Press, 2000.

Boulos, Marc. "It's Functional!" The Ephesus School, https://ephesusschool.org/its-functional/.

HELPS Word-Studies. "1290 diasporá." BibleHub. http://biblehub.com/greek/1290.htm.

Marguerat, Daniel. *Les Actes Des Apôtres (13-28).* Commentaire du Nouveau Testament. Genève : Labor et Fides, 2015.

Sänger, Dieter. "διασπορά," *Diccionario Exegético del Nuevo Testamento.* Edited by: Horst Balz and Gerhard Schneider. Translated by Constantino Ruiz-Garrido. 2 vols. Salamanca: Sígueme, 1996, 1: 940-943.

Tarazi, Paul N. *Galatians: A Commentary.* Crestwood: St. Vladimir's Seminary Press, 1999.

———. *The New Testament: An Introduction*, vol. 2 Luke and Acts. Crestwood, NY: St. Vladimir's Seminary Press, 2001.

———. *The Old Testament: An Introduction*, vol. 1 Historical Traditions. New Revised Edition. Crestwood: St. Vladimir's Seminary Press, 2003.

———. *The Rise of Scripture*. St. Paul: OCABS Press, 2017.

Acts 18:3 – "Tentmakers": A Discussion

Andrea Bakas

In Acts 18:2-3 we have:

And he [Paul] found a certain Jew named Aquila, born in Pontus, who had recently come from Italy with his wife Priscilla (because Claudius had commanded all the Jews to depart from Rome); and he [Paul] came to them. So because he was of the same trade, he stayed with them and worked, for by trade they were tentmakers.[1]

We have that Paul, Aquila and Priscilla were of the same trade. They were tentmakers - σκηνοποιοὶ/skēnopēē. In which sense were they "tentmakers?" What might the meaning of this word be here? I will briefly discuss the word σκηνοποιοὶ and then examine the occurrences of its root word σκηνή/skēnē/tent – in the book of Acts and how these occurrences give us a way to understand the use of σκηνοποιοὶ in Acts 18:3.

The word σκηνοποιοὶ rendered "tentmakers" in English translations appears only once in scripture: in Acts 18:3. It is a compound word comprised of the feminine noun σκηνή/skēnē/tent (tent and tabernacle are used interchangeably in the KJV) and the verb ποιέω/pē-eh-ō – "I do" or "I make". Σκηνή/skēne is from the root "ska" which means "to cover."[2] The word σκηνή/skēnē and its forms occurs 5 times in the book of

---

[1] All scriptural references as written are a mix of the NKJV and NRSV translations. I opted to use more than one English translation because no single translation was adequate. For example, the NKJV translates the word τέχνη (Nestle Greek New Testament 1904) in Acts 18:3 as "occupation," and the NRSV translates τέχνη as "trade." I opted for "trade" over "occupation" because I believe it renders the meaning of the Greek "τέχνη" more accurately.

[2] "Skéné" no. 4633, *Bible Hub Study Tools*, 13 April 2018, https://biblehub.com/greek/4633.htm.

Acts: three times in Acts 7:43-46, once in Acts 15:16 and once in Acts 18:3 in the form of σκηνοποιοὶ.

In order to make sense of the three occurrences of σκηνή in Acts 7:43-46, we need to include verses 47-50 in our reading. In this chapter, Stephen recounts the scriptural story. In verse 41, we have the apostasy of the people of God in their making of the calf and that they "rejoiced in the works of their own hands." Stephen recalls the Lord's rebuke of the people, quoting the prophets. Next, Acts 7: 43-50 reads as follows:

> (43) You also took up the σκηνή/tent of Molóch, and the star of your god Rephán, images which you made to worship; and I will carry you away beyond Babylon
>
> (44) The σκηνή/tent of witness was with our fathers in the wilderness, just as he had directed, speaking to Moses, that he should make it according to the example that he had seen.
>
> (45) Which our fathers, having received it in turn, also brought with Joshua into the land possessed by the nations, whom God drove out before the face of our fathers until the days of David,
>
> (46) Who found favor before God and asked to find a σκήνωμα/tent for the house of Jacob.
>
> (47) But Solomon built him a house
>
> (48) However, the most high does not dwell in temples (made by hands)/χειροποιήτοις[3] as the prophet says (Isa 66:1-2):
>
> (49) Heaven is my throne, and earth is my footstool. What house will you build for me? Says the Lord, Or what is the place of my rest?
>
> (50) Has my hand not made all these things?

---

3 The underlining is mine.

These verses give us the way to understand the meaning of "tentmakers" in Acts 18:3. Acts 7: 43-48 form a dialectic, pitting tents made by the hand of man against tents made by the hand of the Lord, if you will. We have the tent of idols and the house of Solomon versus the tent of Moses and the tent of David – the latter two both built under the Lord's instruction.

Also, Acts 7:44, where we read:

> The σκηνή/tent of witness was with our fathers in the wilderness, just as he had directed, speaking to Moses, that he should make it according to the example that he had seen

is a summary of Exodus 33:7-10, wherein the Hebrew the masculine noun אֹהֶל/ohel/tent (which the LXX translates "σκηνή") – is clearly defined as the abode of the Lord.

A few words about the word אֹהֶל/ohel. The word אֹהֶל/ohel whose root אָהַל/ahal means "to be clear" or "shine," has the connotation of something being "clearly conspicuous from a distance."[4] Jeff A. Benner, in his *The Torah: A Mechanical Translation*, describes אָהַל/ahal as "the shining light of the campfire next to the tent," that can be seen from a distance for those returning home late, just as a star is used as a guide.[5] So according to this interpretation, we have tent which functions as a guide or a beacon. Another possibility is tent as something imposing or mighty, an ironic expression which emasculates the ancient temples. The Lord's tent is more "conspicuous" than a temple of stone.

Exodus 33:7-10 reads:

---

4 "Ohel" no. 0168, *StudyLight Bible Study tools*, 13 April 2018, https://www.studylight.org/lexicons/hebrew/0168.html.
5 Jeff A. Benner, *The Torah a Mechanical Translation*. (Ancient Hebrew Research Center, 2018), e-book, 1548.

(7) And Moses took the אֹהֶל/ohel and pitched it for himself outside the camp, distancing [it] from the camp, and he called it the אֹהֶל/ohel of meeting, and it would be that anyone seeking the Lord would go out to the אֹהֶל/ohel of meeting, which was outside the camp

(8) And it would be that when Moses would go out to the אֹהֶל/ohel, all the people would rise and stand, each one at the entrance of his אֹהֶל/ohel, and they would gaze after Moses until he went into the אֹהֶל/ohel.

(9) And it would be that when Moses entered the אֹהֶל/ohel, the pillar of cloud would descend and stand at the entrance of the אֹהֶל/ohel and he would speak with Moses.

(10) When all the people would see the pillar of cloud standing at the entrance of the אֹהֶל/ohel, all the people would rise and prostrate themselves, each one at the entrance of his אֹהֶל/ohel.

The LXX translates אֹהֶל/ohel in these verses as σκηνή. The heavy repetition of *ohel* in these verses drill in the association of *tent* with God's representative Moses. As Acts 7:44, the summary of these verses attests, God directs Moses's action. It is in this tent that the Lord would speak with Moses. The tent functions as the place where the Lord's word resides. Here we have "tent" defined for us in Exodus 33:7-10 and it is *this* tent that we have in the book of Acts.

The אֹהֶל/ohel of Exodus 33:7-10 has features that are worth mentioning because they add to our understanding of the Lord's preferences. The tent is emblematic of the Lord's anti-city/anti-temple stand. We read in Exodus that God resides in the wilderness where there is no life[6] and he directs Moses to create his tent there. The wilderness is a feature of shepherd culture, as

---

6 Paul Nadim Tarazi, *The Old Testament Introduction, vol 1 – Historical Traditions*, new revised ed. (Crestwood: St. Vladimir's Seminary Press, 1996), 117.

we have learned from Fr. Paul Tarazi: an open space with no walls or divisions.[7] The tent is pitched *outside* the camp. This is repeated four times in verse 7. We have "pitched it for himself *outside* the camp" and then "*distancing* it from the camp" and then "anyone seeking the Lord would *go out* to the tent" and finally "which was *outside* the camp." This emphasis is an illustration of the Lord's approach – he comes from the outside. This brings to mind Luke chapter 4 in which we have that Jesus's ministry begins outside Jerusalem in Galilee. As Fr. Paul explains, Galilee symbolizes the wilderness of the nations[8]. The Lord's "residence" is the wilderness.

"Tent" as a feature of shepherd culture is also shelter, but it is vulnerable to the elements. Men may shelter there, but they are at the mercy of mighty winds, for example. This could be an expression of the fact that the people do not control the tent; they are controlled by it.

The tent is movable and its movement is directed by the Lord. This brings to mind Ezekiel's chariot (Ezek 1:20-21 NRSV). Also, as the tent moves, it leaves no trace of existence, the way an earthly temple would "exist." This feature belittles the stone temples of the Greek pantheon or of Solomon's temple (although we read about this temple later in 1 Kings). We have a good example of this belittling in Amos chapters 1, 2 and 3 where we have the "fortified towers" or "strongholds" of the nations and of Jerusalem condemned by the Lord.

The word אֹהֶל/ohel as the Lord's abode is reinforced in 2 Samuel 7:6 (which is summarized in Acts 7:45-47), where we have a distinction between אֹהֶל/ohel and בַּיִת/bayit.

---

[7] Paul Nadim Tarazi, *The Rise of Scripture* (St. Paul: OCABS Press, 2017), 280.
[8] Paul Nadim Tarazi, *The New Testament Introduction, vol 2 – Luke and Acts* (Crestwood: St. Vladimir's Seminary Press, 2001), 46.

2 Samuel 7:6 reads:

> Whereas I have not dwelt in any בַּיִת/bayit/house since the time that I brought up the children of Israel out of Egypt, even to this day, but have walked in a אֹהֶל/ohel/tent and in a מִשְׁכָּן/mishkan/dwelling place.

Here, the Lord says explicitly that he does not dwell in a house but in a tent. Also here, we have the Lord connected with both an אֹהֶל/ohel/tent and a מִשְׁכָּן/mishkan/dwelling place[9].

Returning to Acts 7 and our accounting of the occurrences of the word σκηνή, we come to the term σκήνωμα in verse 46. Here, we have David who asked to find a σκήνωμα/a pitched tent for the house of Jacob. This σκήνωμα found favor with God as his dwelling because of David's obedience to his will for it. Fr. Paul points out that David kept the tent of witness unaltered, unlike Solomon who, as verse 47 attests, built it according to his own plan.[10]

The final occurrence of σκηνή is in Acts 15:16 in which James makes his case to the council in Jerusalem for God's inclusion of the Gentiles. He quotes the prophets in verse 16 which reads:

> After this I will return and will rebuild the σκηνή of David, which has fallen down and I will rebuild its ruins and I will set it up.

Here the Lord claims the σκηνή of David as his own. He directs its rebuilding. The source for this verse is Amos 9:11, which reads:

---

[9] Ohel and mishkan in this text are not synonyms. There is a distinction made between ohel and mishkan. The exploration of it is deserving of a separate paper.
[10] Tarazi, *New Testament Introduction, vol 2*, 215.

> In that day will I raise up the סֻכַּת/sukkat/booth of David that is fallen, and wall up the breaches thereof; and I will raise up his ruins, and I will build it as in the days of old.

In this verse in Amos, the word used is סֻכַּת/sukkat, usually translated as booth or habitation, not אֹהֶל/ohel. The root of the word סֻכַּת/sukkat connotes a habitation woven together[11], so perhaps this is an added critique of David's house. We have that the booth of David has fallen, but literally, they have come "unwoven" because of their disobedience to the Lord. The LXX renders סֻכַּת/sukkat in verse 9 as σκηνή - τὴν σκηνὴν Δαυὶδ.

So we have established אֹהֶל/ohel in Exodus 33:7-10 as the legitimate dwelling of the Lord. We can see that Moses "makes" the tent of meeting and this tent is where the Lord's word, his teaching, dwells.

We are set up in Acts to associate σκηνή in the same way. Coming back to Acts 18:3 and to the question – in which sense are Paul, Aquila and Priscilla "tentmakers?" Just as the Lord directs Moses and David's tent making, the Lord directs Paul, Aquila and Priscilla's tent making. **It is their preaching of the Lord's word - the gospel - that "makes" the tent of witness**. They "make" the Lord present through Paul's gospel, directed by the Spirit of the Lord. It is not *their* creation. Moreover, Paul's teaching is closely linked with tent here. In Acts 18:3, we hear they were "tentmakers" and then immediately, in the very next verse, verse 4, we have a demonstration of Paul's trade – his teaching.

> And he (Paul) reasoned or preached in the synagogue every Sabbath and persuaded both Jews and Greeks.

---

11 "Sukkah" no. 5521, *Bible Hub Study tools*, 13 April 2018, https://biblehub.com/hebrew/5521.htm.

"Tentmakers" in Acts 18:3 are instruments of the Lord's will – with no other function but to teach the gospel to both Jews and Gentiles.

Hebrew as Literary Language
Dr. Richard Benton

Scholars disagree on the status of the language of the Hebrew Bible. The questions come down to two: (1) whether Biblical Hebrew was a language and (2) when the language might have been spoken, if ever. Paul Tarazi and Gotthelf Bergsträsser agree on the answer to (1), that the Hebrew Bible was written in a single language.[1] For Edward Ullendorf, "Biblical Hebrew" could only be called "no more than a linguistic fragment," because of how much is missing for it to be used in everyday life.[2] It is unclear, however, whether he believed that the language was not spoken at all or that the biblical text represented a small portion of a language spoken by a historical people. Jehoshua Grintz made claims that relate to both (1) and (2) when he wrote that Hebrew "was the main vehicle of speech in Jerusalem and the surrounding country, as well as the language most used for literary purposes during [the late Second Temple] period," which continued from the time of the creation of the Hebrew Bible.[3] Ernst Knauf clearly stated that Biblical Hebrew (1) combined elements from so many different time periods and styles, and therefore, (2) could not have been spoken.[4] Similarly, Tarazi stated that Biblical Hebrew did

---

1 Paul Nadim Tarazi, *The Rise of Scripture* (St. Paul: OCABS Press, 2017), 72; Gotthelf Bergsträsser, *Introduction to the Semitic Languages: Text Specimens and Grammatical Sketches*(trans. Peter T. Daniels; Winona Lake: Eisenbrauns, 1983), 50. This claim, of course, excludes the Aramaic sections of the Hebrew Bible.
2 Edward Ullendorff, "Is Biblical Hebrew a Language?" *Bulletin of the School of Oriental and African Studies* 34 (1971): 254.
3 Jehoshua M. Grintz, "Hebrew as the Spoken and Written Language in the Last Days of the Second Temple," *JBL* 79 (1960): 32. While it goes beyond the scope of this paper, much of the discussion about the "language of Jesus," that is, whether Jews were speaking Hebrew at the time of the writing of the New Testament, assumes that Hebrew was a vernacular language at some point in history.
4 Ernst Axel Knauf, "War 'Biblisch-Hebräisch' eine Sprache?" *ZAH* 3 (1990): 21.

not predate the composition of the Bible and was not spoken at all.⁵ These scholars tend to agree that Hebrew, as written in the Bible, was not spoken, but the precise relationship between the written and spoken languages remains debatable.

Another question that arises from the Biblical Hebrew language is the original meaning of the designation עברי *'ibri* "Hebrew." This question is significant because the term "Hebrew" referred only to people and not to a language in the text of the Hebrew Bible. Julius Lewy wrote that the adjective meant "alien" or "the one from beyond," and was derived from the noun עבר *'eber* meaning "an area outside one's own territory."⁶ According to D. R. G. Beattie and Philip Davies, the term began more specifically as *'eber ha-nahar*, a calque of the Akkadian, *eber-nari*, which was a "clearly-defined territory" in the western part of the Assyrian Empire.⁷ As far as to whom the term refers, Beattie and Davies wrote, "Hebrew is a term used either by foreigners to designate Israelites or Judaeans, or by Israelites and Judeans [sic] when speaking to foreigners about themselves."⁸ Tarazi stated that the term meant "crosser," which comes from the verb of the same root "cross," and refers more specifically to the "itinerant shepherds 'crossing' back and forth through the Syrian Wilderness."⁹ Scholars thus agree that the term derives from the root "cross," but disagree whether it is people from a territory "across" a river

---

5 Tarazi pointed out, "[T]he language that was spoken during the so-called 'Late Biblical Hebrew' period as well as at the height of the so-called 'Standard or Classical Biblical Hebrew' period, is qualified as 'Judean' or 'Judahite,'" so the language of the Bible at some point was seen as different from the language spoken at Jerusalem (Tarazi, *Rise*, 61-62).

6 Julius Lewy, "Origin and Signification of the Biblical Term 'Hebrew,'" *HUCA 28* (1957): 13.

7 D. R. G. Beattie and Philip R. Davies, "What does Hebrew Mean?" *JSS 56* (2011): 78.

8 Beattie and Davies, "What does Hebrew Mean?" 76.

9 Tarazi, *Rise*, 69.

or people "crossing" a territory. The territory, however, seems to be the vicinity of the Syrian Desert "across" the Euphrates.

In this paper I will show that the language in which the Bible was written was called "Hebrew" to identify it with the pastoral "foreigners" of the Syrian Desert, as Tarazi claimed, and those with whom Yhwh identified. I will begin with the basic datum that Biblical Hebrew was the main language of the Tanak; although we have no data that it was spoken in the area. It was originally called "Hebrew" because of its association with nomadism and disconnect from urban life—the home of Yhwh, the main character of the Hebrew Bible. Scripture came from the wilderness, where Yhwh made his home, and the language arose from the same place. In order to grasp what the Bible means by "Hebrew," and so why the translator of Ben Sira would call the language by this name, I will examine the term עברי *'ivri* "Hebrew" in the Hebrew Bible, which appears 34 times, by asking who is using the term, about whom they are using it, and to whom they are speaking. We will see that the term עברי *'ivri* "Hebrew" refers to a super-ethnic group, comprised of the Sons of Israel and multiple pastoral tribes in the Syrian and Arabian Deserts, to whom the Hebrew Bible ascribes Yhwh as the patronal deity. Once we establish these points, we will see that the use of this term to name the written language of the Bible makes explicit that scripture was rooted in the pastoral homeland of the wilderness and intended to cross tribes and did not belong to a single one of them.

Written vs. spoken languages

Based on the paradigm of other languages, we cannot assume that Biblical Hebrew was a spoken language in addition to a literary language. Written languages never reflect spoken vernacular languages perfectly because each serves its own purpose. Marlon Brando's famous line in "On the Waterfront,"

"I *coulda* been a contender," does not follow the rules of correct written grammar. Should he have said, however, "I *could have* been a contender," it would have sounded strange and out-of-place because of his character and the social situation he occupied. This distinction between spoken and written varieties exists in every language with a written variety. As a result of this linguistic dichotomy, biblical and Semitic scholars have debated the relationship between Biblical Hebrew and a spoken analogue.

Societies often include multiple languages and dialects that fill distinct niches. For example, "Arabic," which we often consider a single language, in the modern world occupies a complex space between written and spoken forms. Arabic has terms for each of these varieties of the language: *fuṣḥa* for the literary form (as is used in books and newspapers) and elevated speech (e.g., speeches and sermons), and *'ammiyya* for the panoply of everyday spoken varieties.

The difference between the two creates different social groups. A Moroccan and an Iraqi cannot understand each other when each speaks in his or her distinct, native *'ammiyya.* They are two linguistic groups. An educated Moroccan and an educated Iraqi would both have learned *fuṣḥa,* so they would have no problem understanding the same newscast or magazine article, which their uneducated compatriots could not comprehend. The literary language, therefore, forges the educated of both groups into a single group with its own identity. While varieties of spoken Arabic, *'ammiyya,* belong to distinct social groups, *fuṣḥa* spans multiple tribes and nations.

This linguistic situation is not unique to Arabic. The term "Chinese" refers to both a standard language, Mandarin, taught universally in Chinese schools, as well as to many speakers of mutually incomprehensible but related dialects or languages.[10] All would write with the same language, however,[11] and they may or may not speak Mandarin to each other.[12] Even among German speakers, a rural Bavarian speaking in a local dialect cannot be understood by someone from Saxony without some experience or special training.[13] Yet both could read the same website in common written German or *Hochdeutsch* ("High German"). Written languages unify speakers of various languages into a single social group.

Beliefs about the "Hebrew" language often assume that the authors of the Tanak spoke the very Hebrew in which they wrote, as if they had no choice, and so we do not reflect on the language itself used in this literature. We cannot assume that the scriptural writers spoke the language they wrote in. If we assume that the language of the Torah was only one of multiple possible languages to compose this work in, we must examine the written language as not only the medium but also as part of the message.

The Bible presents a complex linguistic, and thus social, context. First, languages such as Aramaic, Judahite, and Ashdodite are explicitly mentioned in the Bible as being spoken, and among these, only Aramaic is mentioned as written.[14] In other words,

---

10 The language calls itself Pǔtōnghuà, which literally means "common language."
11 Taiwan is one of a few exceptions that uses a different writing system than the mainland, though the language is spoken in mostly the same way.
12 On more than one occasion, I have witnessed native Mandarin and Cantonese speakers speaking English to each other to communicate.
13 I saw a German-language documentary in Germany that featured an elderly Austrian farmer, whose speech was subtitled for other Germans, even though it was technically "German."
14 Evidence of spoken language variation appears in the famous scene in Judg 12:6, where the Gileadites and Ephraimites pronounce the word for "grain" as *shibboleth* and *sibboleth*, respectively. According to the biblical author, the latter showed that "he could not speak it so," that is, he was incorrect. Spoken dialects differed, at least on this subtle level.

while the Hebrew Bible assumes a multilingual environment, it never mentions Hebrew among them. Second, the first time we read of Hebrew as a language is in the Greek Septuagint, when the grandson of Jesus Ben Sira mentioned that the original text he was translating was uttered ἑβραϊστὶ *hebraïsti* "in Hebrew" or "Hebraically" (Sir *Prologue*). His statement raises the question of the nature of this written language and its sociological niche.

Evidence thus points to a unique connection between the term "Hebrew" and the language of scripture, and its distinction from other languages reported as spoken. Since Hebrew in the Tanak only refers to people, we must ask what this term meant before it was mentioned as a language and so what prompted the translator of Ben Sira to call this language by this gentilic adjective.

Identity of the Hebrews

Eberites and the Syrian Desert (Gen 10-11)

Eber (עבר), the eponymous progenitor of all the Hebrews (עברים *'ivrim*), begat the desert-dwelling peoples of the Syrian and Arabian Deserts, to the exclusion of the founders of the great cities of the region. It is only an accident of history that English translates עברים *'ivrim* as "Hebrews" and not "Eberites." The first mention of Eber simply ascribes his children to Shem, son of Noah (Gen 10:21). Over the course of the next three verses, we read that Eber is, in fact, the great-grandson of Shem (Gen 10:22-24). The text singles out Eber as the single, archetypal descendent whose children bear the name of this son of Noah; Eberites are the S(h)emites.

One would expect that this naming would carry special prestige, but the present chapter offers less-than-impressive details about Eber's children, Peleg and Joktan. First, the text only presents the meaning of Peleg's name, "Division," which represents the division of the land (Gen 10:25). Second, the other brother's name is Joktan, which the text does not interpret, but which means inauspiciously, "He/it will be made small." While Joktan bears 13 sons, the Bible only mentions three of them again.[15] We learn little about the totality of Joktan's sons, other than that they dwelt from Mesha to the eastern mountain, Sephar (Gen 10:30). "Division" and "Made Small" dwelling in the wilderness do not inspire awe in the reader.

Furthermore, the sons dwell in obscure places, not the great cities. We only possess general evidence about these locations. Mesha possibly lies somewhere between the Red Sea, Arabian Desert and Persian Gulf.[16] Sephar may be situated on the coast of modern Yemen or may mean "border country" in a more general sense.[17] The biblical text only locates Sephar to "the east." In spite of the number of Joktan's children, the text located these Eberites obscurely somewhere in the desert between the Fertile Crescent and the bottom of the Arabian Peninsula.

The next mention of Eber came after the fall of the Tower of Babel in Gen 11:10, and the text made a genealogical beeline through five generations to bring the focus onto Terah, the father of Abram. This followed the line of Peleg, "Division," whose name acquired additional significance with the story of the Tower and the resulting division of nations. The text did not name the "sons and daughters" who are not the direct ancestors of Abram, but once we arrived at Terah, we learned details about his sons. This clan lived in the land of the Chaldeans, as opposed to their cousins, the sons of Joktan, to the south and west.

---

15 Those mentioned again are Ophir, Havilah, and Sheba, who all bear a relationship to gold.
16 Gary H. Oller, "Mesha," *ABD* 3:708.
17 Oller, "Sephar," *ABD* 5:1098.

If we locate the "Eberites" or "Hebrews" according to Genesis 10-11, they populated the area between Ur and the Syrian and Arabian Deserts. The text contrasts their habitation with that of Eber's city-dwelling great-uncles, who included the eponymous founders of Elam, Ashur, and Aram (10:22). Significantly, the archetypal descendants of Shem who are ascribed to his line were not these founders of great cities, but obscure dwellers of the desert. The text thus presents a special relationship between Shem, son of Noah, and the denizens of the wilderness, including Abram, son of Terah, to the exclusion of the major cities.

Abram, the Hebrew (Gen 14)

Once the narrative sped through the genealogy to land on Terah, it slowed to settle on his most famous son, Abram, in Gen 11. A few chapters later, in Gen 14, we read the first occurrence of the adjective "Hebrew," ascribed to Abram as "*the* Hebrew." Logically, the area would have been filled with Hebrews/Eberites, that is, descendants of Eber, for many generations up to and including Abram's time. Abram, however, is singled out as *the* Hebrew.

The reader must pay attention to the context in which Abram is identified as "Hebrew." He is identified among Amorites when they needed someone with knowledge of the desert when the Amorites were in trouble. Chedorlaomer plundered them and fled northeastward. They called on Abram *the Hebrew* for help. Unless this description contrasts him from the others around him, the addition of this eponym is superfluous; we already knew since chapter 11 that his father descended from the children of Eber. We need to understand, therefore, why the author would have emphasized Abram as *the Hebrew* to be called upon when help in the desert was needed. The Bible introduced the Amorites as

Canaanites, that is, descendants of Ham.[18] Hamites dwelt in the area from Sidon in the North to Gaza in the South, and East to the Jordan (Gen 10:15-16). More specifically, Amorites come from the eastern Mediterranean coast (Gen 10:15-20). Thus, they perhaps lacked the knowledge to pursue Chedorlaomer and his allies to Dan and the area of Damascus (Gen 14:14-15).

Significantly, Abram spent significant time in the Syrian Desert as a typical "Hebrew." The story presented the character of Abram as personally experienced in the desert. First, he emigrated with his father from Ur to Haran, from Chaldean civilization to the provinces (Gen 11:31). He grew up outside the big city. Second, "Haran" literally means in Hebrew "hot (place)," and modern archaeologists locate this city in modern-day southern Turkey, or the northern part of the Fertile Crescent on the border of the Syrian Desert.[19] Third, after living in Haran, Abram turned to the South—the Syrian Desert—to shepherd his sheep, (Gen 13:1-2) before settling down in Hebron, at the Plain of Mamre, with his tent (Gen 13:18). Fourth, Abram lived as a nomad. Over the course of chapters 11 to 14, he moved from Ur to Haran (11:31), from Haran to Canaan (12:5), and to Sichem (12:6), Egypt (12:10), the area of Bethel (13:3), and Mamre (13:18). He thus did not follow the lifestyle of Ham or of Eber's uncles, founders of cities, but as a typical Eberite: a wandering herder, familiar with and at home in the Syrian Desert. Likely his dwelling as a shepherd

---

18 This biblical depiction of the Amorites contrasts with the much older one from Sumerian and Akkadian literature, where the MAR.TU / *Amurru* are depicted—probably satirically—as uncivilized shepherds from the Euphrates Valley, down to W Mesopotamia and the Arabian Desert. From archaeological and linguistic evidence, one can find their influence from Ugarit on the Mediterranean coast to the old cities of Mesopotamia during the first centuries of the second millennium BCE, though they seem to have assimilated into the surrounding cultures by the Late Bronze Age (George E. Mendenhall, "Amorites," *ABD* 1:200-201). The present work, however, focuses on the biblical presentation of the Amorites and their distinction from Hebrews.

19 Yoshitaka Kobayashi locates it about 80 km east of Charchemish ("Haran (PLACE)," *ABD* 3:59).

in the desert earned him the respect of the Amorites when they needed the help of a desert-dwelling "Hebrew."

Sons of Israel among the Hebrews (Gen 39, 43, and 46)

The narrative of Joseph and his brothers' descent into Egypt reveals that "Hebrews" and "Sons of Israel" are not synonyms because the Egyptians were already familiar with Hebrew language and culture before they ever met Joseph's brothers.

The term "Hebrew" had a negative, foreign connotation in this section.[20] Joseph began to live among the Egyptians starting in Gen 39. Soon, however, he rebuffed the advances of Potiphar's wife, and she disparaged him among her house and to her husband by saying that this "Hebrew" was brought in to "mock" them (Gen 39:14, 17). "Hebrew" was the word that identified Joseph and did so in a clearly negative sense.

When the other sons of Israel came down to Egypt for food (Gen 42), they had to identify themselves to the Egyptians, and the Egyptians understood that they were Hebrews without them identifying themselves as such. The brothers introduced themselves as brothers of one father from the Land of Canaan (Gen 42:7, 13). When Joseph concealed himself, he was able to use an interpreter to speak to them (Gen 42:23). This scene takes for granted that the Egyptian court employed someone knowledgeable in whatever language they were speaking, so it was clearly familiar to the officials.

The Egyptians functioned toward Joseph's brothers according to preexisting cultural norms towards Hebrews. On the brothers' second visit, in chapter 43, Joseph offered them food. He did not eat with them, however, because it was an "abomination" for

---

20 Only once do the Egyptians use "Hebrew" in a neutral sense, when Joseph's prison cell-mates described him to Pharaoh as a "Hebrew" and a slave (Gen 41:12).

Egyptians to eat with "Hebrews" (Gen 43:32). Again, we note that the word that designated the sons of this one father was "Hebrews," not "Canaanites" or "Sons of Israel."[21]

We must deduce that this geographic and linguistic information sufficed for the Egyptians to identify their guests as Hebrews. From what they told the Egyptians, Joseph's brothers were Canaanites who spoke a particular language common enough for their hosts that they had a translator on hand. It is not clear if it is *a* Hebrew language or *the* Hebrew language, however. The sons of Israel were Hebrew, so the language must have been connected to that identity in some way, maybe to Canaan. We do not know if the Egyptians considered all Canaanites "Hebrews."[22] Either the Egyptians believed that Canaanites were Hebrews, or the brothers' speech distinguished them from non-Hebrew Canaanites. Whatever the cause, the Egyptians decided that the men were Hebrews and that they could not eat together.

It is likely not a coincidence that the Egyptians held shepherds and Hebrew in contempt, and that the sons of Israel lived as shepherds among them. When Joseph's relatives addressed Pharaoh later in the story, they were to tell him that they were shepherds and that they had settled in the region of Goshen, as they had lived as such in Canaan. Joseph wanted them to tell Pharaoh this because "every shepherd is an abomination to the Egyptians" (Gen 46:31-34). Thus it was either coincidence that the Egyptians held both Hebrews and shepherds in contempt, or they assumed a relationship between Hebrews and shepherds. Based on the origin of the Hebrews, the combination seemed

---

21 Evidently, "Hebrew" is not a genetic designation but a cultural one, since Joseph was surely able to eat with his Egyptian wife (Gen 41:45).

22 The genealogies in Genesis 10 make it clear that Canaanites were sons of Ham, as opposed to the Hebrews, sons of Shem.

inseparable so Egyptian culture likely linked Hebrew and shepherds.

This story clearly distinguishes between "Hebrew" and "son of Israel," because for the Egyptians being Hebrew was a salient characteristic completely separate from their being sons of Israel. Having identified these visitors as Hebrews, the Egyptians followed existing mores to deal with them. Hence the text identifies the sons of Israel as Hebrews, but Hebrews must have included more than just this clan. The text leaves us no choice here but to see Hebrews as a broader category of shepherds to which the sons of Israel belong.

God of the Hebrews (Exod 3, 5)

As we move into the book of Exodus, Yhwh himself distinguished between Hebrews and the Sons of Israel. In Exodus 3, when Moses met Yhwh for the first time, Yhwh introduced himself to him as "the god of your father, the God of Abraham, the God of Isaac, and the God of Jacob" (Exod 3:6). When Moses introduced Yhwh to the Sons of Israel, he was to call him "I am" (אהיה *'ahiyeh*) as well as "Yhwh, the god of your father, the God of Abraham, the God of Isaac, and the God of Jacob" (Exod 3:14-16).

Yhwh was to be introduced differently to Pharaoh. Moses used two appellations for Yhwh in his first actual confrontation with Pharaoh, but he only captured his attention by mentioning the Hebrews. When Moses was to introduce Yhwh to Pharaoh, Yhwh commanded him to call him "Yhwh, god of the Hebrews" (Exod 3:18). Moses and Aaron, in fact, first introduced him to Pharaoh as "Yhwh, god of Israel," which Yhwh never actually called himself up to this point (Exod 5:1). Pharaoh rejected them, stating that he did not know this god and would not let "Israel" go (Exod 5:2). Then, the two added that the "god of the Hebrews" had met with them (Exod 5:3). From that point, Moses and Aaron only called him "God of the Hebrews" when speaking to Pharaoh (Exod 7:16; 9:1, 13; 10:3). Yhwh was therefore the god of Israel *and the rest of the Hebrews.*

To Pharaoh's face, Yhwh reemphasized his identity with the Hebrews, and not exclusively with the Sons of Israel. Significantly, we learned from the previous book that Egyptians reviled Hebrews. The god of Abraham, Isaac and Jacob, identified himself precisely with the shepherds Pharaoh abhorred, and ironically, he forced Pharaoh to allow them to separate and feast separately from the Egyptians.

This claim by Yhwh in front of Pharaoh to be the god of the abominable ones built on the identity of the Hebrews with nomadic desert life outside of major cities. As Yhwh led Israel out of Egypt, he not only was bringing them into the desert where he would speak to them, but where Hebrews belonged.

Do Philistines know who Israel is? (1 Samuel)

A problem arises in the text of 1 Sam 13-14 because "Hebrew" and "Sons of Israel" are both used, but the distinction the author is intending is not immediately clear. Nada Na'aman understood that in 1 Samuel "Hebrew" was an ethnic designation, with more of a negative connotation than "Israel."[23] Ralph Klein similarly believed that "Hebrew" had two definitions: (1) a negative term

---

[23] Na'aman wrote, "It refers mainly to Israelites in the pre-monarchical period and is used to distinguish them from other ethnic groups; it usually appears in unfavorable contexts, thus lacking the halo generally associated with the term 'Israelite'" (Nadav Na'aman, "Ḫabiru and Hebrews: The Transfer of a Social Term to the Literary Sphere," *JNES* 45 [1986]:279). Na'aman further believes that this meaning derives from a development that started long before in the Amarna correspondence, "The Amarna correspondence shows a marked development in the history of the appellation 'Ḫabiru.' On many occasions, the term went beyond its original meaning (i.e., a designation for uprooted people) and became a derogatory appellation for rebels against Egyptian authority" (Na'aman, "Ḫabiru," 275).

for Sons of Israel and (2) mercenaries who could change allegiances.[24]

These claims that equate the term "Hebrew" with "Sons of Israel" assume a change occurred from the usage in Genesis and Exodus, where it encompassed more than the Sons of Israel. No evidence in the 1 Samuel context suggests that such a change occurred, as we can interpret "Hebrew" to continue to designate a larger group than simply the Sons of Israel. Furthermore, the clear negative connotation in Genesis and Exodus does not show up as clearly in 1 Samuel. Just as Egyptians understood the Hebrews to be an ethnic group of which the pastoral Sons of Israel made up a subset, the Philistines likely followed this same paradigm in this book. "Hebrews" was a broad group that the Philistines knew, while "Sons of Israel" was a specific designation for David's subjects familiar to the reader.

Where the narrator used the designation "Sons of Israel," the word in the Philistines' mouths was "Hebrews" in 1 Sam 13-14. For example, the narrator informed the reader that the "men of Israel" hid out wherever they could in 1 Sam 13:6. When they came out from hiding, the Philistines remarked that the "Hebrews" were emerging (1 Sam 14:11). Elsewhere, the narrator told us that there was no smith in the "land of Israel" because the Philistines said they did not want the "Hebrews" to make weapons (1 Sam 13:19). If we assume a continuity in the meaning of this term from the Pentateuch, then this distinction may be one of prestige, that is, the Philistines used a negative term and the

---

24 Klein claimed, "Note that 'Hebrews' is used in two senses in this chapter [1 Sam 14], a) as a pejorative designation for Israelites when Philistines are speaking (14:11; cf. 13:19) and b) as a designation for mercenary outlaws who could choose to fight for hire with either Israel or the Philistines (14:21; cf. 13:3, 7). Victory had a bandwagon effect. Other Israelites, who had earlier hidden on Mount Ephraim (13:6), joined in pursuit of the fleeing Philistines" (Ralph W. Klein, *1 Samuel*, Word Biblical Commentary 10 [Nashville: Thomas Nelson, 2008], 137).

narrator a neutral one, or one of specificity, that is, the Philistines used a general term and the narrator a specific one.

We see this confusion in other scenes, as well. When the Philistines heard the "great shout" from Israel, the former noted that it came from "the camp of the Hebrews" (1 Sam 4:5-6). On another occasion, Israel camped in Jezreel. The Philistine leaders asked about the "Hebrews" there, and one of their own leaders explained that it was "David, servant of Saul, King of Israel" (1 Sam 29:1-3). This exchange indicates honest confusion arising from the fact that to the Philistines, Israel represented one of an indecipherable array of Hebrew tribes or kingdoms. Any negative connotation is less evident.

The biggest challenge to the idea that the terms designated the same group of people is found in 1 Samuel 14:21. We read there that some of the Hebrews with the Philistines went to stand with Israel. The word came from the voice of the narrator, not that of the Philistines, so it would not have the same negative sense. Klein claimed that this is a distinct use of the term, but this distinction is not necessary. They are not necessarily treacherous Sons of Israel. We can understand them as Hebrews who were not Sons of Israel and who decided to align with the Sons of Israel against the Philistines.

The Philistines' perception paralleled closely the Egyptians', even though the latter took place several centuries earlier in the story. The Egyptians created their rules about *Hebrews* not *Israel*. Philistines knew they were in pursuit of *Hebrews* but were less clued into the fact that it was *Israel* until someone from their own group identified the leader as belonging to the latter sub-group. Moreover, the narrator took this distinction as natural when we read about the changing allegiance of a group of Hebrews towards Israel.

The Hebrews in 1 Samuel differed in their cultural attributes from those in the Pentateuch. In Genesis, they were pastoralists from Canaan who spoke a particular language, and in Exodus, the former characteristic played a more important role. In 1 Samuel the Hebrews were not explicitly pastoralists. Therefore, the combination of their language and location likely indicated to the Philistines that they were Hebrews. Whether or not they were still pastoral, they spoke a dialect or language related to those traditional shepherds.

Yhwh and the Hebrews (Jonah 1:9)

In the book of Jonah, the reluctant prophet introduces himself as a Hebrew and one who fears Yhwh, god of the heavens (Jonah 1:9). Significantly, he introduced himself neither as a Judahite nor as an Israelite/Son of Israel. He used the name of a specific deity, Yhwh, in his introduction, as well. The question then arises of why he would use such an unexpected designation for himself.

The data in the above passages depict a world where the Hebrews were known by peoples like the Egyptians and Philistines, but the Sons of Israel were less familiar. The Egyptians knew of Hebrews long before the Sons of Israel entered into their land, and the Philistines knew that they were at war with Hebrews but needed someone to identify the specific kingdom to them. These sailors, who lived far from the Syrian Desert, understood the reference to these people. The specific tribe of Hebrews Jonah came from likely would not have been meaningful.

The sailors also seemed to know of Yhwh, though Jonah had already explained that he had been fleeing this god of his. Like in Yhwh's first revelation to Pharaoh in Exodus 5, Jonah tied together Yhwh to his people, the Hebrews.

The language of the Bible

Since the Bible presented the Hebrews as a super-ethnic group that included the Sons of Israel, this situation must have influenced Ben Sira's grandson's use of the adjective to refer to the language of scripture. More precisely he said that difficulty arose from translating those things "uttered" in "Hebrew fashion" ἑβραϊστὶ *Hebraïsti* (Sir *Prologue*). One could say that as a Greek, perhaps he was over-simplifying the ethnic situation, just like the Egyptians and Philistines and Jonah's sailors, and meant, in fact, the language of Israel or Judah. This grandson, however, was a son of Israel and had access to the Hebrew scriptures, so we cannot believe that he would be capable of this confusion. Hence, if the translator of Ben Sira understood clearly what a Hebrew *person* was, then his appellation of the language points to Hebrew as a language that coincides with this super-ethnic group that included the Sons of Israel.

We know from the Bible itself that people were speaking local, ethnic languages, like Judahite and Aramaic; Hebrew belonged to none of these people-groups and to all of them. Hebrew functioned as a lingua franca, likely never spoken in everyday discourse, but certainly written. Hebrew was the desert *fuṣḥa* to the Judahite, Aramaic, etc. *'ammiyya*. This written language united the disparate groups around not just a common literary language that represented the various desert-dwelling, nomadic, Hebrew peoples, but the language of scripture. For the Egyptians and Philistines, therefore, the Sons of Israel were speaking one of the languages belonging to the "Hebrews." Those modes of speech were closely enough related that Egyptians and Philistines could identify one as "Hebrew."

This evidence leads to the conclusion that literary Hebrew was a broadly-inclusive language and was not exclusive to the children of Israel. It thus paralleled Yhwh's self-introduction to Pharaoh as

God of the Hebrews. Neither Yhwh nor the language of his speech belonged to Israel alone, but both deity and tongue included this tribe within a larger group. Furthermore, scripture belonged to this larger group, as well.

The Tanak supposes that some neighboring nations, most clearly the Egyptians, looked down upon the Hebrews, yet Yhwh chose to identify specifically with them. This identification elevated opposition against the foreign powers of the time. That Ben Sira's grandson called the language of the story "Hebrew" continued the tradition of relating the revelation to these rejected peoples.

While Yhwh chose to reveal himself exclusively to the Sons of Israel at Sinai, the story of the revelation was recorded in a language accessible to all the pastoral Eberite peoples of the Syrian Desert—not of the big cities but of the nomads who inhabited the region and whom the great powers shunned. Those who called Abram, the first one named "the Hebrew," as their father, received this story of revelation in a language that was not "theirs" but extended an invitation to them to be included as Yhwh's people.

Jonah: Do What He Says, Not What He Does

V. Rev. Fr. Marc Boulos

Recently, I had the opportunity to present the book of Jonah to a group of college youth. I was late for the lecture, so I called ahead to instruct the students to read the book aloud to each other and discuss. When I arrived, I asked everyone to share their observations. Universally, each responded that the first part of the book made sense and "fit" with their understanding of Jonah as a paschal figure; but that the last chapter was confusing, because, as one student put it, in that section, "Jonah wasn't very prophetical." Grinning, I explained that although Jonah was a prophet, he was as wicked in chapters one, two, and three as he was in the last. They were unable to hear this in the story, I continued, because their ears were muffled by theology. Jonah was the antagonist in the book, bearing no resemblance to Jesus Christ in the New Testament, except, perhaps, as an evil twin.

The students' confused reaction to the story of Jonah highlights a critical deficiency in popular Christian theological formulae. For the college youth, Jonah's mistakes were less important than his repentance and personal triumph. Even when confronted with Jonah's fatuous behavior in chapter four, the assumption of triumph made it almost impossible for them to connect the dots.

Preconceived notions of death and resurrection, sin and repentance, and, by extension, despair and hope, cripple our ability to hear the teaching of Jonah. These formulae are modeled after a common lie: someone stumbles, makes a comeback, and everything is ok in the end. This paradigm is a lie, because for most of the population of the world (those who are "offline," so to speak) there are no comebacks, no escapes from judgment, and no rays of hope. Entire communities live and die in abject misery. Whether under the boot of a tyrant, afflicted by war, or subsisting in poverty, the more we trust in our own triumph, the dimmer their prospects become.

The seductive power of non-scriptural death and resurrection models stems from our theological preoccupation with the security and comfort of the individual, real or psychological. We bristle at any teaching that undermines this comfort or the certainty of our victory. In place of the specific hope proposed by Scripture, we peddle a false hope, blind to the destruction caused by our pursuit of happiness.

From the beginning of the book of Jonah until its very end, the prophet sought his own comfort, actively working against God: his rejection of the word's mission, the pretense of his so-called "prayer of repentance," the burden placed on God to redeem the city, the prophet's sense of entitlement, and finally, his firm stance, that the extermination of an entire population, including the lowly animals, was preferable to his own discomfort—all these expose Jonah's impressive hypocrisy. This hypocrisy amplifies the agency and self-sufficiency of the word of the Lord. Throughout the book, Nineveh's hope lies not in the prophet, but in the power of the word itself, which can save an entire city from destruction, even when preached on the lips of a rebellious, hypocritical and self-serving prophet.

The word of the Lord

The first and most striking element of the story is the immediacy and primacy of the word's agency:

> The word of the Lord came to Jonah the son of Amittai saying, "Arise, go to Nineveh the great city and cry against it, for their wickedness has come up before me. (Jonah 1:1-2).

The phrase, "the word of the Lord came to Jonah," appears only twice in the entire book. Both occurrences are painful, and the absence of a third is menacing. Painful, the first time, because of Jonah's boldfaced rejection of a direct command from the Lord. Unbearable in the second instance, because gifted a second chance, Jonah persists in his rebellion. Menacing, finally, in its absence from chapter four, since at the end of the book, it is still not clear that Jonah has repented. Should the word appear again, it will be for the last time, since there are no third chances in the Bible. Ignoring all of this, theologians impose a "sin and repentance" paradigm on the story, misreading Jonah's adventure with the fish as a conversion experience, as though his being cast into the sea was a redemptive trial. On the contrary, "The Lord hurled a great wind on the sea" (Jonah 1:4) not to redeem Jonah, but to complete a specific and deliberate mission. The best way to explain, not only the storm, but the desperate rowing of the sailors and the episode in the belly of the fish, is by way of a contemporary example.

Looking around a room full of confused college students, I asked those present if anyone had ever played a real-time strategy game. In such games, the player broods over a live action map. The mission, almost always, is to move the game's characters from a starting position on the map to a specified destination. As the main player progresses, these characters get pulled off course, forcing the player to click the mouse frantically, dragging his or her units back on course toward the goal. Sometimes the player uses obstacles to redirect their character, for example, a storm. They might use other units to destroy or redirect objects, like a boat or a car. Finally, in some games, you can even use strange creatures to pick up your character to get it back on course. Hopefully, you are beginning to see the point: the storm, the subversion of the sailors' rowing and the fish are all elements in a game that the word of the Lord—the main player—uses to get Jonah back on route to his assigned destination on the map. The entire incident has nothing to do with Jonah's self-reflection or supposed repentance. All that matters to the main player is the mission of the game. In this sense, Jonah's prayer borders on total irrelevance, save its value as a literary device.

The agency of the word

Considering his low threshold for discomfort, evidenced in chapter four, the first half of Jonah's prayer exaggerates his predicament. In the depths of the sea, all the while in the Lord's care, Jonah exclaims, "I have been expelled from your sight. Nevertheless, I will look again toward your holy temple'" (Jonah 2:4). This statement is problematic, since the word of the Lord has been with Jonah from the beginning of chapter one, and even now carries him to his assigned destination. "No," Jonah, you have not been expelled, you are being sent, and even now, "the word is very near you; it is in your mouth and in your heart so that you may obey it." (Deut 30:14). If the word is indeed near, to what temple does Jonah supposedly look? It is also noteworthy that the prophet, whom we expect to carry the word to Nineveh, is himself *being carried* by the word.

At the end of the prayer, the Lord asks the fish to vomit—yes, literally, vomit or spew—the prophet up onto dry land for round two of mission one:

> Now the word of the Lord came to Jonah the second time, saying, "Arise, go to Nineveh the great city and proclaim to it the proclamation which I am going to tell you (Jonah 3:1-2).

At last, "Jonah arose and went to Nineveh according to the word of the Lord," (Jonah 3:3) but then something extraordinary happened. Jonah spoke the assigned word, and immediately, *at the first hearing,* "the people of Nineveh believed in God; and they called a fast and put on sackcloth from the greatest to the least of them" (Jonah 3:5). Then, without Jonah's help, the word of the Lord—the primary agent in the story—moved ahead on its own to visit the king of Nineveh, who, like his people (and strikingly, unlike Jonah) repented immediately. Where the prophet was dragged to his duty kicking and screaming after multiple visits from the word, all of Nineveh, from the least to the greatest, both man and beast, repented willingly, again, *at the first hearing*. This positive reaction is foreshadowed by the sailors, who, though they worshipped other gods, chose obedience to the word of the Lord in 1:14, despite their fear of retribution:

> Then they called on the Lord and said, "We earnestly pray, O Lord, do not let us perish on account of this man's life and do not put innocent blood on us; for You, O Lord, have done as You have pleased." So they picked up Jonah, threw him into the sea, and the sea stopped its raging (Jonah 1:14-15).

When the Lord manipulated the "game map" causing a great wind, the sailors struggled to find a way out of danger without throwing Jonah overboard. Though, at this point in the story, the reader understands that God is working to change Jonah's direction (literally, not symbolically) the characters in the story do not. For the sailors, tossing Jonah into the sea during a storm meant his certain death. None of them wanted Jonah to die, but unlike the prophet, they chose to trust in the Lord. It is as though everyone in the story, save the prophet himself, is ready to obey the word Jonah was sent to proclaim.

King, prophet and city

The reaction of the King to the word's agency is notable. In the Book of Jonah, you have familiar biblical characters (king, city, and prophet) acting in unfamiliar ways. In Scripture, a king normally operates as negative function. Here, in Jonah, he seems almost heroic. Not only does he submit to the word when it reaches him, but in accordance with the precepts of the Law, he includes, "beast, herd, and flock," is his proclamation. Both man and beast are to be covered in sackcloth, from the least to the greatest, and man is ordered to call upon God earnestly, so that each man might turn from his wicked way and violence, so that all the inhabitants of the land, including the animals, might be spared. "Whoever is righteous," we read in Proverbs, "has regard for the life of his beast, but the mercy of the wicked is cruel." (Prov 12:10)

Here, it is worth mentioning that Nineveh, located in Upper Mesopotamia, sits on the east bank of the Tigris River. That a king and a people from this region would behave this way lends credibility to Fr. Paul's thesis in *The Rise of Scripture.*

The pouting prophet

Jonah's refusal to turn from his wickedness is as impressive as the King's repentance. No sooner had Nineveh turned, than Jonah became angry. From his perspective, the salvation of Nineveh made his obedience to the commandment pointless:

> Please Lord, was not this what I said while I was still in my own country? Therefore in order to forestall this I fled to Tarshish, for I knew that You are a gracious and compassionate God, slow to anger and abundant in lovingkindness, and one who relents concerning calamity (Jonah 4:2).

The mercy of the wicked is indeed cruel. In carrying out his duty to preach the word for the sake of an untaught people, while the sailors prayed for his survival, Jonah hoped for Nineveh's destruction, if only to make the task worth his time. But who, Jonah, is wasting whose time? How many times was God forced to ask you to go to Nineveh? How much time was lost dragging you across the map? The sailors fought wind and sea for you. Even the fish, a simple animal, answered the Lord's command to assist you. Everyone is willing to help you, to carry you, and to spare your life, Jonah, even as you show no regard for life. Not only would you have preferred the death of Nineveh, but when you did not get your way, you begged God for your own death:

> Therefore now, O Lord, please take my life from me, for death is better to me than life (Jonah 4:3).

Here, Jonah's rejection of life, like his rejection of the word's directive in chapter one, illustrates his betrayal of the specific hope proposed in the story. The word of the Lord is given to safeguard life in totality, of which man, let alone Jonah, is only a small part. Not only does this life include people from other cities and other lands, but everything that is found in the land, both plants and animals. In contrast, Jonah hopes only for and in himself. As readers, we buy into the lie of Jonah's "prayer of repentance," because we, like the prophet, hope not in the word of the Lord for *its* purpose, but in ourselves for *our purposes*. In this way, our "death and resurrection" and "sin and repentance" interpretations forgo the lesson of the text. Instead of preaching this lesson, we amplify and peddle the prophet's sin of self-entitlement. Jonah, the Lord asks, "Do you have good reason to be angry?"

More than anyone in the story, and by his own admission, Jonah benefitted from the grace and compassion of God, who is slow to anger, abundant in lovingkindness, and relents concerning calamity. Willfully seeking and readily accepting this kindness for himself, the same Jonah pouts when kindness and mercy to others causes him mild inconvenience. Holding out for the people's destruction, Jonah sought a comfortable place in the shade, outside the city. There is no small irony here: the word Jonah, in Hebrew, means "dove", a symbol of peace and respite from God's wrath. (Genesis 8:11)

Pauline grace and the Plant

When trying to explain Pauline grace to parishioners and students, almost always, someone asks me why they should do anything at all if their deeds do not matter in the first place. Setting aside Paul's deeper point, that we must fulfill our duty without receiving credit or personal benefit, I usually begin my answer by challenging the assumption that there must always be a reason for necessary actions. When you are hungry, do you need a reason to put food in your mouth? No. When it comes to our own needs, we act on impulse, without reason. The Bible demands that we show the same courtesy to others. By means of its commandment, it trains us to care for the needs of others on impulse. More importantly, it is the commandment itself, not the disciple, that holds agency and deserves credit for the deed. The story of the Lord's plant illustrates this point.

Jonah showed compassion for a living thing that served his needs but cared nothing for the life of an entire city. In contrast, throughout the entire story, God labored *against* Jonah to save a people whom he created with his own hands, by the sweat of his own brow. Unlike Jonah, the Lord has good reason to be angry. God did all the work, stands to lose the most, and is the only one who cares for Nineveh. It is God, not Jonah, who deserves credit for their repentance and salvation. Again, the Lord asks Jonah, "Do you have a good reason to be angry?"

Conclusion

I have argued that preconceived theological models for redemption, resurrection, and hope blind us to the genuine hope proposed in Scripture, which applies not to the individual, but to the totality of the Lord's creation, "living things both small and great" (Ps 102). When our theology wrongly interprets Jonah as a model of repentance, we either ignore or find ourselves confused by his hypocrisy. Worse, we teach our confused students to embrace this hypocrisy. When we make Jonah our protagonist, we ignore the agency of the word in the story in order to glorify a hypocrite, whose hope is rooted in the destruction of others. In this way, we are worse than Jonah, who, once restored to his mission, and despite his abhorrent behavior, faithfully pronounced the words that God commanded him to speak, verbatim:

> Yet forty days and Nineveh will be overthrown (Jonah 3:4).

It is we, not Jonah, who by our theology, add false words of human hope and triumph to the Lord's decree, abandoning the most vulnerable among us to that cruel, abusive, and merciless tyrant: our own comfort.

Earlier in the story, when the poor, kindhearted sailors were trying to figure out which god they had so angered as to threaten their ship, they cast lots, and the lot fell upon Jonah. When asked about the cause of the storm, his occupation, his origins, and so on, Jonah boasted "I am a Hebrew, and I fear the Lord God of heaven who made the sea and the dry land" (Jonah 1:9). It is an odd statement at this point in the story, since Jonah, who claims to acknowledge that God made both the sea and the land, still behaves as though he can escape the Lord by means of the sea. More interesting, however, is the irrelevance of the prophet's identity. Its only value in the story is to demonstrate that it has no value at all. Whoever Jonah is, wherever he comes from, and however he rebels has no bearing whatsoever on the efficacy of the word. It is the word that is the main player in the game. It is the word that holds all agency. It is the word to which all credit is due. It is the word, Matthew will explain much later, that is the only sign afforded the prophet. Jonah need only speak this word, as directed, and we, together with the Ninevites, need only obey:

Then Jesus spoke to the crowds and to His disciples, saying: 'The scribes and the Pharisees have seated themselves in the chair of Moses; therefore all that they tell you, do and observe, but do not do according to their deeds; for they say things and do not do them' (Matt 23:1-3).

Hard, Fat and Dull Hearts: The Function of Divinely Induced Obduracy in Exodus 4-14, Isaiah 6 and Matthew 13

V. Rev. Dr. J. Sergius Halvorsen

For the contemporary reader, scripture seems to say that man both has, and does not have, free will. From the sin of the first parents in Genesis to the sin of Ananias and Sapphira in Acts, there are any number of instances of people making bad decisions; committing sins and disobeying the commandments of God. Instances of people choosing to violate God's commandments tend to support the idea that human beings are conscious, free-willed agents. Some contemporary Christians feel compelled to embrace an idea of free will even more enthusiastically in order to correct for the (real or imagined) influence of the doctrine of divine predestination and the frightful notion that human beings are mere automata that have been set in motion by God to mindlessly dance their way to a predetermined location in either heaven or hell. For a contemporary reader with a robust notion of free will, the places in scripture that speak of God hardening someone's heart can be very difficult. This paper examines the function of divinely induced obduracy in Exodus 4-14 and in Isaiah 6 as well as how the passage from Isaiah is used in Matthew 13.

In Exodus 5-10 there are over two dozen references to a hardening of Pharaoh's heart. Scott Langston, in his diachronic study of the use of the Exodus motif, notes, "In both early Christian and Islamic discourse the hardening of Pharaoh's heart continued to be understood in terms of disobedience."[1] Origen provides one of the first accounts of how these texts were drawn into a debate regarding free will, and Cesarius of Arles notes that the Manicheans used the image of Pharaoh's divinely hardened heart as an argument against the Old Testament.[2] Since the Reformation any number of debates have arisen over free will and predestination, one of the most well-known being that between Luther and Erasmus.[3] The image of Pharaoh's hard heart was used by Confederate leaders during the American Civil War to describe the northern opposition to secession, and it was used as recently as 2001 by a columnist in Zimbabwe who likened President Mugabe's intransigence to Pharaoh's hardened heart.[4] The narrative of Exodus 1-20 is central to Jewish and Christian traditions and God's hardening of Pharaoh's heart is a uniquely captivating element of that story.

Pharaoh, the King of Egypt, is an outsider, an enemy and oppressor of God's people who not only made their lives "bitter with hard service" but also commanded the midwives to kill the male Hebrew children (Exod 1:14, 16). The brutality that Moses witnessed of an Egyptian taskmaster beating a Hebrew was the direct result of Pharaoh's command to oppress the Hebrews with hard labor (Exod 2:11). When God first calls Moses, God says,

> I have seen the affliction of my people who are in Egypt and have heard their cry because of their taskmasters; I know their sufferings and I have come down to deliver them out of the hand of the Egyptians, and to bring them up out of that land to a good and broad land, a land flowing with milk and honey, to the place of the

---

[1] Scott M. Langston, *Exodus Through the Centuries*, (Oxford: Blackwell Publishing, 2006), 85.
[2] Langston, *Exodus Through the Centuries*, op. cit *On First Principles* 3.1.7-14, 86.
[3] Langston, *Exodus*, 87.
[4] Langston, *Exodus*, 88.

Canaanites, the Hittites, the Amorites, the Per'izzites, the Hivites, and the Jeb'usites. (Exod 3:7-8)

Egyptian acts of injustice against God's people are the stated reason for the Exodus, and Pharaoh, the King of Egypt, is the personification of Egypt's injustice. Pharaoh has chosen to oppress God's people long before there is any discussion of hardening hearts. In other words, Pharaoh is not an innocent bystander; he's not some well-intentioned person who happens to be the unfortunate recipient of a divinely hardened heart. Pharaoh is not a neutral character whose free will has been divinely abrogated.[5] In his analysis of divine hardening of hearts in Isaiah, John McLaughlin notes that God hardens the hearts of those who have already committed injustice.[6] The point of hardening the hearts of those who do wicked deeds has nothing to do with free will, per se. Divine hardening of the heart of the wicked functions in the narrative in the same way that a surveillance camera functions in crime drama. The camera catches the perpetrator in the act, and "hardening" the record in such a way that the villain cannot deny his evil deed. In Exodus, Pharaoh has already committed injustice, he has already done something worthy of divine punishment, so the divine hardening of heart is not a loss of free will.

In Exodus, and throughout scripture, Pharaoh is the personification of the unjust king who oppresses God's people

---

[5] A sympathetic attitude toward the character of Pharaoh in Exodus is comparable to a sympathetic attitude towards the swine in the accounts of Jesus's healing of the demoniacs in the synoptic gospels. Nobody who eats pork or has a fondness for pigs wants to drown a perfectly good herd of swine, but in scripture swine function as an unclean abomination that are potentially harmful. For the contemporary reader, the swine are equivalent to a field of opium poppies or a meth lab; things that should be destroyed to protect others from harm.

[6] John L. McLaughlin, "Their Hearts Were Hardened: The Use of Isaiah 6,9-10 in the Book of Isaiah" *Biblica* 75, no. 1 (1994): 6.

subject to divine punishment.⁷ Pharaoh is the enemy of God's people, the obstacle to God's will. Echoes of this divine hardening of the heart, or spirit, of the gentile outsiders are seen in Deuteronomy when God hardens the spirit of Sihon the King of Heshbon (Deut 2:30) and in Joshua when God hardens the hearts of all the kings so that they would not make peace with Israel but would go to battle "in order that they should be utterly destroyed, and receive no mercy but be exterminated as the Lord commanded Moses" (Josh 11:20). However, in Isaiah it is no longer the gentile, outsiders who are caught in the act of wickedness. Now it is God's people who are caught in the act of doing the kind of wickedness that previously was done by Pharaoh. The Lord tells the prophet,

> Go, and say to this people: "Hear and hear, but do not understand; see and see, but do not perceive." Make the heart of this people fat, and their ears heavy, and shut their eyes; lest they see with their eyes, and hear with their ears, and understand with their hearts, and turn and be healed. (Isa 6:9-10)

Like the divine hardening of Pharaoh's heart in Exodus, there is a harsh quality to the message that might evoke a certain kind of outrage in the contemporary reader. God is doing something to the people that makes them incapable of understanding, repenting and being healed. While it may seem like an abrogation of free-will, it is not. The people of Israel had already rejected God and disobeyed God's commandments in manifold ways. John McLaughlin observes, "[D]ivine hardening takes place so that the people may not repent, which implies they have actually done something of which to repent."⁸ Like Pharaoh, the people of Israel have been caught in the act, their wickedness frozen not in

---

7 Augustine argues that God's hardening of Pharaoh's heart is divine punishment for Pharaoh's treatment of God's people. Langston, *Exodus*, 86.
8 McLaughlin, "Their Hearts," 6.

surveillance camera footage, but in the eyes of the God who delivered them from slavery in Egypt.

God's word in Isaiah is all the more scathing inasmuch as it echoes God's hardening of Pharaoh's heart in Exodus, and the hardenings in Deuteronomy and Joshua. What is striking here is that God is now acting against his own people in a way that he had heretofore only acted against the outsider. It is as if God is now saying to his people, "Because of the injustice and suffering that you are bringing upon the widow and the orphan, and because of your worship of false gods, you are no better than the Egyptians that oppressed your fathers or any of the other gentiles."

Francis Landy defines Isaiah 6:9-10 as the metapoetics of the book, "in other words a statement of the book's own status as poetry. It is a key to how to read or not to read the book, to the author's intentions, and to the primal encounter, whether one of opposition or of congruity, between the prophet and God."[9] The divine hardening—or fattening—of the hearts of the people, the "catching them in the act," such that they cannot evade God's justice might be initially shocking to pious sensibilities. Walter Brueggemann summarizes it this way:

> The intention of the decree of Yahweh is that Judah and Jerusalem should be narcoticized so that they will not be healed. God wills an unhealed people! This is not what we might expect, but of course prophetic assertion is most often not what is expected. This is indeed a countermessage, countering official religious assumptions that God always wills good.[10]

---

[9] Francis Landy, "Paradoxes of Prophetic Language in Isaiah" in *The One Who Reads May Run: Essays in honor of Edgar W. Conrad* ed. Roland Boer, Michael Carden & Julie Kelso, (New York: T&T Clark International, 2012), 30.

[10] Walter Brueggemann, *Isaiah 1-39* (Louisville: Westminster John Knox Press, 1998) 61.

For the time being, God wills that the wicked should be frozen under the harsh lights of divine justice. In fact, the hardening of hearts in Isaiah should be scandalous. It is meant to stun the reader into a reverent silence before a God who is willing to apply the same chastisement to the chosen people as God had applied to the wicked outsider. God's treatment of the wicked insider lays the groundwork for a much deeper and more authentic spirituality. McLaughlin notes that this inability for repentance, this being caught in the act, demands a much deeper response, "The people themselves are not able to turn to God in order to seek forgiveness and salvation and therefore they call upon God to take the initiative in restoring their covenantal relationship."[11] If one is incapable of repenting on one's own, and requires God's action to make repentance and reconciliation possible, then one is much more likely to understand that repentance is a gift from God. Ironically, a divine hardening of the heart prevents one from a more diabolical form of pride in which one congratulates oneself for being intelligent and pious enough to figure out how to repent. According to Isaiah, even when one does repent, the glory is not due to the penitent, but the glory is due to God who has made repentance possible. In this way the divine hardenings in Exodus and Isaiah are remarkably similar in that they both ultimately lead to God being glorified.

However, in Isaiah, unlike the armies of Pharaoh in Exodus, the people of Israel are not condemned to total annihilation. After criticizing those who look to the Egyptian armies with their horses, chariots and horsemen for salvation, (Isa 31:1) Isaiah speaks of the redemption of Israel and "a king who will reign in

---

11 McLaughlin, "Their Hearts," 17.

righteousness" (Isa 32:1). In these days there will be a reversal, or undoing, of the hardening that God calls for in chapter 6.[12]

> Then the eyes of those who see will not be closed, and the ears of those who hear will hearken. The mind of the rash will have good judgment, and the tongue of the stammerers will speak readily and distinctly. The fool will no more be called noble, nor the knave said to be honorable. (Isa 32:3-5)

In Isaiah, God proclaims that authentic repentance—clear sight, sharp hearing, good judgment, and right speech—cannot be the result of human cleverness or self-righteous piety. Human beings cannot take responsibility for their repentance any more than a mere mortal can take responsibility for the reign of the divinely appointed king.[13] Repentance and reconciliation are solely a gift from God.

God's action in Isaiah 6:9-10 is a divine initiative for human repentance. While the divinely imposed fat heart, the heavy ears and shut eyes prevent the people from turning and being healed, the overall function of divinely imposed obduracy is to prevent the individual from thinking that he or she can do anything apart from God's mercy. Another way to put this would be through a creative reading of verse 10b.

> Make the heart of this people fat, and their ears heavy, and shut their eyes; lest they ***think they can*** see with their eyes, and hear with their ears, and understand with their hearts, and turn and be healed ***by their own power.***

As many commentators note, the narrative of Isaiah does not provide much opportunity for repentance. Fr. Paul Tarazi

---

12 Mc. Laughlin, "Their Hearts," 18.
13 This particular comparison is remarkably difficult to understand within the context of a 21st century democratic government, when people take immense pride in electing their chosen candidate.

observes, "The purpose [of Isaiah's mission] was not to convince [the people of Israel] to change their ways; it was only to show them the justice of the Lord's decision to punish them!"[14] However, the book of Isaiah interprets the defeat and exile of Israel in a way that is instructive for people who are no longer in the same geopolitical drama. Francis Landy notes, "If the primary audience was meant to be baffled by the vision, subsequent readers, who had before them the entire book, were intended to understand it."[15] Isaiah 6:9-10 provides the reader, or hearer, with a unique opportunity to interpret his or her own situation in terms of God's previous action.

The authors of the New Testament "repurpose" Isaiah 6:9-10 in a number of ways. All three of the Synoptic Gospels refer to Isaiah 6:9-10 in the context of Jesus's telling of the parable of the sower. In all three instances, the reference to Isaiah is part of Jesus's response to the disciples's questioning.[16] In Luke the disciples ask what the parable of the sower meant, (Luke 8:9) and in Mark they ask more generally, "concerning the parables" (Mark 4:10). But in Matthew they ask Jesus "why do you speak to them in parables." In Mark and Luke, Jesus alludes to the text of Isaiah, but in Matthew, Jesus explicitly refers to Isaiah,[17]

> To you it has been given to know the secrets of the kingdom of heaven, but to them it has not been given. For to him who has will more be given, and he will have abundance; but from him who has not, even what he has will be taken away. This is why I speak to them in parables, because seeing they do not see, and hearing they

---

14 Paul Nadim Tarazi, *The Chrysostom Bible, Isaiah: A Commentary* (St. Paul: OCABS Press, 2013), 76.
15 Landy, "Paradoxes," 28.
16 Matt 13:1-23; Mark 4:1-20; Luke 8:1-15.
17 "This is the only example where a Matthean fulfillment quotation is uttered by Jesus himself." Craig A. Evans, *To See and Not Perceive: Isaiah 6.9-10 in Early Jewish and Christian Interpretation*, JSOT v.64 (Sheffield: Sheffield Academic, 1989), 110.

do not hear, nor do they understand. With them indeed is fulfilled the prophecy of Isaiah which says: "You shall indeed hear but never understand, and you shall indeed see but never perceive. For this people's heart has grown dull, and their ears are heavy of hearing, and their eyes they have closed, lest they should perceive with their eyes, and hear with their ears, and understand with their heart, and turn for me to heal them." But blessed are your eyes, for they see, and your ears, for they hear. Truly, I say to you, many prophets and righteous men longed to see what you see, and did not see it, and to hear what you hear, and did not hear it. (Matt 13:11-17)

Perhaps the most obvious exegetical challenge to this text from Matthew is the potential for self-righteous misinterpretation. If one focuses narrowly on this text, it is possible to fall into the trap of thinking that the hearers—those to whom it has been given to know the secrets of the kingdom of heaven—are vastly superior to the outsiders, those who see but don't see, and hearing don't hear. However, this would be a catastrophic misreading. Perhaps the disciples have been given to know the secrets of the kingdom of heaven, but it does not appear to have done them much good. In Matthew 15, shortly after being told that he has been allowed to know the secrets of the kingdom of heaven, Peter asks Jesus to explain another parable and Jesus wonders, "Are you also still without understanding?" (Matt 15:15-6) There is also Jesus's stunning rebuke of Peter: "get behind me Satan" (Matt 16:23). So clearly, the disciples and the hearers of scripture are still far from perfect even though they have been given to know the secrets of the kingdom. The continuing fallibility of those who "have been given to know" is seen most clearly in the betrayal, denial and faithlessness of the disciples during the passion narrative. Clearly, Jesus's use of Isaiah 6:9-10 in Matthew is not meant to lead the hearer into self-righteousness. Yet, how does one make sense of the insider/outsider dynamic that Jesus sets up so clearly in terms of those who have been given to know the secrets of the kingdom and those who see yet do not see and hear yet do not understand?

Commenting on Isaiah 6:9-10 Francis Landy notes, "The secret is a temptation, since once [the hearers] know that there is a secret hidden in the words they will attempt to unveil it."[18] In Matthew 13 something similar is going on with the parable of the sower, and the subsequent discussion between Jesus and the disciples. The hearer of this text is given a chance to listen in on a private discussion between Jesus and his disciples. A "discourse overheard" is a powerful rhetorical strategy to gain the attention of the hearers because it plays on innate human curiosity. If we overhear a conversation where someone says to someone else, "Listen, this is for your ears only…" the instinctive reaction is to eavesdrop all the more eagerly, because everyone wants to know a secret; everyone wants to be part of the privileged in-group. It is also interesting to note that in Matthew 13:10-17 the outsiders—the ones to whom Jesus speaks in parables—are never clearly defined. The disciples ask Jesus why he speaks to "them" in parables, and Jesus responds that knowing the secrets of the kingdom have been given to "you" but not to "them."

Contextually, the outsiders would be the "great crowds" that had gathered to hear Jesus teach (Matt 13:2) but still, crowds are notably generic. Those to whom it has not been given to know the secrets of heaven are not specifically the Pharisees, nor any of Jesus's notable opponents. It is also important to note that as soon as one hears Matthew 13:1-23, as soon as one is made privy to Jesus's "insider teaching," he or she is no longer a member of the ignorant crowd, but someone who has been privileged to hear the "secrets of the kingdom." So, on one level, Isaiah 6:9-10 has a purely rhetorical function in Matthew. It sets up the rhetorical context of a "discourse overheard" in order to gain more attentive hearing from the reader or listener. Whenever we hear that someone is going to reveal something secret to a select group, it is

---

18 Landy, "Paradoxes," 34.

human nature to want to overhear the discourse directed towards the select group.

However, there is greater complexity to Matthew's use of Isaiah 6:9-10. While a self-righteous interpretation of the text is impermissible, Matthew uses the tendency towards self-righteousness as a lure to snare the hearer. As soon as the hearer is enticed to listen in on a "discourse overheard," in order to be part of the "in group," the hearer is treated to what appears to be a delicious helping of *schadenfreude*. Not only does Jesus say that "they" neither hear nor understand, but he goes on to quote Isaiah fully: dull hearts, heavy ears, closed eyes. And then Jesus really heaps it on when he says, "But blessed are your eyes, for they see, and your ears, for they hear. Truly, I say to you, many prophets and righteous men longed to see what you see, and did not see it, and to hear what you hear, and did not hear it." At this point, the hearer is probably really feeling good about himself, "I thank you Lord that you did not make me like that ignorant crowd, hearing and not hearing, seeing and not seeing." However, Jesus pulls the rug out from underneath our pharisaical feet when he says, "Hear then the parable of the sower."

If I am indeed so blessed, and so honored to hear and see what the prophets and righteous men longed to see, and if I am so enlightened as to not have a dull heart and eyes and ears, then why do I need to listen to Jesus's explanation at all? My ignorance of the parable's meaning and my desire to hear the explanation of the parable actually are a stark reminder of my own ignorance. To say that someone is blessed to hear and understand before he has heard and understood is a persuasive use of prolepsis. It is like telling the smoker about how wise and smart he is for quitting, and talking about the pathetic masses who are ignorant of the dangers of tobacco, and going on to praise the smoker for achieving something truly remarkable and healthy…all while he is still smoking a cigarette. The praise for the hearer is entirely proleptic, it is praise for something that has yet to occur, and as such functions as a powerful strategy for persuasion. So, the thoughtful hearer of Matthew 13 realizes that he is, in fact, very much part of the crowd that does not yet understand.

However, one may still wonder how Jesus's teaching is supposed to function among the broader public, the nations whom Jesus later commands the hearer to teach and baptize (Matt 28:19-20). Mark Achtemeier summarizes the question, "If Jesus's use of parables is a response to the dullness of his listeners, a key question for understanding the passage will be how that response is supposed to function: What does Jesus intend the parables to do for (or to!) his audience?"[19] Once the hearer recognizes that he is, in some important ways, part of the ignorant crowd, he is also given some insider information into the meaning of the parable. Jesus explains that it is all about the spreading of the word of God, and that the different soils are the different kinds of hearers, most of which do not yield fruit. A common approach to Jesus's explanation is for the hearer to ask, "Well then, which soil am I?" This is not a particularly helpful approach, since one can either be the good soil, or one of the bad soils. To identify with the good soil—and for that matter, to self-identify with any of the "good guys" in scripture—is normally a recipe for pride and self-righteousness. However, to identify with the poor soil—an interpretation that is much more in line with Jesus's call to repent for the kingdom of heaven is at hand (Matt 4:17)—is also problematic, since it creates a very difficult image conflict. If I am bad soil, how do I become good soil? Yes, there are ways to till up bad soil, or fertilize it, and improve its suitability, but this parable (unlike Jesus's parable in Luke 13) does not say anything about soil improvement. A much better exegetical approach is to consider that Jesus is commanding us to be the "prodigal sower"

---

19 Mark P. Achtemeier, "Matthew 13:1-23." Interpretation 44, no. 1: 61-65 (1990) 61.

who goes out and sows the seed of the Word of God on all soils, and keeps doing so, no matter how some efforts might fail. The parable of the sower is not about soils, it is about sowing. The parable is meant to persuade the hearer to step into the shoes of Isaiah, the one who is commanded to go out and preach to a non-understanding people. Having been blessed with the explanation of the parable, we are now commissioned to minister to, serve and even die for, the people who have not heard and understood. In this way the overall message of Matt 13:1-23 conforms well to the overall trajectory of Isaiah which Fr. Tarazi describes as the three act structure of Isaiah: "(1) Israel's disobedience leads to (2) its punishment in the form of its people being scattered among the nations, which in turn results in (3) the gathering of the nations together with the redeemed of Israel"[20] To hear God's message is to be scattered, so that God may, in his time, gather his faithful along with the nations.

Commenting on Matthew 13, Mark Achtemeier observes, "The text lends more support to the hypothesis that the parables were intended to cause blindness and deafness among the crowds."[21] One of the most nettlesome problems facing people who have attempted to follow the God of Abraham, Isaac and Jacob, the Father of our Lord and Savior Jesus Christ, is the hiddenness of God. This rebellious sentiment reaches its horrifying climax in Jesus's passion:

> Those who passed by derided him, wagging their heads and saying, "You who would destroy the temple and build it in three days, save yourself! If you are the Son of God, come down from the cross." So also the chief priests, with the scribes and elders, mocked him, saying, "He saved others; he cannot save himself. He is the King of Israel; let him come down now from the cross, and we will believe

---

20 Tarazi, *Isaiah*, 33.
21 Achtemeier, "Matthew 13:1-23," 62.

in him. He trusts in God; let God deliver him now, if he desires him; for he said, "I am the Son of God."'" (Matt 27:39-43)

In the 2017 film by Nathan Jacobs, "Becoming Truly Human," a young woman speaks regretfully about how she lost the Christian faith of her childhood. She says, "I'm sad because I want to believe there is something but there is nothing showing me that there is....When you die you just go in a box and you're done....I want to personally see for myself the hardcore evidence." In the face of such heartbreaking testimony, one is tempted to ponder the seeming irony of a deity who not only ascends into heaven after his death and resurrection, but who also seems to cloak his teaching in parables. One feels a strong affinity for the disciples who are eager to hear Jesus speaking plainly and not in figures (John 16.29).

As to the apparent contradiction of a God who comes into the world to save the lost, but who at times seems to be so obscure, it is important to note the role that idolatry has played and continues to play. Speaking about the messianic reign of the king that will open eyes and ears, bringing understanding, Isaiah says in that in that day everyone shall cast away the idols of silver and gold "which your hands have sinfully made for you" (Isa 31:7). Before Jesus, the people of Israel ceaselessly struggled with the temptation to fashion and worship idols and false gods. But here it must be noted that the great sin of idolatry is not necessarily the reverence for an object. Rather, it is the sin of worshipping a god of one's own creation; being obedient to a god who commands only what I want. Idolatry, at its heart, is blasphemy: it is making oneself into a god, or into the maker of gods. It is interesting to note the parallels between the Psalmist's description of idols, and the sinful people of Israel whose hearts are hardened by God.

> They have mouths, but do not speak;
> eyes, but do not see.

> They have ears, but do not hear;
> noses, but do not smell.
> They have hands, but do not feel;
> feet, but do not walk;
> and they do not make a sound in their throat.
> Those who make them are like them;
> so are all who trust in them. (Ps 115:5-8)

The final verse is striking in how it connects with Isaiah 6:9-10. Those who worship deaf dumb and blind idols are themselves made deaf dumb and blind.

Jesus's rebuke against Peter, (Matt 16:23) Peter's ultimate betrayal of Jesus, and the scattering of the other disciples at Jesus's passion reveal that the disciples were people with dull hearts, heavy ears and closed eyes. They saw in Jesus what they wanted to see: a military, political messiah who would use worldly force to beat the worldly powers, and most important of all, would then allow Peter and the others to enjoy the worldly success and wealth of their oppressors. It could be said that the disciples made an idol out of Jesus, worshipping the messiah of their imaginations, which was little more than worshipping themselves. Mark Achtemaier, commenting on Jesus use of Isaiah 6:9-10 notes "Jesus' aim is not to cause blindness in his hearers but rather to illumine a previously existing condition of blindness of which they are unaware."[22]

The God of Abraham, Isaac and Jacob, the Father of Jesus the Christ is always, in some ways hidden, and those of us who confess faith in this God, are always in some ways blind and deaf because of our idolatry. As was the case for Peter and the other disciples, this idolatry is particularly nefarious when we call that idol "Jesus" but in fact worship a messiah of our own imagination that commands us to do exactly as we please. In the end, from the perspective of finite, sinful human beings standing before the

---

22 Achtemeier, "Matthew 13:1-23," 62.

infinite, perfect God, perhaps there is never a "plain speaking" of the Word of God. Like children learning new concepts in math and science, where the truth might initially appear incomprehensible or contradictory, perhaps the Word of God is always obscure and difficult to comprehend for us. Maybe the desire for a simple, straightforward, non-challenging word from God is merely the desire of a sinful and adulterous nation. Instead, as we struggle to hear and understand God's Word, we are continuously reminded that our hearts are fat, our ears are heavy and our eyes are closed. Ben Witherington notes, "Jesus is unveiling apocalyptic secrets about the coming of God's eschatological reign. To understand such mysteries requires close attention and an open heart."[23] Perhaps God's most precious gift of sight and hearing is the wisdom to know just how blind and deaf we truly are.

---

[23] Ben Witherington III, "Jesus the Sage and His Provocative Parables" in *Jesus and the Scriptures: Problems, Passages and Patterns*, ed. Tobias Hagerland (London: Bloomsbury T&T Clark, 2016), 170.

Stones Rolled and Rolled Away: Kerygmatic Structures in Mark 15:40-16:8

Rev. Duane M. Johnson

It was in the year 2000 that a parishioner asked me about what we were to understand as being the real ending of Mark's gospel. He had taken note that the earliest complete manuscripts of Mark ended with 16:8, and that this gospel's later manuscript history included what could be regarded to two other endings, a "shorter ending" and a "longer ending."

The former consists of what is most likely an editorial expansion of 16:8, an addition specifically intended to let any hearer of Mark know that these same women who had originally fled from the tomb in a trembling, astonished state and kept silent about what happened there eventually reported it to "Peter and those with him." It tersely tells of how "Jesus himself sent out by means of them, from east to west, the sacred and imperishable proclamation of eternal salvation." (RSV)

The so-called "longer ending," versified as 16:9-20, and in some instances placed right after the "shorter ending," is a post-resurrectional filling-out of the original Markan ending whose content appears to owe not a little to the Lukan tradition. The parishioner was concerned to know if the abruptness of the original Markan ending was evidence that an original "longer ending" had perhaps been lost. I explained to him that, given the complete lack of evidence even to suggest such a possibility, it was better to focus on what Mark's original ending was doing. In other words, if the author of Mark had intended his gospel to end that way, then it was worthwhile to ask ourselves why.

If anything, this parishioner was simply reading Mark with historically literal eyes: if those women had fled from the tomb too frightened to say anything about what they had experienced there, first how could Mark have written about it, and second, how could we in turn know about it? Because he was reading the text as a piece of historical reporting, he naturally wanted to know what was going on here when Mark ends his story by telling us "And when they went out, they fled from the tomb, for trembling and astonishment had taken hold of them, and they did not say anything to anyone because they were afraid."

I remember drawing his attention to what preceded 16:8, to the way the abruptness of the ending functioned as a way for the author to emphasize exactly what was announced at the tomb "very early on the first day of the week." At the time I assured my parishioner that Mark's literary instincts must have included a unique combination of the evangelistic and the dramatic, that a story as important and as life-changing as the one he is telling us would be better served when told in ways we would be less likely to forget. It was my way of saying that Mark—as the text stood in its original form—was exactly what the author intended and that there was no reason to consider it otherwise. Corollary to this way of understanding the text *as we have it* is the proposition that, if Mark is telling us everything he wanted us to know, then what are we supposed to know?

In order to know what Mark is telling us, it is necessary that we hear the whole story. Thus, the basic storytelling structure of beginning-middle-ending cannot be ignored, and how those elements fit together coherently, is urgently relevant when it comes to understanding the gospel attributed to Mark. The canonical text is *his text*, that is, it contains the whole of his authoritative communication to us. We therefore have no liberty to understand its elements and details in isolation from each other because to hear with faith means to hear all of what a text contains.

In this paper I am focusing on some features contained in the way Mark's gospel ends.[1] These are found in the passage 15:40 through 16:8, from the point when we hear that the Galilean women had watched the crucifixion at a distance, to when the text ends with three of them fleeing from the tomb of Jesus "because trembling and astonishment had taken hold of them." The passage contains what are two conversations. The first is the three-way exchange between Joseph of Arimathea, Pilate, and his centurion. The second is what occurs among the three women at the tomb and when they encounter there a certain "young man" who has something to tell them.

I am presenting these two conversations as "kerygmatic structures," and here I only seek to highlight their kerygmatic function. I am understanding kerygmatic function in terms of the ways in which the two conversations are (1) dramatically linked and have parallel aspects, and (2) how their relative sequencing is the way in which Mark structures his gospel and brings his *kērygma*, that is, his proclamatory narrative to its memorable conclusion.

Mark has a gospel attributed to him. We know that this word – gospel - is used in different ways. For example, we have four canonical gospel books in the New Testament, and, as whole books, each is a different Jesus-narrative. Each aims to tell the story of who Jesus is and what his death and resurrection are supposed to mean. Thus, one sense of the word "gospel" refers to what has become a *de facto* genre, a type of literature or a written form characterized by certain elements. Matthew, Mark, Luke, and John are four different "gospel" accounts of Jesus, but each

---

[1] All translations from the Greek New Testament or Septuagint, unless otherwise indicated, are my own.

one differs slightly in the way that it presents what it means to believe in Jesus as the Christ. This is what brings us to the other, broader New Testamental/Pauline sense of the word, i.e. that the gospel is—in what amounts to the most basic sense of the word—the proclaimed message that Jesus is the Christ. The easiest way to understand the difference between these two meanings of the word gospel is to think of the former kind of messaging as consisting of the formal, canonically authorized account of Jesus and his life, while the latter is the spoken/taught/lived, etc. form of belief in Jesus.

But how any story ends depends very much on how it begins. If the gospel of Mark is the story of Jesus, and, since our English word "gospel" is explained as meaning "good news," why would this word—aside from what would be plain semantic associations—be chosen as the designation for the Christian good-news message? After all, Christians did not invent the word εὐαγγέλιον. It had a pre-Christian usage in the Greco-Roman literary world, and this usage—such as we encounter it in the sources of antiquity—is consistent enough to provide a clue for its apostolic appropriation.

The Greek word εὐαγγέλιον consists of two elements. The first is the prefix εὐ-, which denotes something good or well, with the clear implication that the proximity of anything εὐ is beneficial. The second element is the noun ἀγγέλιον, which refers to a message sent to inform others. Up to a point we can understand why this Greek word, transmitted to us via its Anglo-Saxon rendering as *gospel*, should come to mean "good news" or "glad tidings," but those phrases are too anodyne to capture the thrust of the classical contexts in which it occurs. Specifically, when the word εὐαγγέλιον is used by Cicero, Plutarch, or Josephus, it is to denote a military victory: how an emperor, a king, a regional military governor, or even a chieftain has triumphed over his enemies. Thus, the εὐαγγέλιον is the declaration of victory, the announcement that the king is still the king and remains the king by virtue of triumphing over his enemies. When the εὐαγγέλιον arrives either by herald or dispatch, the understanding is that the people receiving the news are to celebrate it joyfully and with gladness because it is the notice that *their* enemy has been defeated.

This was the imperial Roman context for the official, that is, both the written and the spoken use of the word εὐαγγέλιον. Thus, it had a highly specific valence, a semantic resonance, such that when people in the first century A.D. heard the word that, when used in Christian literature, we habitually translate as "gospel," it would have had non-gospel associations. I assume that Mark would have known such things, and therefore he constructed his account of Jesus as εὐαγγέλιον, as the proclamation of how God has defeated his enemies.

English translations of Mark keep it simple. The RSV renders 1:1-3 with a straightforward faithfulness to the Greek vocabulary and syntax:

> The beginning of the gospel of Jesus Christ, the Son of God.
> As it is written in Isaiah the prophet,
> "Behold, I send my messenger before thy face,
> who shall prepare thy way; the voice of one crying in the wilderness:
> Prepare the way of the Lord, make his paths straight—"

When rendered in this fashion, it is easy to reckon Mark 1:1 as functioning like a title. The phrase ἀρχὴ τοῦ εὐαγγελίου Ἰησοῦ Χριστοῦ is thus a statement announcing that what you are hearing is the beginning (ἀρχή) of what is going to be the written εὐαγγέλιον about Jesus who is the Christ. The word ἀρχή is translated in the RSV et al. as a nominative-case noun and presented as such ("The beginning of..."), but what if the word is operating textually in a more verbal fashion?

This possibility hinges on reading 1:2-3 as being what forms the content of the verbal action inherent in the noun. The phrase καθὼς γέγραπται is what notifies us of this content, and, more specifically, that the content of everything that Mark is about to tell us can be traced back prophetically to what the book of Isaiah declares. It is thus that I translate Mark 1:1-3 in this way:

> ¹The victory declaration about Jesus as the Christ, as the son of God, begins
> ²just as it stands written in the prophet Isaiah:
> "Look and see, I am sending my messenger ahead of your presence, he who will prepare the way for you;
> ³the voice of one crying out in the wilderness,
> 'Make ready that way the Lord will come,
> straighten out his paths.'"

On the one hand, there is the human reality of Jesus, but, on the other hand, and perhaps more importantly, the man Jesus—and what will be claimed about him—was foretold as being what God would will for the sake of our salvation. The claim is that the εὐαγγέλιον Ἰησοῦ Χριστοῦ begins, most properly, with what God himself declares about him by means of his word. The focus here is on Isaiah 40-55, and, more specifically, on the figure of the suffering servant, and thus it is no accident that Mark's composite citation in vv. 2-3 should be attributed to the prophet Isaiah.

The dominant scriptural image throughout the New Testament is that of the Isaianic suffering servant. Everything else in the Old Testament ends up being invoked in one form or another—creation, fall, captivity, exodus, covenant, obedience, and salvation—but, when it comes to the way God's will for our salvation comes to pass, all shall depend on the *impossible necessity* of the person who

> bears our sins, and for us he is made to suffer pain,

and we reckoned him to be distressed, afflicted, and ill-treated.
And he was wounded on account of our sins,
and he has been stricken due to our lawless actions;
our lesson in peace came upon him, by his bruising we have been healed. (Isa 53:4-5)

The four suffering servant songs occur in Isaiah 40-55, in a portion of the book that has come to be known as the "Book of Consolation" due to the way those middle chapters of the book presuppose a context of Babylonian exile: the idea is that these 15 chapters form a scriptural message of "consolation" for the chosen people of God suffering in exile. Isaiah 39 closes with the prophet's blunt pronouncement that, even though God had saved Hezekiah's Jerusalem from the Assyrian menace, the seeds of Judah's demise at the hands of the Babylonians were sown when that same king took the liberty of showing the contents of his kingdom to Babylonian ambassadors. The prophetic word is introduced in Isaiah 40:1-2 with the admonition (RSV):

> Comfort, comfort my people, says your God.
> Speak tenderly to Jerusalem, and cry to her
> that her warfare is ended,
> that her iniquity is pardoned,
> that she has received from the LORD's hand
> double for her sins.

The Septuagint rendering of 40:1 is παρακαλεῖτε παρακαλεῖτε τὸν λαόν μου, λέγει ὁ Θεός. The verb παρακαλεῖν is often translated as "comfort" or "console," and it is used in contexts to render—as needed—the ideas of imploring, exhorting, requesting, or asking for something, but let it be said that the more basic meaning of the word is "to make an appeal to someone." It is with this in mind that I have translated the Septuagint Greek of 40:1-3 in the following fashion to highlight the evangelistic nature of Isaiah's middle section:

> Appeal, oh appeal to my people, says God.

> You priests, speak to the heart of Jerusalem,
> appeal to her, for her humbling is complete,
> her sin has been loosed,
> for she has received from the hand of the Lord double for her sins.
> The voice of him who cries out in the wilderness:
> "Prepare the way (ὁδόν) of the Lord,
> make straight the paths of our God."

The cumulative message is a pure prophetic simplicity: Israel's lack of covenant faithfulness has placed her in exile, that is, far from the presence of God's *mišpaṭ* (the sustaining rule of his righteousness), and how he plans to right the wrong of her situation shall be the direct reflection of his holy will, and, when it happens, it will astound all who hear of it. The following passages outline the gist of what the prophet proclaims:

> For this reason my people shall know my name on that day
> because I am he who speaks.
> I am present like springtime in the mountains,
> like the feet of him who announces (εὐαγγελιζομένου) the glad tidings of peace,
> like he who declares (εὐαγγελιζόμενος) good things,
> for I will make your salvation to be heard, saying,
> "O Zion, your God shall reign as king,"
> because the voice of those who guard over you has been raised up,
> and they shall rejoice together in one voice;
> for their eyes shall see in unison when the Lord will have mercy on Zion.
> Let the desolate places of Jerusalem burst forth with joy,
> because the Lord has had mercy on her,
> and he has rescued Jerusalem.
> And the Lord will reveal his holy arm before all the nations,
> and all the ends of the earth shall see the salvation that comes from our God. (Isa 52:6-10)

> See for yourself, my servant shall understand,
> and he will be exalted, and he will be glorified greatly.

Just as many will be astonished (ἐκστήσονται) at you,
so shall men disparage your appearance,
and likewise the sons of men your glory.
So shall many nations stand in wonder of him,
and kings will keep shut their mouths;
for they to whom nothing was declared about him shall see,
and the ones who did not hear will understand.
Lord, who has believed what we made men hear?
And to whom has the arm of the Lord been revealed? (Isa 52:13-53:1)

For my wishes (βουλαί μου) are not like your wishes,
nor are your ways (ὁδοὶ) like my ways, says the Lord.
But as far away from the earth is the sky,
so too is my way far from your ways,
and your thoughts are distant from mine. (Isa 55:8-9)

What is to note here is the way in which the image of the ὁδός frames Isaiah 40-55. Mark 1:3 is the citation of Isaiah 40:3, the announcement that the ὁδὸς Κυρίου is what shall be prepared, and that the "paths of our God" (τρίβους τοῦ Θεοῦ ἡμῶν) are to be "made straight." After all, if Israel stands in exile, there is only one reason for her condition: she has been unfaithful to the covenant. If it is God himself who is going to act, just as scripture declares him to have done in the Exodus; if the Lord is the universal God who oversees the affairs and actions of all the nations, what is certainly the prophetic vision of the deity; and if God is the only true λυτρούμενος/ῥυσάμενος Hebrew *go'el*) of his people, what the Old Testament asserts from start to finish about how God is the sole redeemer, then how God will do that is foretold in the scriptural word concerning the enigmatic figure of the suffering servant. Salvation is thus only ever a matter of what happens when God "wins," that which constitutes scripturally the true meaning of the Hebrew *yešū'āh*.² It is thus no accident that this middle portion of Isaiah concludes with what we find in the last verses of chapter 55:

> For as the rain or the snow comes down from the sky,
> and it does not return until it has watered the earth,
> and has brought forth things, and has made them to blossom,
> and has given seed to the sower, and thus there is bread for food,
> So too shall be my word (ῥῆμα), whatever goes forth from my mouth,
> It does not return until whatever I have willed is fulfilled,
> and I will furnish your ways (ὁδούς σου), and execute my commandments.
> For you shall go forth in gladness, and in joy will you be taught;
> for the mountains and the hills will exult in joyful expectation of you,
> and all the trees of the field shall hail you with their branches.
> And instead of the shrub there shall arise the cypress,
> and instead of nettle there shall up the myrtle;
> and the only name will be that of the Lord,
> an enduring sign that shall not fail. (Isa 55:10-13)

The prophetic ῥῆμα is the scriptural word of God. If Isaiah 40:3 declares that there shall be the voice of one crying in the wilderness because of what the Lord has planned to do in accordance with what he has devised by his own counsel (40:13-14), then vv. 4-8 tell us that its purpose is so that "all flesh" (πᾶσα σάρξ) might see what will be the Lord's glory on the day when he comes to execute salvation (*yešū'āh*/σωτήριον) not just for Israel but for all the nations:

> Every valley shall be filled, and every mountain and hill will be brought low;

---

2 Paul Nadim Tarazi, *The Chrysostom Bible—Isaiah: A Commentary* (St. Paul: OCABS Press, 2013), 146-158.

and the glory of the Lord will be seen,
and all flesh will see the salvation (σωτήριον) of God,
because the Lord has spoken it (ὅτι Κύριος ἐλάλησε).
The voice of the one who says, "Cry out!"
And I said, What shall I cry out?"
All flesh is grass, and every human glory is as the flower of grass.
The grass withers, and the flower fades away;
but the word of our God (ῥῆμα τοῦ Θεοῦ ἡμῶν) remains for ever.
(Isa 40:4-8)

In order to understand just how Isaiah 40-55 is a "book of consolation" we have to keep in mind the calamitous condition of foreign exile prophesied by Isaiah at the close of chapter 39. If the prophetic word is going to function as a message of consolation for Israel in captivity, then it must be a declaration of what God will one day accomplish in order to end the exile of his people. In other words, the Lord's words will serve as a *consolation* for those who "stand firm/patiently endure" in him (40:31, 49:23, 51:5) by remaining true to the core of the prophetic *appeal*. God's saving actions will be a mixture of him presented as king, warrior, shepherd, and redeemer—images that figure prominently in the scriptural narrative of deliverance *par excellence*, that of the Exodus.

The British biblical scholar Rikki E. Watts proposes that there is an underlying thematic unity between the Exodus tradition and Isaiah, that the latter deliberately framed portions of its message in ways that invoke and/or echo what the book of Exodus tells us about Israel's delivery from bondage in Egypt.[3] The shared schema consists of the sequence *deliverance, journey,* and *arrival* at the place where God is present (ranging from Sinai to Jerusalem/Zion, and encompassing the Jerusalem Above). It is thus possible to think of Deutero-Isaiah as the idea of the Exodus being recycled,

---

3 Rikki E. Watts, *Isaiah's New Exodus in Mark* (Grand Rapids: Baker Academic, 2000), 50, 81-82, 90.

that is, as being appropriated once again in order to cast the Isaianic message of a renewed hope in Israel's salvation in ways deliberately evocative and allusional. Deutero-Isaiah was never supposed to have functioned as a proof (*Beweis*) for what God wishes to communicate to those listening in exile, but rather we have it as a scripturally informed (*schriftgemäß)* cornerstone of the biblical tradition, simultaneously influenced and influencing.

What sets the stage for the closing of Mark's "victory declaration" is the story of Jesus and his messianic reception in Jerusalem, his usurping of the temple and its sacrificial operations, his replacement of the latter with his personal teaching about what God wants from those who would come to sit at his table, the paschal significance of the Last Supper, and finally, his betrayal, trial, and crucifixion. It is a tightly woven narrative that ultimately centers on God's relationship with the temple, that man-made structure built no less from man-hewn stone.

It is thus no accident that when Jesus executes his "cleansing" of the temple in Mark 11:15-17, in effect halting its sacrificial apparatus, that he quotes Isaiah 56:7 in Mark 11:17:

> And he taught and he was saying to them,
> "Does it not stand written, 'My house
> shall be called a house of prayer
> for all the nations?'
> And you have made of it a lair for robbers." (Mark 11:17)

Jesus shuts down the temple and calls not so much for the reform of its operation as he does for its replacement. His teaching is the replacement, and, in classic Old Testament prophetic form, he halts the sacrifice in order to become the sacrifice. What frames the teaching of the tribulations in Mark 13 is the initial prophecy of the temple's physical destruction—how in 13:2 Jesus says that "there will not be one stone left against another (λίθος ἐπὶ λίθον), that will not be torn down," and in 13:31 he seals this vision of human transience by declaring that "The sky and the earth shall pass away, but my words will not pass away."[4]

What should be noted here is the image of the stone, the λίθος, and how it figures in the messaging of Mark's εὐαγγέλιον. It is an obvious symbol of permanent strength and power. Men build cities and houses, temples and palaces, with the hope that they will endure. God, however, by his scriptural word reminds us that neither these structures nor the plans on which they are based are truly durable. What does endure is what the biblical text teaches us. Jesus invades the temple, and within its enclosures he proclaims the lasting validity of God's word while simultaneously pronouncing the passing of what men are want to reckon as permanent.

Beginning in Mark 11, the two scriptural symbols for this Babel-esque impulse in man—this persistent tendency to place worldly ambition over obedience to God—are naturally the Jerusalem temple and the Roman praetorium. These two monumentally stone edifices cooperate in what ends up being the judicial murder of Jesus, and what, by many might estimate, would be the plain and simple end of the story.[5] Jesus dies on the cross, and what

---

[4] There is also the lithic image of the "alabaster jar of ointment of pure nard" with which the woman anoints Jesus when he is at the house of Simon the Leper in Bethany (Mark 14:3-9): she breaks the jar and pours its contents on Jesus both as a prefiguration of his upcoming burial and as an anticipation of the post-burial anointing of Jesus planned by the women who go to his tomb. The woman anoints Jesus in faithful hope (the stone is broken), while the myrrh-bearing women go to anoint him in reverent grief (and encounter what they suppose will be an unmovable stone).

[5] This association is most explicitly developed in John's gospel. The passage 19:12-16 tells of the final decision being made to put Jesus to death, and v. 13 describes the setting for what amounts to the joint judgment against Jesus: "When Pilate heard these words, he brought Jesus out and sat down on the judgment seat at a place called The Pavement (λιθόστρωτον), and in Hebrew Gabbatha." (RSV)

happens on Golgotha is witnessed by some women in Mark 15:40-41:

> And there were also women who were looking on from afar,
> and among them were Mary the Magdalene,
> and Mary the mother of the younger James and of Joses,
> and Salome,
> they who, when he was in the Galilee, had been following him
> and serving him;
> and many other women who had come up along with him to Jerusalem.

This sets the stage for the way in which Mark structures the remainder of his text in terms of two basic settings and the conversations that occur in them. The first centers on the actions of Joseph of Arimathea, and the second tells of what the myrrh-bearing women encounter when they go to the tomb of Jesus. There is also a mirrored reversal of the directions of movement. Mark 15:43-47 begins in Jerusalem and moves to the tomb's location outside of the city, while 16:1-8 begins with movement outside the city toward the tomb and then implies a movement back into the city.

The first setting revolves around the figure of Joseph of Arimathea, who is described in the text as a "noted member of the council" (εὐσχήμων βουλευτής), meaning that he is presumably a member of the Sanhedrin (15:1). We hear that he "was himself also living in expectation of the kingdom of God," and the phrase προσδεχόμενος τὴν βασιλείαν τοῦ θεοῦ suggests, while perhaps not outright discipleship to Jesus as Matthew and John indicate, then at least a more sympathetic attitude toward Jesus than the rest of the council has exhibited.[6]

What is most significant about Mark's identification of Joseph is not so much whatever notability (εὐσχήμων) he may have possessed, but just the mere fact of his belonging to the council (βουλευτής). He may have been "living in anticipation of the kingdom of God," but we are still left with the question of what kind of kingdom was he anticipating. Did he have any idea of what the crucifixion of Jesus was going to signify? Here I would assume that he had no idea at all, but, as a man who most likely entertained some degree of hope about Jesus of Nazareth, all of that anticipation must have been shattered when he received word of the crucifixions underway outside the city gates.

Joseph may have been βουλευτής, a member of the council, but he was not a member of the divine council. This is a *Leitmotiv* running through Deutero-Isaiah: first, that no man is privy to God's will prior to his showing it (40:13-14, 46:11), and second, that the imaginings of mere men are no match for what the Lord devises (55:8-9).[7] In this sense Joseph is no "counselor" (σύμβουλος) of the Lord, and, with his hope condemned to death, there would have been only one thing left to do.

He took courage (τολμήσας) and went before Pilate to ask for the body of Jesus. Joseph thus represents traditional Israel caught up in transition. Knowledgeable of the law and schooled in the

---

[6] The evangelist Luke indicates this more explicitly in his description of Joseph in 23:50-51: καὶ ἰδοὺ ἀνὴρ ὀνόματι Ἰωσὴφ βουλευτὴς ὑπάρχων καὶ ἀνὴρ ἀγαθὸς καὶ δίκαιος — οὗτος οὐκ ἦν συγκατατεθειμένος τῇ βουλῇ καὶ τῇ πράξει αὐτῶν — ἀπὸ Ἁριμαθαίας πόλεως τῶν Ἰουδαίων, ὃς προσεδέχετο τὴν βασιλείαν τοῦ θεοῦ. Cf. the description of the elder Simeon in Luke 2:25 as δίκαιος καὶ εὐλαβὴς προσδεχόμενος τὴν παράκλησιν Ἰσραήλ.

[7] Isaiah 41:21-25 indicates what is necessary for inclusion in the divine council: "say to us, declare to us those future things of the end (τὰ ἐπερχόμενα ἐπ' ἐσχάτου), and we will know that you are gods." (v. 23)

prophets, he had nursed messianic hope in his heart even though Judea was under Roman rule. In addition, Joseph goes to Pilate, who, because he stands for the grim reality of Roman imperial domination, operates symbolically as the embodiment of Israel's stalled messianic hope. He goes to Pilate to collect the body of Jesus, who in turn had embodied—however variously—the renewed immediacy of that hope.

Their conversation, as indicated in Mark 15:42-45, proceeds schematically in this way:

> Joseph: Grant to me the body (σῶμα) of Jesus.
> Pilate: Is he dead?
> **Centurion: Jesus is dead [let the world know that Jesus is dead].**
> Pilate: You may have the body (πτῶμα).
> Joseph: He silently prepares Jesus for burial.

Pilate is the obvious embodiment of Roman rule, and, as the passage opens, Joseph must seek out Pilate if the body of Jesus is to be obtained for burial. Jesus has been crucified and is now most likely dead, but Pilate must verify the latter before the body can be released. Roman punishment must be completed for the sake of Roman rule's continuity.

Mark 15:46 details the steps taken by Joseph to bury Jesus: note that when Pilate releases the "corpse" (πτῶμα) of Jesus to him, the Markan narrative no longer refers either to a σῶμα or a πτῶμα, but simply as "him." Joseph places him in a tomb, "one that had been hewn out of rock (ἐκ πέτρας); and he rolled a stone (λίθος) against the door of the tomb." This first section is set in the remaining hours of Friday. Joseph's movement to the tomb coincides with the setting of the sun. Joseph places the body of Jesus in the tomb, he rolls the stone against the entrance, and entry into the tomb as well as exit from it are blocked. There is no mention of what will happen to the body of Jesus: all is silence with not a word uttered. There is now nothing but what a single stone rolled into place signifies.

Just as the Galilean women were looking on from afar at the crucifixion in Mark 15:40, so too there are the two women (Mary the Magdalene and Mary the mother of Joses) who are witness to Jesus being placed in the tomb. Both 15:40 and 15:47 use the verb θεωρεῖν to describe the matter-of-factness of what the women are seeing. The verb will be used again in 16:4 when the myrrh-bearing women "see that the stone had been rolled away," but from that point on the regular verb form for seeing (ὁρᾶν) is used.

The second conversation forms the heart of what happens at the tomb "very early on the first day of the week…when the sun had risen." It is structured like this:

Women: Where is the body of Jesus?
Young man: He has been raised (i.e. he is alive). Go and tell the others!
Women: They say nothing because he has been raised.

Opposite declarations are at the center of each conversation: in the first, the centurion asserts that **Jesus is dead**; in the second, the young man tells the women that **Jesus has been raised**, that he is in effect alive! Both Joseph of Arimathea and the women went off to tend the body of Jesus, but the results were quite different: Joseph prepared a corpse for burial; the women wished to finish tending to the corpse according to funerary custom but they found no corpse.

Up to a point Joseph and the myrrh-bearing women represent the same frustrated but persistent hope: Joseph rolls a stone in place at the door of the tomb and thus he placed a seal of quiet finality on what had been a wild hope; the women go to the same sealed tomb, but, after worrying about who will roll away the stone and thus allow them access to the body of the crucified messiah in whom they too had hoped, they become witnesses to the unexpected "ways" (ὁδοί) of God. Yet, by way of contrast, their action begins when the sun has risen. The women expect to find the body of Jesus still in the tomb, the large stone blocking the entrance, and no one able to move it. One by one, each of these expectations turns out otherwise: the stone has been rolled away, entrance into the tomb is possible, the body of Jesus is gone, and the young man (νεανίσκος) announces to them what has happened.

The first section ends with the women "seeing where he was laid" (ἐθεώρουν ποῦ τέθειται), that is, they saw where the body of Jesus had been placed; but central to the second section is the young man's indication to the women "see the place where they laid him" (ἴδε ὁ τόπος ὅπου ἔθηκαν αὐτόν). In other words, what was declared as final in the first section is contradicted and fantastically overturned in the second.

Who is the young man dressed in a white robe? While pious tradition is content to regard him as a comely angelic being sent to announce what is—for now, at any rate—not so much the good news as it is the improbable news, there is a more likely literary explanation both for his appearance and what he wears. He is often linked to the νεανίσκος who is mentioned in Mark's account of the arrest in Gethsemane (13:51-52). A "certain young man" who had been following Jesus up to that point flees with the rest of the disciples once Jesus is arrested. He is dressed in nothing but "a linen cloth (σινδών) wrapped around his naked body," a garment that Jesus's arresters are left holding in their hands as the youth fled from the scene. When this figure reappears in 16:5, he sits on the right side of the tomb when the women enter (the opposite of flight); he is "dressed in a white robe," a στολὴ λευκή, that is, what a public herald (κῆρυξ), or, for that matter, what a baptizand might wear, and thus it is a far cry from the coarser funerary wear that Joseph used to wrap the presumably unclothed body of Jesus (15:46); and now, instead of nakedly fleeing, he sits in a position of authority in order to declare that Jesus has been raised and that "he is going before you to the Galilee."

Are these two νεανίσκοι the same character? No, for the simple reason that they function differently. If the first νεανίσκος represents well-intentioned failure (the opposite of the ὑπομονή commended by Isaiah in 40:31, 49:23, and 51:5), then the second νεανίσκος is—in contrast to the earlier necessary image of human vacillation—the declaration of God's power and purpose.

The larger question throughout this paper has been the nature of the relationship between Mark and Isaiah. Did the author of Mark, whom—I would say—we can safely assume was familiar with the Isaiah text, deliberately construct his Jesus narrative by basing it, to greater or lesser degrees, on the figure of the suffering servant, seeing in what the prophet wrote an ancient prophesy now realized in the person of Jesus of Nazareth? To what extent did Isaiah's fragmentary and often elusive portraits of the suffering servant supply a template for Mark in constructing his portrait of Jesus? It is impossible to say with any certainty which text guided which and in what way, but yet it should not matter one way or the other because what does count is the richly oscillating degree of intertextual resonance we can discern between the two.[8] Why quibble over historical, theological, or even exact lines of literary causation when we can discern echoes of Isaiah 53:6-7 in the way Mark describes the silence of Jesus before Pilate in 15:4-5?

> Like sheep we have gone astray; by himself man has gone astray;
> but the Lord has handed him over to our sins,
> and even though he is ill-treated, he opens not his mouth;

---

8 This is what N. T. Wright means when he writes about hearing different texts "with biblically attuned ears" in *How God Became King: The Forgotten Story of the Gospels* (New York City: HarperCollins, 2012), 213-214.

> like a sheep he was led to the slaughter,
> and just as a lamb is silent before the shearer, so too he opens not his mouth.
>
> And Pilate asked him again, saying,
> "Why do you make no answer?
> See the many things of which they are accusing you!"
> And Jesus made no other answer, so that Pilate was left in wonder.
> (Mark 15: 4-5)

The point is rather that, given the range of thematic links between them, the two texts stand in relation to each other in a fully *schriftgemäßig* fashion, that is, it becomes nearly impossible to understand one without reference—at some point—to the other. We can hear and/or read each one separately from the other, but in order to understand each text, it is eventually necessary to refer to the other.

Mark consciously structures the end of his "victory declaration" in the form of these two conversations. The first one announces that Jesus is dead, and the second one is the declaration that the dead and buried Jesus has been raised, that his tomb is empty, and that he has gone before his disciples to the Galilee: the οὐκ ἔστιν ὧδε announced by the young man in the empty tomb in 16:6 is transformed into the ἐκεῖ αὐτὸν ὄψεσθε of 16:7.

And the final troubling detail of 16:8, namely, that "when they went out, they fled from the tomb, for trembling (τρόμος) and astonishment (ἔκστασις) had taken hold of them, and they did not say anything to any one because they were afraid," this can be understood with reference to Deutero-Isaiah. The same word for trembling (τρόμος) occurs in 54:11-14, a long passage filled reference to stones:

> Lowly and outcast, you were not comforted;
> see for yourself, I am preparing carbuncle for your stone,

> and your foundations to be of sapphire,
> and I will make your battlements of jasper,
> and I shall set your gates in crystal stone,
> and your enclosure will be of precious gems;[9]
> and all your sons will be taught by God,
> and your children will live in great peace,
> and in righteousness shall you be built up;
> remove yourself from the unrighteous one, and be not afraid (μὴ φοβηθήσῃ),
> for trembling (τρόμος) will not come near to you. (Isa 54:11-14)

In the same way the term for astonishment (ἔκστασις) appears in Isaiah 52:13-15, the first three verses of the fourth suffering servant poem:

> See for yourself, my servant shall understand,
> and he will be exalted, and he will be glorified greatly.
> Just as many will be astonished (ἐκστήσονται) at you,
> so shall men disparage your appearance,
> and likewise the sons of men your glory.
> So shall many nations stand in wonder of him (θαυμάσονται ἐπ' αὐτῷ),
> and kings will keep shut their mouths;
> for they to whom nothing was declared about him shall see,
> and the ones who did not hear will understand.

If Mark tells us that the myrrh-bearing women fled in this fashion, that "they did not say anything to any one because they were afraid," it is because Mark himself has already told us everything we need to know. The *kērygma* of Mark is complete as its stands.

---

9 Cf. the catalogue of stones that make up the building materials of the New Jerusalem's walls and their foundations in Rev 21:18-21.

The Last Discourse – John 13-17

V. Rev. Timothy Lowe

The Gospel of John is organized around several discourses, that is, several long teaching sections which are unique only to this gospel. The discourses themselves reflect the ongoing issues the Johannine communities are facing both externally within the greater Roman Empire as well as internally with their fellow Jews and their relationship with the synagogue. In many ways, the Gospel of John is an apology of faith over and against the Judaism of its day focusing on the person of Jesus as the long-awaited messiah.

The Last Discourse is the longest of these. A last discourse is not unusual in the Bible as it is a common literary technique as a main figure is facing death. There are examples of Jacob, Moses, Joshua, Samuel, and even Paul in the New Testament.[1] I will examine the content and issues of Jesus's last discourse in the gospel of John, focusing on its pastoral themes as it relates to the context of the emerging post-apostolic community and a blueprint for future leadership in the Johannine communities if they are to survive and be faithful to the gospel of the crucified messiah as they face persecution from within the Roman Empire, excommunication from the synagogues, and divisions within their own communities.

One of the different things with the Gospel of John is that there is no account of the last supper in comparison with the other gospels, no Passover meal and no establishment of a new covenant. What replaces it is the washing of the feet in chapter 13. Hence, we must pay close attention to this seminal chapter and its focus

---

1 Gen 49; Deut 32-33; Josh 24; 1 Sam 12; Acts 20.

and message to the Johannine community at the end of the first century and beginning of the second one.

While the Passover is mentioned as coming, they are gathered together two days beforehand where Jesus announces that his "hour has come to depart out of this world to the Father" and that he has loved his "own to the end" (13:1). The Greek word here is "telos", a word meaning "end" as in reaching a goal or the finality of death. And in this case, the two are the same. This is our context for the last discourse chapters 13-17. This is the overarching rubric to understand them.

In chapter 13, verse 4, Christ symbolically lays aside his garments before he washes the feet of his disciples and we must connect this action with his coming death, the laying aside of his life for them. He then begins to wash his disciples' feet. In the ancient world no male would do this to another male.[2] The job was for slaves, women or children. Hence Peter's objection is not without merit in verse 6 and leads to an important dialogue and a needed message for the Johannine churches.

After Peter's first objection to Christ humiliating himself in such a way, Christ responds with a strange prophetic statement: "What I am doing you do not know now, but afterward you will understand!" (13:7) In other words, the meaning of the symbolic action expressing the content of Christ's coming death on the cross can only be understood after the event and not beforehand. This is clear by Peter's response of rejecting the washing altogether because he does not understand it. Or to put it differently, he cannot know beforehand the full implication of Christ's death on the cross until after the event, until after the first cleansing. Hence

---

2 Charles H. Talbert, *Reading John* (New York: Crossroad Publishing Company, 1992), 191.

it requires an act of trust on his part to be "done unto" and then have the weight of the action on his shoulders.

After Peter's rejection of the washing, Christ says clearly that he must receive it or be cast aside because only through the washing does he have an inheritance. The Greek word is "meros" which reflects the Hebrew word, "helek" and refers to one's personal inheritance from his father, or the Ancient Hebrews and their portion of the land.

Apparently, Peter has a problem of constantly telling Christ what to do whether it be expressed as an act of arrogance (knowing better than the master himself) or piety (not just my feet but my hands and my head as well), it is all the same thing despite calling him Lord. This is important because he is considered the religious leader par excellence, a "type" so to speak and his behavior is constantly being contrasted with that of Christ's in the text. It is one of misguided zeal, grandiose gestures, and narcissism the likes of which is hard to tame.

After the dialogue with Peter and the completion of the act of humiliating service, (loving them to the end to hearken back to verse 1 of our chapter) Christ puts his clothes back on, reclines again and gives them a teaching moment: "Do you understand what I have done to you?" (13:12) The text does not give us their reply, but we know that they are clueless. In the gospel of John no one understands the condescension of love vis-à-vis the arrogance of the human being.

The text squeezes the disciples by confronting them with their own piety: "You call me 'Teacher' and 'Lord,' and rightly so, for that is what I am" (John 13:13). It is at this point that the game is over and the weight of confession of faith is now the sword of Damocles hanging over everyone's head because the issue now becomes one of hearing and doing as students of the master:

"Once you know these things, you will be blessed if you do them" (13:17).

So now the disciples must wash each other's feet as the seminal expression of obedience and love of Christ, as proof that they have an actual inheritance from him, an inheritance of teaching and example as a deposit towards eternal life. I take the text here to mean not disciples in the general broad sense, but specifically relations between the leaders of the churches, for the example must always start there. Bishops and priests, the appointed shepherds, must be committed to this kind of service to each other lest the sheep themselves wander away. If you will, this is basic Christianity 101, the heart of Christ's final hour, the consummation of his teaching and cross. If we fail on this point, the whole thing collapses. This is why the episode of the washing of the feet is, in my opinion, more powerful than the Last Supper accounts and critical to the post-apostolic age until the present time as it expresses the fundamental attitude leaders must have with each other and their common witness to their flocks.

In chapter 13, verse 18, we have a second reference to the coming betrayal of Judas and John's gospel will spend 13 verses on this topic which means it is a key centerpiece like the washing of the feet that needs our close attention. Is it just a stumbling block to be explained, "How could someone from Christ's disciples betray him?" John references it as both something known to Christ and the fulfillment of Scripture and is sharing this knowledge beforehand so they will be prepared and understand the larger picture of his humiliating shameful death and its root causes. The passage is brilliant and has a shocking element as Christ is deeply troubled and testifies generically at the beginning that one of the 12 is going to betray him.

We are all acquainted with the word "testify," or to bear witness and we know it is technical and legal and not just opinion. What is even more odd is John 13:22: "His disciples stared at one another at a loss to know which of them he meant." The point is one of shock and horror. If Christ washing their feet was disturbing enough, now they have a brother betrayer in their midst! And yet Christ tells them beforehand so that they will not be "unmade" by the scandal! So is not this the message? In the larger context of Johannine communities and leadership, the point is that betrayal will constantly be with us and on the same level of handing over Christ to his enemies! Scandal will come from the highest levels of leadership and we should be prepared for such. And we should teach and prepare our people for such as well, and in the gospel of John the source is money/greed/earthly power, pure and simple. No one is safe from the seduction of money, greed and power. This section ends with Judas heading out into the night to do his business, showing his allegiance to the darkness of the evil one, and the text makes it clear that the others still had no idea what was going on around them even though they have been told.

In chapter 13, verse 31, Jesus exclaims: "Now is the Son of Man glorified and God is glorified in him." The movement of the chapter has been one of washing the feet, ushering Judas forward to his appointed task and now the above exclamation. We are all acquainted with the biblical word "glory," the very weight of God's presence as he expresses his power in a victorious conquering of his enemies. And yet where is this "glory" that Christ proclaims is being visibly demonstrated, for glory cannot be hidden? Is it Christ's mere acceptance of the divine plan/will which leads to the cross? Or has the full content and meaning of the cross already been functionally demonstrated in the washing of the feet making the second act of the crucifixion functionally anticlimactic for those of us who have been "done unto"?

While Jesus tells the remaining eleven that he is leaving them and they cannot come with him at this time, he sandwiches this cryptic saying between a key verse:

> A new commandment I give you: Love one another. As I have loved you, so you must love one another. All men will know that you are my disciples if you love one another. (John 13:34-35)

So the glory of Christ is demonstrated in acts of love and these demonstrations of power are now referential as a singular commandment and identifying mark of being his disciple. Again, notice that the emphasis continues to be on the inter-relations of the future leaders. Not only must they humiliatingly serve each other but they must do it out of love without grinding their teeth in the process.

The chapter ends with Peter again trying to preempt the process with his own bold self-assertions: "I will lay down my life for you," he exclaims (John 13:37). Christ is not asking Peter to do anything other than serve his fellow brothers with love, and Peter himself wants to focus on Christ's own coming death. If he cannot die to himself, he will end up denying Christ altogether when put to the test. This is the whole point: "I tell you the truth, before the rooster crows, you will deny me three times!" (John 13:38) Are we the next Judas, the lover of money? Are we the next denier? Are we the next one to reject the washing of the feet? These are questions posed to the Johannine community as they are kicked out of the synagogue and create divisions among themselves, if the historical context is to be believed by current scholars.

Chapter 14 continues the last meal discourse begun in chapter 13 and the break for the new chapter is artificial. The chapter is clustered around a series of three questions from the mouths of Thomas, Philip and Judas (not Iscariot). If we understand the questions, we understand the chapter.

After the final disturbing news of chapter 13, "Where I am going, you cannot follow now, but you will follow later," (John 13:30) Christ tells them not to have troubled hearts over this for he goes to prepare a place for them and thus will return later to gather them (John 14:1). This leads to our first question placed in the mouth of Thomas: "Lord, we don't know where you are going, so how can we know the way?" (John 14:5) Sadly this comes after Christ announces that they know the way, so there is a clash and disconnect. You would think that Christ would repeat his examples of laying aside his garments and washing their feet as betrayal looms and yet the point of Thomas's ignorance is to demonstrate the difficulty of truly accepting the message of the cross and the end of an earthly messiah and an earthly kingdom. One of the quagmires of pastoral work or teaching is the assumption that the hearers and/or students actually understand what you are saying and then believe it. Thomas here does not get anything and that is the point which allows Christ to clarify again who he is and what he actually is doing.

> "I am the way, and the truth, and the life. No one comes to the Father except through me. If you knew me, you would know my Father as well!" (John 14:6-7)

In other words you cannot dismiss the previous chapter once you have been "done unto" by Christ as I am calling it. In fact, Christ gets nastier by following up with the statement: "From now on, you know him and have seen him" (John 14:7).

Philip, not to be undone in stupidity by his counterpart Thomas, responds with, "Lord, show us the Father and that will be enough for us" (John 14:8). This leads into a long monologue of patient discourse: "Don't you know me, Philip, even after I have been among you for such a long time?" (John 14:9) The answer is of course, "no." Speaking as a priest of 35 years, this is most telling because enduring cluelessness is part of our landscape.

We speak and speak and speak. We teach and teach and teach and still our words fall on a lot of deaf ears. Finally, Christ tells Philip to look at the works themselves that he has done as vindication that there is more going on here than empty talk. And here we must hearken back to the previous chapter as the culmination of "his works" in symbolic washing as expression of his consummate love and death on the cross.

What follows now is the whole notion of doing greater works than Christ by asking them in his name since he will now be able to answer prayer just as the Father has answered his requests. If you will, it has taken the aura of a talisman, the magical formula of power for Christian success: "In Jesus's name. In Jesus's name. In Jesus's name." And so the text traps us again because the formula often does not work and thus we stand condemned for our own failure and unbelief! But the corrective comes in the next verse, "If you love me, you will do what I command" (John 14:15). Think back to the previous chapter where Christ gives them a new commandment, which is now repeated.

Having said this, you would think it would be enough, but Christ continues and talks about another lawyer, the Spirit of truth to be with them forever, coming from the Father. This means they will have no excuse whatsoever if they are unbelieving, unknowing, unfruitful and weak. Christ sums his actions up in the phrase: "I will not leave you orphans" (John 14: 18). So the disciples, leaders of the next generation and those beyond have been given the tools to do the job at hand. Therefore, we are all left without excuses, and this is the whole point.

Now notice how the argument circles back around again at the end to the commandments:

> Whoever has my commandments and obeys them, he is the one who loves me. He who loves me will be loved by my Father, and I too will love him and show myself to him. (14:21)

In the end, "the way" is the way of Christ's commandments, so we should not drift too far from them, let alone get excited by any other signs or wonders, as they may in fact be temptations, or at least, distractions.

This means we have come to our last foil with a question from Judas noted as "not Iscariot": "But, Lord, why do you intend to show yourself to us and not to the world?" (14:22) This serves again to emphasize in boring repetition the issue of love of Christ being synonymous with obeying his teaching: "If anyone loves me, he will obey my teaching…he who does not love me will not obey my teaching" (14:24). If this was not enough, Christ claims that these words come directly from the Father so there is no room for discussion or negotiation. Again, reference is made to the coming lawyer, the Holy Spirit, who will remind us of all that has been taught which means that it is singularly an issue of obedience and nothing else.

Verse 29 brings again the technique which we have heard twice previously, "I have told you now before it happens, so that when it does happen you will believe." So, these two chapters which open the last discourse are designed to strengthen our belief in the gospel of the crucified messiah and not be ignorant of the commandments flowing from his side, to use a later Johannine image from chapter 19. Christ closes the chapter with the singular positive reference to the world when all of his work is accomplished: "The cosmos must learn that I love the Father and that I do exactly what my Father has commanded me" (14:31). This means there can be no longer any confusion or misunderstanding about who he is. The meal summarily ends, "Rise now, let us leave from here" (14:31).

Chapter 15 begins a new meditation that is distinct and disconnected from the two previous chapters. There is no departure despite the reference above. It opens with the statement: "I am the true vine and my Father is the gardener." Isaiah 5:1-7 is the clear reference in the background where the vineyard is the rebellious house of Israel which is about to pass through judgment and destruction. This chapter has a clear dimension of judgment for those branches extending from the vine that are not fruitful. They will be cut off by God the Father and thrown into the fire to be burned. Those branches/disciples that are fruitful will be pruned so as to bear more fruit. Without fruitfulness, we are worthless.

What is important is to understand the clear hierarchy in this meditation: God the Father is the gardener; Christ is the vine and the disciples are the branches. It is a hierarchy we saw in the previous chapter as well when Christ says that no one can come to the Father except through him. So, we are connected to God only through Christ and therefore we bear fruit solely by remaining/abiding in him. We can do nothing on our own. This point is repeated twice in verses 4 and 5. Later in verse 7 he references as well, his "words" remaining in the disciples as the key. In verse 10 he further clarifies that they must obey his commandment in order to remain in his love. It should not surprise us that love is primarily expressed as faithfulness to his commandments in view of the biblical Israel's all-encompassing sin of harlotry.

He completes this thought by referencing his personal joy through faithfulness and sharing it with them and thus making it richer and more complete. Finally, they are told again to love each other as he has loved them but then interjects a novel idea found only here:

> I no longer call you servants/slaves, because a servant does not know his Master's business. Instead, I have called you friends, for everything that I learned from my Father I have made known to you. (John 15:15)

In other words, they are given a unique status based on disclosed knowledge that brings with it the burden of mutual love because they share in this knowledge of the teaching of Christ. Again, the focus is on mutual relations within the community and in repeating this point again in verse 17, "This is my command: Love each other," we can surmise elsewhere, e.g., in the epistles of John, that the community was tearing itself apart with strife and disagreements.

John 15:18-25 addresses the issue of rejection and persecution that the disciples will face. The gospel of John lives in a black and white world both within the context of the Roman empire and rejection by the Jewish community. In 3rd generation Christianity, the apparent audience of the gospel of John, Christ still is the epiphany and forerunner in all things:

> If the world hates you, remember it hated me first. If they persecuted me, they will persecute you also. If they obeyed my teaching, they will obey yours as well. (John 15:18-20)

But then there is an odd but key insertion in verse 21: "They will treat you this way because of my name, for they do not know the one who sent me." The case in the gospel of John is that his opponents do not know His Father and that he is not acting in his own name or with his own words. Therefore, they hate both of them. In the gospel of John, it is inconceivable that there could ever be any marriage between the teaching of Christ in the nascent community of believers and the Roman Empire. This would undo all that they knew and understood of the gospel itself and its teaching. John 15:22 says it concisely, "If I had not come and spoken to them, they would not be guilty of sin. Now, however, they have no excuse for their sin."

In the end, Christ concludes that he has been hated without reason but nonetheless as he leaves the earthly community, he will send the Spirit of truth from his father to continue the testimony in future generations. The promise of the coming Spirit and the ongoing teaching are the links between the apostolic witness and all future generations.

Up to this point I have said nothing about the overall unity of the last discourse chapters. A case could be made that they are in fact a patchwork of discourses put together with repetitions of theme and thought so that there is no real literary unity at all. At the end of Chapter 14 when Christ closes and says mealtime is over, let us go from here, the narrative starts all over again. Peter and Thomas ask Christ where he is going in chapters 13 and 14 and then in the chapter 16:5, Jesus says that no one asks him where he is going. All of this is to state that chapter 16 opens up again with the theme of persecution and the cause of the persecution is ignorance of the Father and therefore Christ himself.

But the principle in the gospel is quite simple, since you have been told everything beforehand, you will be prepared for the ensuing persecution (excommunication) and hatred (martyrdom) of the Roman authorities or the misguided zeal of your fellow monotheists, the Jews. All of this is put under the rubric of Christ's imminent departure and so he will no longer be able to protect them. The counterweight though is the promise of the Spirit who will both continue and complete the teaching of Christ as his agent. Just as Jesus was the agent of the Father, so the Spirit will now be the agent of Jesus: "He will take of what is mine and declare it to you" (John 16:14).

What is a constant underlying conviction and belief about the gospel of John is that no one really can understand Jesus until after his resurrection, after his final glorification and the coming of the Spirit. This again puts the squeeze on the community who live post-resurrection and post-Pentecost. The haplessness of the disciples is temporarily excused because Jesus is still with them, but the haplessness of the disciples afterwards, their unbelief and barrenness is inexcusable. The hour of scattering is no longer in play as the peace of Christ; his glorification has conquered the world. Our job is to do the commandments focused solely on the menial tasks of loving service with clarity in understanding the manner in which we share in the "hour" of Christ.

Like many elements of the Gospel of John, chapter 17 has nothing to compare itself with. The entire chapter is a long prayer and can be divided into three parts: Verses 1-8 where Jesus prays for himself, verses 9-24 where he prays for his present disciples and future generations, and verses 25-26 where he restates his work and mission. Similar to the washing of the feet which replaces the episode of the Last Supper and the breaking of bread, this episode replaces the agony in Gethsemane of the Synoptics. The previous chapter ended with the declaration: "Be of good cheer, I have overcome the world" essentially moving us beyond this synoptic point of crisis and submission to the divine plan of suffering.

Chapter 17 opens up with Jesus's declaration, "Father, the hour has come. Glorify your son, that your son may glorify you" (verse 1). Jesus realizes that it is only his father who can make him appear victorious to all and the time has come for that to happen and only then can he in return glorify his father. Jesus declares he has been absolutely faithful to his mission and in verse 5 makes the request to return to his original status:

And now, O Father, glorify me together with yourself, with the glory which I had with you before the world was. (John 17:5)

I am not going to talk now about the "pre-existent" Son, but rather the manner in which Christ assures his disciples of the majesty of God and the comfort and assuredness of the divine plan expressed in the hyperbolic phrase, "before the world was." In other words, no small thing is happening in front of the eyes of the disciples.

In John 17:6, the prayer focuses solely on the disciples as the ones specifically set aside by the Father to receive the "deposit of word" that is the teaching given to them by Jesus as the very words coming from the Father.

The second section begins Jesus's intercession for his disciples. The opening verse, John 17:9, is odd because it states that Jesus is solely praying for those who have been faithful and not for others in the world. It is here that we must remember the larger context of Jesus's departure from them and therefore he can no longer take care of them in the manner his physical presence allowed. So he asks the Father to look after them while they remain in a very hostile world. He does interject a new thought that He will be glorified in them and this hearkens back to verse 1 and glorification happening through faithfulness to the teaching and mission of Christ. It is this common faithfulness to teaching and mission that unity is revealed and experienced as a oneness both with the Father and Jesus his Son and agent. As Christ has faithfully and successfully trained the 12 minus the son of perdition, so now the process must continue forward giving future generations the same assuredness of the original disciples themselves.

So, living according to the deposit of words, means that the disciples are no longer of the world because they have been formed from above: "They are not of the world, just as I am not of the world" (John 17:16). In verse 17, Jesus requests that the Father "sanctify them in truth", that is make them completely holy and set apart by the truth that is the word of the Father.

John 17:18-19 continue the hierarchy of Father to Son, and Son to disciples: "As you sent me into the world, I have also sent them into the world. And for their sakes I sanctify myself, so they also may be sanctified by the truth." So it is in being wholly set aside to the word of truth that the disciples can glorify Christ which according to this gospel will include persecution and hatred from the outside as well as the call to humble service to others.

The focus of John 17:20-23 now changes to future generations, which means everyone gets squeezed by this gospel. So the hierarchy of order continues, Father to Son to first disciples and then subsequent generations. This has nothing to do with the silliness of apostolic succession but is word/teaching based. The unity of verse 21, "That they all may be one, as you, Father are in Me, and I in You" is not a theoretical ontological based unity, but a functional unity of keeping the commandments of God, the obedience of genuine love. While we can acknowledge that the issues of doctrine and creed provide a structure of external unity, in the gospel of John it is the confession that Jesus has come from the Father, revealed the will of the Father and has returned to the Father and provided all things for his community left behind to continue faithfully in the same service and love.

In fact, the unity in John's gospel is so powerful as to be a profound witness to the hostile world because it is not manufactured by human hands. Or to put it another way, the world will recognize in some fashion the truth of the teaching when they see the powerful witness of unity that flows from the well of keeping the commandments in love. So, unity is more about the question of entering into the unity that exists between the Father and his Son Jesus, a unity based upon Jesus's complete and perfect obedience and love of his Father's will.

John 17 ends with a repetition of Jesus's earlier declaration that the world is ignorant of the Father, but he is not. He has now shared this intimate knowledge of God with his disciples, and that they have accepted the fundamental truth about who Jesus is. The unity of the three in love, Father, Son, and disciples is his final petition, and therefore it is his final legacy and warning to us, especially anyone in a leadership position. We are now held responsible for the deposit of teaching and the gift of washing. Yes, we are no longer fighting with fellow Jews over who Jesus is, or being excommunicated from the synagogue and being persecuted by the Roman authorities. Perhaps all theological apologies have largely ended within our church.

What remains for us is the teaching of Christ, focusing on the commandments themselves and our acceptance of humble service to each other, specifically any of us in positions of authority. While the gospel does focus on theological correctness about the person of Jesus, it balances this out with greater emphasis on obedience in love and humility. This is how we are called to witness as a community of faith to the outside world. This is how Jesus is glorified in us and thus how God himself is glorified. If the behavior does not match the confession of faith, then we become fruitless and are worthless branches cut off and burned. Therefore, we must heed the warnings of the last discourse and realize that we have no excuse for faithlessness for we have been "done unto" by Christ in teaching, washing, and the gift of the Holy Spirit, according to the Gospel of John.

Becoming Enlightened: The Healing of the Blind Man at Bethsaida

Rev. Fr. Dustin M. Lyon

Introduction

The pericope of Jesus healing a blind man at Bethsaida is, perhaps, one of the more intriguing healing stories in the Gospel of Mark (8:22-26). When Jesus and his disciples arrive at Bethsaida, a blind man is brought to him (v. 22). However, instead of restoring his sight in the village, Jesus leads him out of the village, puts saliva on his eyes, and lays his hands on him (v. 23). Jesus is able to heal the blind man, but only partially at first. When Jesus asks the man what he sees, he says that he sees people, but they are like walking trees (v. 24). Again, Jesus lays his hands on the man. This time, Jesus is able to successfully heal him so that he sees everything clearly (v. 25). In the end, Jesus tells him to go home, but with the warning to not go back into the village (v. 26).

At worst, it seems that Jesus is a failed healer. At best, it seems he still needs time to learn how to master his craft. But that isn't the only question the text raises. Why would Mark tell us that Jesus had come to Bethsaida, only for him to lead the blind man out of the city? Why does Jesus heal with saliva? What is Mark trying to point out by mentioning that the man sees trees walking around? Is there significance in the second healing touch? And, finally, why would Jesus send this man home, but then specifically tell him not to go back into the village where he most likely makes his home?

This isn't the first healing episode in Mark. Jesus has already healed a paralytic man (2:1-12), a man with a withered hand (3:1-

6), a demoniac in the country of the Gerasenes (5:1-20), Jairus's daughter from death (5:21-24a, 35-43), and a woman with hemorrhages (5:24b-34). What makes this pericope unique, though, is that on the surface Jesus's first attempt doesn't seem successful. Before the blind man is able to see with clarity, Jesus has to reach out and touch him again. As strange as it may seem to modern readers, Mark's account is a tightly woven unit that speaks volumes.

Mark includes this episode in his Gospel for two reasons. The first is to develop the theme of the disciples's ignorance. Time and time again, they had failed to understand both the meaning of the gospel and their mission to carry that gospel into the world—both to the Judean and then the Gentile. They are the true "blind man" who are in need of clear vision. The second reason Mark includes this story is to illustrate how that very same gospel confronts the powers of this world. In this confrontation, Mark shows that only God, not Rome or Caesar, can truly heal our blindness. This is the sign of Israel's renewal—the coming eschaton that the prophets had foretold.

Bethsaida as a reminder of the disciples's blindness

The pericope starts when Jesus and his disciples arrive in Bethsaida. Jesus had set out for this destination earlier (6:45) but didn't reach it. Some historians have identified Bethsaida as the city on the east bank of the Jordan River where it enters the Sea of Galilee,[1] and later renamed Julias by the tetrarch Philip Herod.[2] However, archaeologists have been unable to say whether or not this is the precise location of the miracle. To make the matter

---

[1] Chad Myers, *Binding the Strong Man: A Political Reading of Mark's Story of Jesus* (Maryknoll: Orbis Books, 1988), 240.
[2] Josephus, Antiquitates judaicae XVII, ii, 1.

more complicated, other scholars have suggested different locations.

However, Mark isn't interested in precise historical locations or details. For him, every story, parable and word has a deeper, more mystical meaning. This is to draw the reader into the kingdom of God. Mark is clear about this:

> And when [Jesus] was alone, those who were about him with the twelve asked him concerning the parables. And he said to them, "To you has been given the secret of the kingdom of God, *but for those outside everything is in parables; so that they may indeed see but not perceive, and may indeed hear but not understand*, lest they should turn again, and be forgiven." (Mark 4:10-12 RSV)

Historical details, as interesting as they may be for modern readers, miss the point of what Mark is saying. By beginning the miracle at Bethsaida, Mark is inviting the reader to find a deeper meaning in the village's name.

On the surface level, "Bethsaida" means "House of Fish" or "Fishing House."[3] But on a much deeper level, this reminds the reader of the disciples's original calling. "And Jesus said to them, "Follow me and I will make you become *fishers* of people.""" (1:17 RSV altered). Jesus takes them under his wing, teaches them (4:10-13, 33-34; 7:18b-23), and commissions them to heal, cast out unclean spirits and preach repentance (6:6b-13). The whole world has become a "house of fish" in which the disciples can cast their net.

The connection between fish and the disciples's calling becomes stronger as the disciples struggle to carry out their task. In both the feeding of the five thousand (6:30-44) and the feeding of the four thousand (8:1-10), the disciples are given an opportunity to

---

3 Michael M. Homan, "Bethsaida," EDB 1:174.

truly become *fishers of people*. Though both incidents are set in a deserted place—a *barren* location—Jesus asks *the disciples* to *feed* the people. He wants to them to teach the gospel, but the disciples don't get it.

> But [Jesus] answered them, "You give them something to eat." And [the disciples] said to him, "Shall we go and buy two hundred denarii worth of bread, and give it to them to eat?" (Mark 6:37)

> And his disciples answered him, "How can one feed these men with bread here in the desert? " (Mark 8:4)

The disciples think that Jesus wants them to deal with the physical hunger of the people. But what Jesus really wants, is for them to feed the people in a mystical way. Only when Jesus intervenes are the fishers of people able to "feed" the people with "five loaves and two fish" (6:41), and, in the second account, "a few small fish" (8:7). The fish and bread are metaphorical, though. Jesus makes this clear in a later conversation with his disciples.

> And his disciples answered him, "How can one feed these men with bread here in the desert?" (Mark 8:4)

> And they discussed it with one another, saying, "We have no bread. " And being aware of it, Jesus said to them, "Why do you discuss the fact that you have no bread? Do you not yet perceive or understand? Are your hearts hardened?" (Mark 8:16-17)

> "When I broke the five loaves for the five thousand, how many baskets full of broken pieces did you take up?" They said to him, "Twelve." "And the seven for the four thousand, how many baskets full of broken pieces did you take up?" And they said to him, "Seven." And he said to them, "Do you not yet understand?" (Mark 8:19-21)

Jesus is teaching them that the "fish" they are to feed people with, even when they are in the desert, is the instruction already given to them. Yet, the disciples remain obdurate. As a result, Jesus constantly rebukes them for their lack of understanding (4:10, 13, 41; 6:37, 52; 7:17-18; 8:4, 14-21), and Mark describes their hearts as hardened (6:52; 8:17). To put it another way, the disciples are the blind man, lacking clarity about their role as disciples.

The fact that Bethsaida is more than a historical footnote is corroborated by the fact that Jesus leads the blind man out of Bethsaida right away. The actual location doesn't matter. By taking the man out of the village, Jesus is, in other words, taking this man into the wilderness—a deserted place. This, of course, is no accident. It recalls the feeding of the five thousand and the feeding of the four thousand, both of which had taken place in the desert (6:31-36; 8:4). Away from civilization, it's clear it's the power of God, not human power, that's at work. Jesus is shown to embody God so that here, in the desert, bread and fish are more than just bread and fish. This is a theme that Mark develops even further when Jesus leads the blind man out of Bethsaida.

Taken by the hand into the desert

Jesus takes the man out of the village "by the hand" (Mark 8:23). This is not yet the healing touch the reader expects. The detail is not surprising, since the man was blind, but it's more than a comment about how Jesus guides the blind in unfamiliar surroundings.[4] Throughout his Gospel, Mark has been careful to show that Jesus is the embodiment of the Yhwh, the God of Israel.[5] Like Yhwh, Jesus is called Lord (Mark 1:3b, quoting Isa 40:3), forgives sins (Mark 2:1-12; cf., Exod 34:6-7), shepherds Israel (Mark 6:30-44; cf., Ezek 34:11-15), and walks on the sea (Mark 6:45-52; cf., Job 9:4-11). The wording of our passage continues to show this embodiment through two specific

---

4 Myers, *Binding the Strong Man*, 417.
5 Richard B. Hays, *Reading Backwards: Figural Christology and the Fourfold Gospel Witness* (Waco: Baylor University Press, 2014), 18-28.

scriptural motifs: 1) Yhwh leading his people by the hand, and 2) Yhwh instructing his people in the desert.

Yhwh freed the Hebrews from slavery in Egypt so that he could lead them into the Sinai desert. It is there that God gave them his Torah, making them his people. And God did this "by the hand."[6]

> And Moses said to the people, "Remember this day, in which you came out from Egypt, out of the house of bondage, for by *strength of hand* the LORD brought you out from this place…" (Exod 13:3)

Then, after Israel fell to the Assyrians and Judah to the Babylonians, they were exiled out of the Promised Land. Foreign countries become their "desert." It's here that the prophets wrote about how God would again take them by the hand in order to renew his covenant.

> Behold, the days are coming, says the LORD, when I will make a new covenant with the house of Israel and the house of Judah, not like the covenant which I made with their fathers when *I took them by the hand* to bring them out of the land of Egypt, my covenant which they broke, though I was their husband, says the LORD. (Jer 31:31-32)

> I am the LORD, I have called you in righteousness, *I have taken you by the hand* and kept you; I have given you as a covenant to the people, a light to the nations. (Isa 42:6)

Jesus steps into the role originally played by God in scripture: taking people's hands in the desert to instruct them and make them God's people. It's here, away from the city, that Jesus will take his disciples—represented by the man—by the hand, open their eyes, and heal their blindness. Mark emphasizes this to show that Jesus doesn't do this as a human with special powers, but as

---

6 M. Eugene Boring, *Mark: A Commentary* (Louisville: Westminster John Knox Press, 2006), 233.

the embodiment of Yhwh. The same God who was at work in the Old Testament is still at work looking after his people. Yet, if the people disobey God, he will set them straight. After being led out of the village and touched by Jesus, the man will, at first, only see trees walking around. This is a warning. If the disciples continue to go astray, they will be cut down as trees in the forest.

The warning of walking trees

Mark depicts the healing in two stages. The first stage only results in partial sight. After Jesus puts salvia on the man's eyes and lays his hands on him, he asks the man what he sees. His response is unexpected, "I see people; but they look like trees, walking" (Mark 8:24b altered). This startles many modern readers. Is this to be understood as a failed miracle?

As mentioned above, this pericope is about the blindness of the disciples, who have had their hearts hardened. Like the man, whose vision is now only partly restored, the disciples's vision is partial and distorted. Jesus fears that if they don't learn to see clearly, they will be misled by the religious and political authorities of their day, who are blind themselves.

> And [Jesus] cautioned [the disciples], saying, "Take heed, beware of the leaven of the Pharisees and the leaven of Herod." (Mark 8:15)

It's no secret that Jesus and the Pharisees clashed over how to understand the Law (Mark 7:1-22). In addition, Jesus and Herod didn't see eye-to-eye either (Mark 6:14-29). Both authorities opposed Jesus, and, as such, represent in Mark an old and disobedient Israel that is no longer relevant. Isaiah and Ezekiel had compared such an Israel to a tree that's about to be cut down and burned.

> When [a tree's] boughs are dry, they are broken; women come and make a fire of them. For this is a people without discernment;

therefore he who made them will not have compassion on them, he that formed them will show them no favor. (Isa 27:11)

Therefore thus says the Lord GOD: Like the wood of the vine among the trees of the forest, which I have given to the fire for fuel, so will I give up the inhabitants of Jerusalem. And I will set my face against them; though they escape from the fire, the fire shall yet consume them; and you will know that I am the LORD, when I set my face against them. (Ezek 15:6-7)

Matthew also draws on this imagery and compares the religious and political authorities of Jesus's day to an ill-fated tree.

... and do not presume to say to yourselves, "We have Abraham as our father"; for I tell you, God is able from these stones to raise up children to Abraham. Even now the axe is laid to the root of the trees; every tree therefore that does not bear good fruit is cut down and thrown into the fire. (Matt 3:9-10)

The disciples's partial vision has led them to "see" like the Pharisees and Herod, a group of leaders that are, essentially, trees doomed to be cut down and thrown into the fire. Mark links the disciples's blindness, those that are leading them astray, and "trees, walking." As the prophets had forewarned, the disciples had better start bearing fruit or their fate will be no better off than that of the Jewish authorities.

Other interpreters, such as Orthodox iconographer Jonathan Pageau, have suggested that walking trees are a common motif in the ancient world.[7] In these cases, "walking trees" represent an "uprooted" humanity. If one pulls a tree out of the ground and turns it upside-down, then it looks like a person with wild hair. Of course, an uprooted tree is no longer connected to a nutrient source. To be a "walking tree," then, is to be disconnected and cut

---

[7] Jonathan Pageau, "The Symbolic World," n.p. [cited 29 August 2018]. Online: https://www.youtube.com/user/pageaujonathan/videos.

off. Whether Mark draws from scriptural images of Israel as a tree, or ancient motifs of "walking trees," the idea is the same. It's a warning. The disciples had better heed to the teaching given to them by Jesus. If they don't, their blindness could lead them to their demise. But, because Mark presents his Gospel as shrouded in mystery, he gives us a chance to be touched by Jesus again, take a second look, and have our vision completely cleared.

The second stage of healing

It's the second stage, when Jesus lays his hands on the man's eyes again, that true clarity is given. It bothers contemporary readers that full healing doesn't happen immediately. However, this fits the larger pattern of Mark's Gospel: everything is veiled in secrecy. As mentioned above, Mark set the stage in chapter 4. To the disciples, and the reader, everything is given in secret. Unlike the Gospel of Matthew, Mark doesn't explain the meaning of parables he tells, let alone the deeper meanings. The result is that the disciples, along with the readers, often don't get it. This pattern follows through all the way to the end of Mark's Gospel, which finishes on a strange note.

> And [Mary Magdalene, Mary the mother of James, and Salome] went out and fled from the tomb; for trembling and astonishment had come upon them; and they said nothing to any one, for they were afraid. (Mark 16:8)

Scribes, uncomfortable with this ending, have added two different endings over the centuries: a shorter ending with only one additional verse, and a longer ending with 10 additional verses. However, the original ending, veiled in mystery, is in line with the rest of Mark's Gospel. Upon coming to the end, we are invited to go back and reread it. This time, we have to carefully study and search for the hidden, secret meaning. Jesus laying his hands on the blind man a second time foreshadows both Mark's modus operandi and the ending to his work. A second touch, a second read through the Gospel text, is needed to see the Kingdom of God. But once we have clarity of vision, we must take care not to blind ourselves by turning away from what we learned.

Going home, but not to the village

Now that the blind man is fully healed, Jesus tells him to return home, but not to go back into the village. This seems like a strange command—presumably, the man's home *is* in the village. Again, Mark is inviting us to search for a deeper meaning.

Because healing is a good thing, the man is sent home (*oikos*), presumably, to tell his friends and family all that Jesus had done for him. This is implied from previous passages. The man who was healed by Jesus of an unclean spirit at the Gerasenes was also told to "go home" (*oikos*). In that case, he was specifically told to tell his friends " . . . how much the Lord has done . . . " (Mark 5:19). The disciples are also given a similar command to go into "houses" (*oikos*) and spread the gospel (Mark 6:6b-13). In both cases, to "go home" comes with the responsibility to spread the good news.

However, once healed, one shouldn't return to an old path or be led astray by the Pharisees or Herod (Mark 8:15), and so the man is told not to go into the village. Fr. Paul Tarazi points out that the only other place "village" occurs in the singular is in Mark 11:2.[8] In this instance, it either refers to Jerusalem or a village very near Jerusalem. In either case, it represents the Pharisees and Herod whose center is Jerusalem. This serves a warning in the same manner as the trees had been previously. The disciples are not to follow the path of scriptural Israel, which had disobeyed

---

8 Paul Nadim Tarazi, *The New Testament Introduction, vol 1 - Paul and Mark* (Crestwood: St Vladimir's Seminary Press, 1999), 186.

God and had been exiled. After all, the power of the gospel confronts the powers which had previously enslaved us.

Healing and power

If the overall theme of the pericope has been the blindness of the disciples, the mode of healing demonstrates the power of the gospel message. To heal the blind man, Jesus puts saliva on his eyes and lays his hands on him. To modern ears, this sounds very magical. But cloaked in this description is a demonstration of the power of Jesus's teaching—one that hits at the very heart of the political powers of the day.

Healings, such as this one, were common in the ancient world. In the first century, there were many Hellenistic magicians who performed all sorts of healings, including restoration of sight.[9] The most famous healing place was the Temple of Asclepius in Epidaurus, Greece. People from all over the Mediterranean flocked there to be healed from all sorts of maladies. Typically, the inflicted spent the night in the abaton hoping that the cure for their disease would be revealed to them in their dreams.[10] If a person was healed, a metal votive or small sculpture of the restored body part was dedicated to the god Asclepius. In addition, many patients also dedicated inscriptions at Epidaurus to praise the god who had cured them. One such inscription is remarkably similar to Mark 8.

> Alcetas of Halieis. This blind man saw a dream. It seemed to him that the god came up to him and with his fingers opened his eyes, and that he first saw the trees of the sanctuary. At daybreak he walked out sound (Inscription 18).[11]

---

9 Boring, *Mark*, 232.
10 S.E. Iakovidis, *Mycenae-Epidaurus* (Athens: Ekotike Athenon S.A., 2002), 138-9.
11 Quoted in Adela Yarbro Collins, *Mark: A Commentary* (Hermeneia NT 4; Minneapolis: Fortress Press, 2007), 392.

Though Mark doesn't say that Jesus used his fingers to open the man's eyes, he does mention that Jesus stretched out his hands. And, even though this inscription doesn't mention saliva, it does say that the blind man originally saw trees walking around.

In addition to using the Hellenistic magician as a basis for the healing of the blind man, Mark also had a political motive in mind. Mark's Gospel starts, "The beginning of the *gospel* of Jesus Christ, the Son of God" (1:1). This beginning is a direct confrontation to the Roman authorities.[12] Just a few decades earlier, the empire had been in chaos. Following the death of Julius Caesar, the empire endured a bloody civil war. Finally, with the defeat of Marc Anthony and Cleopatra by Octavian at the battle of Actium in 31 C.E., the empire entered into its "Golden Age." The *Pax Augusta*, the "Peace of Augustus," had begun. Octavian became Augustus Caesar and he was hailed as a cosmic savior and a messiah. Augustus brought stability, security, and economy prosperity to the empire. For the Romans, this was the "gospel."

Augustus began a "divine" dynasty of Roman emperors who not only ensured peace in the empire but had the power of healing. Right before Mark wrote his gospel, the empire again found itself in a civil war.[13] Nero had committed suicide and the empire didn't have a clear successor. This was the "Year of Four Emperors." In the end, Vespasian rose to power, beginning the Flavian dynasty and Rome had a new "savior." However, he needed legitimacy that would solidify his rule in the people's eyes. One such story helped do this:

---

12 N.T. Wright, *Simply Jesus: A New Vision of Who He Was, What He Did, and Why He Matters* (New York: HarperOne, 2011), 29-30.

13 Nancy H. Ramage and Andrew Ramage, *Roman Art: Romulus to Constantine* (3d ed.; Upper Saddle River: Prentice Hall Inc., 2001), 154-6.

Vespasian as yet lacked prestige and a certain divinity, so to speak, since he was an unexpected and still new-made emperor; but these also were given him. A man of the people who was blind, and another who was lame, came to him together as he sat on the tribunal, begging for the help for their disorders which Serapis had promised in a dream; for the god declared that Vespasian would restore the eyes, if he would spit upon them, and give strength to the leg, if he would deign to touch it with his heel. Though he had hardly any faith that this could possibly succeed, and therefore shrank even from making the attempt, he was at last prevailed upon by his friends and tried both things in public before a large crowd; and with success. (Suetonius *Vespasianus* 7.2-3)[14]

The story gives Vespasian the support he needed. Not only was he able to heal the blind, a sure sign that he was the "Son of God" as Caesar Augustus had been, but the god Serapis had predicted Vespasian's magical touch.

This is the same period in which Mark writes about Jesus healing the blind man by spitting in his eyes. And, just as the emperors are hailed as "messiahs" and the "Sons of God," Mark hails Jesus as a "messiah" and a "Son of God" (1:1). Mark sets Jesus up as an alternative to Vespasian and his rule.[15]

In addition, Mark wrote with the prophetic expectation of a new age: through the prophets, God promised to draw Israel, along with all the other nations, to himself as one people of God. The tension between Caesar and Christ becomes even more powerful in this case. For the first century Judean, healing blindness is equated with the release of Israel and Judah from exile and captivity. Only when the blind receive their sight would this new age be ushered in.

---

14 Quoted in Yarbro, *Mark*, 392.
15 Brian J. Incigneri, *The Gospel to the Romans: The Setting and Rhetoric of Mark's Gospel* (Boston: Brill, 2003), 171.

In that day the deaf shall hear the words of a book, and out of their gloom and darkness the eyes of the blind shall see. (Isa 29:18)

Say to those who are of a fearful heart, "Be strong, fear not! Behold, your God will come with vengeance, with the recompense of God. He will come and save you." Then the eyes of the blind shall be opened, and the ears of the deaf unstopped. (Isa 35:4-5)

... the LORD opens the eyes of the blind. The LORD lifts up those who are bowed down; the LORD loves the righteous. (Ps 146:8)

Scholars have pointed out that within first-century Judaism, only God could heal the eyes of the blind.[16] So, Jesus is more than just another person with claims to an imperial throne. Because Jesus has the power of Yhwh himself, it's a sign that God's "golden age" is beginning. By being able to heal blindness, Mark shows that Jesus is the embodiment of the God of Israel, who has the power to bring about Isaiah's vision of a restored and renewed Israel. It's this kingdom that is in direct competition with Rome. Perhaps, Vespasian is a "savior" who has the power to cure blindness, but it's Jesus who brings about the eschatological restoration and new creation.

Conclusion

In telling the story of Jesus healing the blind man at Bethsaida, Mark highlights the disciples's failure to comprehend their calling. Like the Pharisees and Herod, the disciples seem stuck at only understanding the "secrets of the kingdom" on a superficial level. They don't understand that the gospel, which is being taught to them by Jesus, is news of the renewal of Israel, the calling of all nations to God, and the coming of the new age written about by Isaiah and the other prophets. They don't seem to understand this

---

16 Ben Witherington III, *The Gospel of Mark: A Socio-Rhetorical Commentary* (Grand Rapids: William B. Eerdmans Publishing Company, 2001), 239.

gospel is an alternative to the gospel offered to them by Rome. Though the disciples are starting to see, their vision remains cloudy. They only see trees when they should be seeing people.

In many ways, this pericope isn't just about the blindness of the disciples. It's also about our blindness. Like those early readers of Mark's Gospel, we too are being offered an alternative gospel. Politicians, modern medical marvels, technology, and all sorts of social programs promise to usher in a new age. They offer comfort, stability, and prosperity. But Mark reminds us that these gospels can't feed us in the desert. Our sight deceives us. To be cured, we are invited to admit that we only see trees walking around and receive a second healing touch from Jesus.

Bibliography

Boring, M. Eugene. *Mark: A Commentary.* Louisville, KY: Westminster John Knox Press, 2006.

Collins, Adela Yarbro. *Mark: A Commentary.* Vol. 4 of *Hermeneia: A Critical and Historical Commentary on the Bible.* Minneapolis: Fortress Press, 2007.

Freedman, David Noel, ed. *Eerdman's Dictionary of the Bible.* Grand Rapids, MI: Eerdmans, 2000.

Hays, Richard B. *Reading Backwards: Figural Christology and the Fourfold Gospel Witness.* Waco, TX: Baylor University Press, 2014.

Iakovidis, S.E. *Mycenae-Epidaurus.* Athens: Ekotike Athenon S.A., 2002.

Incigneri, Brian J. *The Gospel to the Romans: The Setting and Rhetoric of Mark's Gospel.* Boston: Brill, 2003

Myers, Chad. *Binding the Strong Man: A Political Reading of Mark's Story of Jesus.* Maryknoll, NY: Orbis Books, 1988.

Pageau, Jonathan. "The Symbolic World." No pages. Cited 29 August 2018. Online: https://www.youtube.com/user/pageaujonathan/videos

Ramage, Nancy H. and Andrew Ramage. *Roman Art: Romulus to Constantine*. 3d ed. Upper Saddle River, NJ: Prentice Hall Inc., 2001.

Tarazi, Paul Nadim. *Paul and Mark*. Vol. 1 of *The New Testament: An Introduction*. Crestwood, NY: St Vladimir's Seminary Press, 1999.

Witherington III, Ben. *The Gospel of Mark: A Socio-Rhetorical Commentary*. Grand Rapids, MI: Eerdmans, 2001.

Wright, N.T. Simply Jesus: A New Vision of Who He Was, What He Did, and Why He Matters. New York: HarperOne, 2011.

Biblical Interpretation In Between Science and Worship

Dr. Merja Merras

To be able to define the way of Biblical interpretation during the centuries one has to determine the reason why and when Scripture was written. It is the target the interpreter aspires to, or should be, at least. There have been several attempts to find the answer, but I found most sensible the answer Paul Tarazi has found, namely that the Old Testament[1] was written intentionally in opposition to the Hellenistic cult of deities, heroes and cities which had spread into the Near East with the occupation of Alexander the Great and his successors. The purpose was to strip them of their power in the minds of the people, and to manifest how deities, heroes and kings are futile.[2] The Scripture such as we know it seems not to have been written earlier than in the Hellenistic era, 3rd or 2nd century BCE. Another competing view points to the Persian period (ca. 550-330 BCE). Some stories might have been known before that in oral form, and some even written, though we do not possess any document of it. If there was no Scripture, there could be no interpretation either.

Interpretation in the Greek world

As soon as the Scripture - or at least a part of it, the Torah – was in written form, there came out soon also interpretations, which tried to figure out what does this mean for us who now hear it. The surrounding world was Greek with its own methods of interpretation. The methods applied by Jews and later Christians to their Holy Scriptures had already been highly regarded for a

---

[1] The "Hebrew Bible" is not apt because it omits the tight cohesion of both Testaments.
[2] Paul Nadim Tarazi, *The Rise of Scripture* (St. Paul: OCABS Press, 2017), 33-39; 42-44.

considerable time in the Hellenistic philosophical schools. The Iliad and Odyssey of Homer and Theogony of Hesiod were the basic books of instruction in the gymnasium during the Greek-Hellenistic era. The platonic presupposition of words signifying something other than what is said became a given. *Allegory* was a common method, originated in the divine world, and it transmits a concealed meaning that possesses a deeper sense. In the Hellenistic period, the allegorical method of interpretation was maintained by the leading philosophical schools. Another method was *etymology,* which means determining the meaning of the word from the same letters written elsewhere and was widespread in antiquity. This type of etymological derivation was considered to be an art in antiquity and continued to develop in the later philosophical school.[3]

Philo of Alexandria, born from Jewish parents, enjoyed a comprehensive Greek education, but was well versed also in the Holy Scripture, though through the Septuagint. He was a prominent interpreter of Scripture in the first century CE and his influence is found in Biblical exegesis many centuries forward. He was a follower of the allegorical method. The image of humanity in Philo corresponds to his dualism that speaks of two parts: the carnal as the lower sphere and the spiritual sphere of the *nous* (reason) as the seat of knowledge. Methodologically, Philo prepared the instrument by which the first Christians could interpret the Old Testament in the sense of salvific events which were seen in the life of Jesus Christ. Certainly there were also opponents of the allegorical method. The grammarians Eratosthenes and Aristarch who lived in Alexandria in the 3rd and 2nd centuries BCE founded the *philological-grammatical*

---

3 Henning Graf Reventlow, *History of Biblical Interpretation, vol. 1: From the Old Testament to Origen*, trans. Leo G. Perdue (Atlanta: SBL, 2009), 36.

Merras, Biblical Interpretation

approach to exegesis.[4] This won followers in the Biblical interpretation far to the modern times.

Jewish interpretation

The one who begins to interpret the original written Hebrew text, especially the Torah, must master the Hebrew language. Ezra is regarded by the Jews as the founder of scriptural exegesis (Neh 8). People evidently would not have understood a reading which was completely out of touch with the currents of thought of their time or in conflict with their collective aspirations and traditions. In their attempt to make people understand the reading, Ezra and his associates had to build bridges between the past and the present. Thus the *Midrash* took shape – orally at first. Rabbi Hillel the Great, who was active at the shift of the common era, left a significant legacy with his teachings: "What is hateful to you, do not do to your fellow: this is the whole Torah; the rest is the explanation; go and learn!"[5] He also formulated the seven rules according to which the Biblical text must be explained. One of the methods, *derash* means inquire or seek the comparative midrashic meaning, as given through similar occurrences. One has to hear a certain sentence in comparison with other passages where the same root appears and try to find the connection. The other much used method *qal wachomer* means that from lighter matters one can draw conclusions to heavier matters. G*ezerah shawah* means that two passages with the same lingual parity can be united.[6]

Ancient Jewish exegesis is known from the Qumran scrolls as early as from the 2nd century BCE. The community of Qumran undertook its exegesis by using views and concepts that were

---

4 Reventlow, *History*, 39-45.
5 *The Babylonian Talmud*, 1.tract. Shabbat 31a. Translated by Michael L. Rodkinson. Also an e-book.
6 James Trim and Herbert Bateman IV, "The Seven Rules of Hillel," http://www.yashanet.com/studies/revstudy/hillel.htm.

common in early Judaism. However, these presumably were not actually of a Jewish origin, but rather went back to the Hellenistic way of interpretation, which was the common and only way to deal with texts.

The most flourishing period of midrashic activity was in Palestine in the 3rd and 4th centuries CE when the spiritual life found its only refuge in the Synagogue in which the Torah was taught and sermons delivered. The letters of Scripture were intended as containers ever to be filled with the wine of a good, new vintage. *Halakhah,* representing the religious rules of practical life and *Haggadah,* embodying the philosophy of the generation, existed side by side in a complete unity. *Halakhah* was restricted to seven rules, whereas *Haggadah* had a greater scope. Rabbis began to comment on each other and all discussion was written down. Haggadic Midrash continued to express the ideas, aspirations, hopes, fears and collective thoughts of the Jewish people. It is a fundamental characteristic of Midrash that it keeps its gates open. It is neither categorical nor exclusive, and it never closes a debate. Jewish Midrashic activity found its way also to the writings of Church Fathers: Eusebius, Ephraem Syrus, John Chrysostom, Augustine and Hieronymus.[7]

Bereshit Rabba is a running commentary on Genesis, verse by verse, and often even word by word, whereas the others are homiletic Midrashim and do not comment on each verse separately. The rabbis were not concerned with elucidating the meaning of the Biblical text according to the strictly scientific canons of scholarship, but rather to find in it teachings and messages so as to address the problems which they encountered in

---

7 *Midrash Rabba.* Translated into English with notes, glossary and indices under the editorship of Rabbi Dr. H. Freedman and Maurice Simon with a foreword by Rabbi Dr. I. Epstein. 1. vol. (London: The Soncino Press, First Edition 1939, Third Impression 1961), XIV-XVII, XX-XXI.

their own days. Thus the text was seen through the spectacles of contemporary thought. The story of Jacob and Esau reflects the struggle between Judea and Rome, Esau symbolizing the military might of the Roman Empire and its ruthless conquest of the peoples.[8]

Though rabbis were well acquainted with Hebrew they did not comment on the proper names which were often key to understanding the message of the story. In this they were equal with Christian interpreters. The information hidden in names is almost untapped everywhere. The name Abel, *hebel* in Hebrew, from Gen 4, is also used in Ecclesiastes (1:2) and translated there as *vanity*. The rabbis have not paid attention to this, though they often seek similar expressions in different books of Scripture.[9]

As an example of the way that rabbis find analogies might be the following:

> (Gen 8:8) *And he (Noah) sent a dove…but the dove found no rest*, etc. Rabbi Judah ben Nahman said in the name of Resh Lakish: Had it found a place of rest, it would not have returned. Similarly, *she dwelleth among the nations, she findeth no rest* (Lam 1:3): but had she [the nation] found rest, they would not have returned [to God]. Again, *And among these nations shalt thou have no repose, and there shall be no rest for the sole of thy foot* (Deut 28:65): but had they found it, they would not have returned.[10]

Sometimes rabbis found in Hebrew words similarities that led them to interesting deductions, such as:

> (Gen 9:13) *I have set my bow* (kashti) *in the cloud:* that means, My likeness (kishuthi), something that is comparable to Me (like in

---

8 *Midrash Rabba*, XXVIII.
9 The Abel – *Hebel* connection is explained in *The Rise of Scripture*, p. 162: "The human being is a mere *hebel* (vanishing breath) and should never endeavor to become a king 'like God'".
10 *Midrash Rabba*, 265.

Ezek 1:28). Is that really possible? In truth, [the bow resembles God] as the straw resembles the grain.[11]

The ancient Jewish interpretation strives through haggadic and halakhic interpretation to help hearers to adjust the teaching to their own lives.

The Septuagint in its original form is a typically Jewish translation. Scholars have recognized this in the more recent period. However, this translation originated in a Hellenistic milieu. Rabbinic Judaism rejected the Septuagint due to the fact that the Christians had made the Old Testament Septuagint *their* Scripture and interpreted it according to their own understanding. For instance, the transcendence of God is emphasized in Septuagint. The translation *Pantocrator* (Almighty) differs from the ancient Hebrew title *Sabaoth* (Lord of Hosts) or *Shaddai* (the Almighty), thus making these expressions attune to Greek ears. On the whole, one can observe a development throughout the Septuagint of a spiritualization of the concepts of God. Even so, not all of the human images for God are removed.[12]

Besides the Greek translation there was also an Aramaic translation, Targum. Hebrew was read first in synagogues and then the Greek or/and Aramaic translations followed. The original text always had the supreme authority.

The New Testament written according to the Old

The Old Testament was the Scripture of the Christians before the New Testament came out. The first written documents of the New Testament were the Pauline letters which were written to explain the Old Testament and especially the concept of Messiah

---

11 *Midrash Rabba*, 283.
12 Reventlow, *History*, 21-22.

there. The proclamation of Jesus as the Christ, who was the Messiah expected by the Jews, took place according to Scriptures, it means according to the Old Testament. The conversion of the non-Jews to the Christian faith signified at the same time that they had to accept the Old Testament as authoritative. Paul held in common with those with whom he communicated, from both contemporary Judaism and the early Christian communities, the position that the Scriptures were undeniably addressed, not to the past, but rather to the contemporary hearers. Allegory is found only three times in Pauline letters, 1 Corinthians 9:9; 1 Corinthians 10:1-13 and Galatians 4: 21-31. One Corinthians 10: 1-13 wherein Paul speaks about the behavior of the ancestors in the wilderness, is rather an analogy, which Paul sets forth before the community of Corinth as a warning. This form of the comparison of an episode from the salvation history of the past with the present comes close to a method that one designates typology. *Typology* involves the comparison of events and persons in an earlier time to those in later periods. The best-known Pauline typology is that between Adam, the first man, and Christ, the Adam at the end of time. It is clear that Paul is intimately familiar with the characteristic interpretations of his Hellenistic Jewish environment and that he goes along with their methodological approaches. However, the Torah is for Paul a valid expression of God's will.[13]

Scholars usually begin the interpretation of the New Testament from the Gospels thinking that the words of Jesus written in the Gospels were first, and Paul and other disciples with their explanations are later. Yet we do not possess any authentic words of Jesus. Scholars are used to refer to the Q-source, a collection of Jesus's words, which they thought has been a basis for the gospels. However, we do not possess any manuscript or other documents to prove this theory. On the other hand, all of Jesus's teachings are

---

13 Reventlow, *History*, 61-66. One Thess 4:2-8.

present in the Pauline letters. Therefore, it is sensible to think that the Gospels are crafted from the Pauline teaching using the Old Testament as much as possible. This is especially seen in the Gospels of Mark – the first one - and Matthew. The four Gospels and Acts represent the five books of the Torah, the letter corpus represents the Prophets and the book of Revelation represents the Writings, focused towards the coming world.[14]

Theological visions

The teaching of Scripture continued in churches and synagogues through antiquity and the Middle Ages giving instructions for human behavior and giving consolation and hope for a better future. Its purpose was the same as it was at the time of Ezra. No other radical interpretation was needed. The sermons tried to adapt the message of the passages which were read to the common life of the audience.

However, the Greek style scholarly interpretation of the Bible was carried on by the Church Fathers, well trained in Greek philosophy, as well as among Jewish scholars. Allegory, typology and philological-grammatical methods were continued in those circles as before, and even developed further. Also, the chiastic pattern commonly found in ancient literature was found anew. In the great theological debates of the early centuries there was an intense appeal to Scripture. Biblical interpretation was not separated from the Christian dogma.[15] The fourth gospel, especially, provided content for the speculation about Jesus's being the "Son of God." The Christian creed was formulated

---

14 Paul Nadim Tarazi, *The New Testament: An Introduction, vol.4 Matthew and the Canon* (St Paul: OCABS Press, 2009), 85-106. Tarazi, *Rise*, 383-385.

15 Frances M. Young, "Interpretation of Scripture," in *The Oxford Handbook of Early Christian Studies*, eds. Susan Ashbrook Harvey and David G. Hunter (Oxford: Oxford University Press, 2008), 850.

according to the Biblical vocabulary, the only exception being the word *homoousios* which reflects the influence of Greek philosophy and was used by Gnostics. This word impacted Christian theology, distancing it from the original simple world view. Intentionally or unintentionally Greek philosophy became the basis for Christian theological discussion: *Philosophia ancilla theologiae.*

Scientific studies

The Enlightenment in Europe and in America brought strong growth to the natural sciences and new perspectives in scholarly study. The naturalistic world view questioned religion. The divine origin and the historical authenticity of Scripture were seen with skepticism, though the cultural meaning of the Bible was not questioned. All biblical studies should be critical and further it is not possible to argue that the history of humankind is dependent on greater powers. All mythical explanations should be rejected, and religious text should be explained from natural premises. The result was that notions of Biblical announcement, the Incarnation, God's active function, the reality of metaphysics, etc. vanished from the sight. The historical-critical method was adjusted to explain Scripture. However, the term historical-critical is made by theologians themselves to emphasize that they are "critical." All interpreters made their own view the basis on which this "historical-critical" method was to be understood.

The first "historical-critical" interpretations of the Bible tried to adjust texts and Christianity into the new worldview: there is nothing supernatural and all Biblical stories must be explained being events of the natural history, and Scripture should be studied according to the same historical study as all literature of the Antique. There must be reliable sources to understand what really happened. And yet there might be several different views to interpret the sources. This method did, however, foster the development of new kind of studies. The most powerful was Julius Wellhausen's theory (1883) of how and when the Old Testament had been composed. According to him God's different names in the Old Testament meant that the text is assembled from different layers. This theory of sources ("Quellentheorie")[16] had an influence on scholars many decades after him, even now somewhere, although it has been replaced by new views. The interpreters were eager to write the history of ancient Israel and Judah according to the Biblical data. This *maximalist* view lasted long, but it led to the *minimalist* view in the 1990's. This view argued that we can really know very little about Israel's history, because archeological finds support only a few details, and the stories in the Bible are just stories and there is very little evidence that they reflect real events.[17] Jewish scholars especially resisted this and made the archeological evidence support their views, for archeological finds can be interpreted in different ways.

The study of Israel's past has now moved beyond the maximalist/minimalist debate. In our time the narrative method has gained much favor. Scholars have learned that both the Old and the New Testament contains edifying stories which try to teach us something. This teaching is the most important result we can get from those stories, not the historical accuracy. The storytelling tradition has lived anywhere where people sit around a fireplace in the evenings. Stories should be entertaining, but they had to have elements of the experience of life, too, for the benefit of young people. Stories were written down when there was capacity to do that. Most scholars have until now understood that Scripture should be treated as literature rather than as history. "The Bible's language is not a historical language. It is a language

---

[16] Julius Wellhausen, *Prolegomena zur Geschichte Israels* (Berlin: De Gruyter, 1883).
[17] Thomas L. Thompson, Philip R. Davies, Lester L. Grabbe and Israel Finkelstein are examples of minimalist scholars.

of high literature, of story, of sermon and of song. It is a tool of philosophy and moral instruction," as Thomas L. Thompson wrote in his pivotal study *The Mythic Past* in 1999.

The special methods for Biblical interpretation came out first in the 1960s and 1970s. They were Textual criticism, Form, Source and Redaction criticism, Rhetorical and New literary criticism and finally Feminist criticism in the 1980s. They produced many new valuable results, but also turned the focus away from some old views, such as typology. When I as a student expressed my interest in typology my professor said that those studies belong to the history of Biblical interpretation.

The connection between the Old and the New Testament

The New Testament has its own exegetical difficulties. There have been attempts to write a history of Jesus and his disciples according to the Gospels but without success, since the stories are contradicting. Whether or not Jesus's words are authentic or falsified by one or more sources, is a cause of heavy debate. The stand that Jesus said something which was preserved in a Q source, was and still is valid, though there are no written documents of this source. This view prevented scholars from seeing that the first written "Christian" documents, the Pauline letters, cover in teaching the entire body of Gospel literature. Without Paul there were no Christian teachings at all. His interpretation of the Old Testament is the only way to access the right Christian teaching. Therefore, understanding Paul's teaching is the key to understanding the whole Scripture, both Old and New Testaments.

How the Old Testament serves the New Testament even today, we can take as an example 2nd Corinthians where Paul has written:

And to keep me from being too elated by the abundance of revelations, a thorn was given me in the flesh, a messenger of Satan, to harass me, to keep me from being too elated. (2 Cor 12:7 RSV)

In the book of Job, we find something similar:

Satan went forth from the presence of the Lord, and afflicted Job with loathsome sores from the sole of his foot to the crown of his head... Then Job answered the Lord: "I know that thou canst do all things...therefore I despise myself, and repent in dust and ashes." (Job 2:7; 42:2, 6)

There is a connection between these two stories and together they teach us that whatever happens to us it is in God's plan to guide us to the desired destination. No scholarly study can tell us this result. Only a story can.

Academic dead languages

Throughout the history of Biblical scholarship, there has been a strong conscience that the original language of the Old Testament is Hebrew. The language of the early church was for practical reasons Greek and its Scripture was first the Septuagint and later the New Testament literature. The language of higher education was for a long time Greek, because of the great philosophers and authors. Latin came in tandem along the history. Hebrew was left to the use of the clergy thinking their possibility to read the original text and transmit its contents to the audience. In almost all European universities there was a theological faculty and a professor of Hebrew and Greek language. Did they really study the original texts to transmit it to others? I doubt it. Some professors were interested in the old manuscripts of the Bible, and their work yielded notable results in defining the age and value of the manuscripts. The study of Septuagint Greek brought knowledge of the translation techniques. It is understandable that European (and American) scholars could not have maximum use of Hebrew because their own languages were totally different. Hebrew is not a spoken language and all words must be learned from the dictionaries, made by Western scholars. Greek has almost the same situation because spoken Greek was totally different from the Biblical Greek. The Biblical languages were truly dead languages, and even professors – who knew the grammar very well - could not promote their deeper understanding of it. To get full benefit from Hebrew one has to have a close language as a mother tongue. The spoken Arabic language unlocks many Hebrew sayings such as they were first meant.

The good knowledge of Hebrew and Greek has resulted in the writing of several translations of the Bible into the vernacular beginning from the 17th century. Translators did their best to capture the original meaning of the text for the readers. But they failed in many passages because they did not know the ultimate purpose of the text. The western world is trained in the Greek philosophy and unintentionally or intentionally , translators have adapted its visions. Scripture, however, is written from a totally different worldview. One example is from the Gospel of John: Ἐν ἀρχῇ ἦν ὁ λόγος, καὶ ὁ λόγος ἦν πρὸς τὸν θεόν, καὶ θεὸς ἦν ὁ λόγος (John 1:1). Why does the last *theos* have no article? It should be there if one translates the sentence as the RSV does: *and the Word was God*. But if one understands that *theos* without the article means divine, the sentence takes on a new meaning: In the beginning there was the word – meaning God's message for the people – and this word was God's word, being and coming from him and this word was divine – meaning the only message from God to humankind.[18]

---

18 Paul Nadim Tarazi, *The New Testament: An Introduction. Vol. 3 Johannine Writings* (Crestwood: St Vladimir's Seminary Press, 2004), 131-134.

Much effort, less attainments

The Society of Biblical Literature was founded in 1880 for the promotion of Biblical studies in America. It is the oldest and largest learned society devoted to the critical investigation of the Bible from a variety of academic disciplines. It has grown to be international and has taken under its wings many newcomers as well as distinguished scholars to meet in local or international conferences. The network of Biblical scholars throughout the world strived to better understand the details of Scripture. But there is no consensus as to why this literature was written and how to understand its function. The answer could neither be to get information from the religious thinking of the past nor to satisfy the appetite of the scholars concerning the forms and histories of the text. Jesus Ben Sirach has the same mindset:

> Not only the readers must needs become skilful themselves, but also they that desire to learn be able to profit them which are without, both by speaking and writing.[19]

But if we do not find its real purpose, this book has no meaning for humanity today. Ever more people seem to think so. According to the scholarly exegetical rules it is forbidden to study this literature as having a message from the Creator of the world even for today. According to the teaching of the worldwide Christian Church this literature is God's word to humankind. If we agree on the first proposition, we can continue the study and demolish Scripture to pieces and be as content as a child after he or she has demolished a tower he or she just had built. This brings us to a dead end in the interpretation of Scripture. If we agree on

---

[19] "The Book of Sirach," Prologue in *Septuagint Job, Proverbs, Ecclesiastes, Song of Songs, Wisdom, Sirach: The Greek Old Testament*, George Valsamis (Athens: Elpenor, 2018), 143.

the other proposition there is always a danger that we began to interpret it according to our own penchants.

Sheep and shepherds

However, there is still one way to proceed. In the Greek world people admired the ideal world and following this, the western world constructed a theology of the Bible. However, according to Paul Tarazi, the Biblical world presents us only a shepherd with his flock. We are compared to sheep. If a sheep goes its own way, it is going to perish in the wilderness. A sheep has to follow the shepherd to survive. No one asks the sheep where it wants to go and what it wants to do. No vote, no democracy, only following instructions. This was what Jesus did. According to the New Testament he was just a son of man, a human being, who had no power of his own. He had to follow the Father and his will, and in so doing he becomes what he is – a true shepherd, the Messiah, a winner.[20]

If we see Scripture as literature, full of edifying stories, which demonstrate the best way of living, namely respecting God and his law and serving other people, it has a meaning even for today. Scripture offers as an example the life of shepherds who have all they need, if God who masters nature gives rain and sunshine sequentially. The Greek deities are futile, kings seek only their own prosperity and the life in cities is unnatural, luring men to vices. There is no need for metaphysical or philosophical explanations. Scripture guides people to live here and now under the law of the Creator. There is always the possibility for those interested, to study the form of the Scripture, its language and its manuscripts, but Scripture is not written for that reason. It is a common heritage for humankind to guide them to understand what is a good life and what is the ultimate goal of all living.

---

20 e.g. Matt 4:1-11, 26:53-54 and John 10:25, 11:40-44. Tarazi, *Rise*, 49-55.

Scripture says to the shepherds: "Ho, shepherds of Israel who have been feeding yourselves...but you do not feed the sheep." "Feed my sheep!" (Ezek 34:2-3; John 21:17)

The Desert as Image of God
Dr. Robert D. Miller II, OFS

From an early period, biblical authors perceived the South as God's domain. In particular, note five closely related poetic fragments in the Old Testament scholars have frequently read together (Fig. 1). The first is Deuteronomy 33, which gives five locations from which God has come: Sinai, Seir, Paran, "peak sanctuary," and the mountain slopes. This is not about the revelation of the Law. As we shall see, only this variant mentions Sinai, and the rest are clear in referring to Israel's southeast, not southwest. In any case, God does not come from Sinai in Exodus; he comes to Sinai, to deliver the Law. Then Judges 5 and Habakkuk 3 introduce a new term, Teman, which can simply mean "south,"—that is the Latin at this place—although the Septuagint interprets it here as a geographic proper name. While Ezekiel 25 uses the expression "Teman to Dedan" as a merism for the whole of Edom, which suggests southern Palestine, the mention of Midian in Habakkuk might put Teman even further south, into northwest Arabia. Psalm 68:8-9 also has no allusion to the Exodus. The people moving could easily refer to movement into battle with God at their lead. A comparable "Hadad went before me" appears in the Tel Dan Stele.

Since GOD MARCHED FROM THE SOUTH is the basic theme, we have a very early tradition that God has at one time resided in the south, in order for him to be able to come from there. This is not about Sinai. First, there is no tradition that has God dwelling on Mount Sinai. God arrives at Sinai from the heavens above: Exod 19:11 (J), "the Lord will come down upon Mount Sinai," and Exod 24:16 (P), "the glory of the Lord settled on Mount Sinai." Second, nothing is said about the Law in these variants. This means "The Desert South" needs to be reckoned with as itself a divine abode. From the desert south, God has approached Israel. This is, therefore, a horizontal theophany. The south is not a place where one can worship God or where he can be encountered.

So important was Yahweh's connection with the South that he was venerated elsewhere as "Yahweh of Teman" or "Yahweh of the South." The title "Yahweh of Teman" is found at Kuntillet Ajrud, a small, single-period site situated between the southern Negev and the eastern Sinai Peninsula, dating to the 8th century BC. "Yahweh of Teman" is found in several inscriptions, once with the definite article, "Yahweh of the Teman," which might translate as "Yahweh of the South." "I have blessed you by Yahweh of Teman," and "May he bless you by Yahweh of Teman." It is also on a Wall Plaster: "Recount [praises] to Yahweh of Teman… Yahweh of the South did good…set the vine…Yahweh of the South (or of the Teman) has …." My friend Jeremy Hutton misses the point by assuming this was southerners' "locally indigenous worship of Yahweh of Teman." The fact that Kuntillet Ajrud is in the south is a red herring. Since the site belonged to the Northern Kingdom of Israel, since stylistically and petrographically its pottery is Judahite, and since it also mentions "Yahweh of Samaria" far from Samaria, such an explanation is unnecessary. Yahweh of Teman is the national God Yahweh, again described as "of the South."

In addition, Late Bronze Age Egyptian texts mention a place named "Yahweh" in this same location, evidence that historically it was Yahweh's domain, either divine abode or landscape sacred to him.

Regardless of what this says about the origins of Yahwism—and I argue elsewhere that it does—it is a theological statement. Making the South God's domain says something about the divine nature. The evidence of Kuntillet Ajrud grounds this theological claim not only in the biblical text but in ancient Israelite religious practice, as well. The biblical association of God with the South, including Edom and Midian, endured in multiple texts in spite of overwhelming onerous against both of those places, not only because it may reflect a historical reality, but because it made a theological claim biblical authors would not do without.

In this essay, I want to elucidate that claim, explaining what it means that Yahweh is "of the South." My argument is not about origins, but about biblical theology, first in the sense of the theology *of* the Old Testament. That is, the traditions of the God of the South—regardless of their origin—are an important part of the theological claims of the Bible, and for all the diachronic development in the history of Israel they can be elucidated as a fixed piece.

There is a second sense of the term "Biblical Theology" that I am also after, and that is theology *from* the Bible. To that end, the use of the desert archetype by Christian spirituality throughout the centuries, read historically, is of great value both as representations of the kinds of religious thinking that shaped the text itself, but also as ongoing representations of the spiritual experiences that shaped the text. This move, therefore, goes beyond the History of Interpretation or Reception History, which are post-exegetical, because seeing what the mythic value of the desert archetype is for Christian tradition helps us understand the theological intention of the biblical authors.

First, let me make two caveats. One, I am not suggesting the Old Testament sets up a "desert ideal," a favorite nostrum of older scholarship.¹ The Bible does not present desert life as an ideal and or advocate a return to nomadic spirituality.²

Secondly, one can conflate "the South" in those biblical passages and at Kuntillet Ajrud with "the desert" of Psalm 68. For an Israelite living in Israel or Judah, the South would be a homogenous concept, bringing to mind the mountainous desert of today's Negev, Aravah, Wadi Rum, and Hejaz.

Biblical writers used the desert landscape as a symbolic resource because the natural world is open to being treated symbolically, as the French philosopher Jean Borello notes, something concomitant with religion.³ To unpack this, I begin with cognitive science, the interdisciplinary study of the mind.⁴ When bearing upon literature, cognitive science understands meaning as what the linguist Bidisha Som calls "the stuff that mental processing is made of; it involves the basic relation between mental content and the experience of the world."⁵

Mental dispositions depend on bodies.⁶ Somatic sensations and physiological responses are the resources for cognitive processes to

---

1 Samuel Nyström, *Beduinentum und Jahwismus* (Lund: C. W. K. Gleerup, 1946), 109; Shemaryahu Talmon, "The 'Desert Motif' in the Bible and in Qumran Literature," in *Biblical Motifs*, ed. Alexander Altmann, Studies and Texts 3 (Cambridge: Harvard University Press, 1966).

2 Nyström, *Beduinentum und Jahwismus*, 163; Talmon, "The 'Desert Motif' in the Bible and in Qumran Literature."

3 Jean Borella, T*he crisis of religious symbolism ; & Symbolism & reality*, trans. G. John Champoux (Kettering: Angelico, 2016), 43.

4 Jay Friedenberg and Gordon Silverman, *Cognitive Science: An Introduction to the Study of Mind*, 2. ed (Los Angeles: SAGE, 2012), 2, 11. It is thus far more than just neuroscience.

5 Bidisha Som, "Toward a Cognitive Linguistics Understanding of Folk Narratives.," *Lokaratna* 4 (2011): 58; cf. Borella, The crisis of religious symbolism, 46, 385.

6 Veikko Anttonen, "Landscapes as Sacroscapes," in *Sacred Sites and Holy Places: Exploring the Sacralization of Landscape through Space and Time*, ed. Sæbjørg Walaker Nordeide, Studies in the Early Middle Ages 11 (Turnhout: Brepols, 2013), 19.

filter through cultural meanings.⁷ So we must consider ancient Israelite bodies that because of travel for trade or military service would have experienced deserts.

The deserts of Israelite bodily experience are real deserts. Average annual rainfall near Kadesh Barnea is 87 mm.⁸ And archaeology and geomorphology show that environmental conditions were similar to those of today.⁹ Although my focus is deserts *in literature*, literary deserts of the Old Testament, nevertheless, the literary depends on the physical.¹⁰ Actual places both dictate language and are in turn defined by language.¹¹ So while constructivists rightly insisted that language gives shape to our understanding of space, that there is no unmediated place,¹² more recent theorists like Keith Basso realize elements of

---

7 Troy E. Hall and David N. Cole, "Immediate Conscious Experience in Wilderness," in *Wilderness Visitor Experiences*, ed. David N. Cole, USDA Forest Service Proceedings, RMRS-P-66 (Missoula: US Department of Agriculture, 2012), 38.
8 T. Littmann and S. M. Berkowicz, "The Regional Climatic Setting," in *Arid Dune Ecosystems: The Nizzana Sands in the Negev Desert*, ed. Siegmar W. Breckle, Aaron Yaʻir, and Maik Veste, Ecological Studies 200 (Berlin: Springer, 2008), 54.
9 A. Yair, "The Ambiguous Impact of Climatic Change at the Desert Fringe," in *Environment Change in Drylands*, ed. A. C. Milington and K. Pye (New York: John Wiley & Sons, 1994), 199–227; Y. Avni, N. Porat, and G. Avni, "Pre-Farming Environment and OSL Chronology in the Negev Highlands, Israel," *Journal of Arid Environments* 86 (November 2012): 12–27.
10 Christopher Y. Tilley, *A Phenomenology of Landscape: Places, Paths, and Monuments*, Explorations in Anthropology (Oxford: Berg, 1994), 31.
11 Sten P. Moslund, "The Presence of Place in Literature," in *Geocritical Explorations: Space, Place, and Mapping in Literary and Cultural Studies*, ed. Robert T. Tally (New York: Palgrave Macmillan, 2011), 31–35.
12 Randi Haaland and Gunnar Haaland, "Landscape," in *The Oxford Handbook of the Archaeology of Ritual and Religion*, ed. Timothy Insoll, Oxford Handbooks (Oxford ; New York: Oxford University Press, 2011), 25; Ernst Cassirer, *Language and Myth (1925)* (New York: Dover, 1953), 9–11; Belden C. Lane, *The Solace of Fierce Landscapes: Exploring Desert and Mountain Spirituality* (New York: Oxford University Press, 1998), 16.

topography are agents in their own sacrality.[13] Language depends on the sensual, so the literary desert depends on the physical desert. But since language also defines the desert, I will eventually return to the literary desert.

Deserts are foreign to everyday life of the biblical authors, who were not nomadic pastoralists. To the rarified environment of Jerusalem scribal culture, the desert was "desolate and still and strange…," "barren, howling" in Deuteronomy's words. The desert was the opposite of their urban environment. Studies find that cognitive engagement with wilderness involves focused attention on small, varied details.[14] For Israel, from what was learned through trade and travel, compounded by imagination, the desert was "unfamiliar and often grotesque in its forms and colors, inhabited by rare, furtive creatures of incredible hardiness and cunning…"[15]—snakes and scorpions, owls, porcupines, hyenas, and wolves. Biblical writers knew the desert was "sparingly colonized by weird mutants from the plant kingdom …as spiny,

---

[13] Anttonen, "Landscapes as Sacroscapes," 13; Guy Davenport, *The Geography of the Imagination Forty Essays* (Boston: David R. Godine, 2005), 4; Jaana Kouri, "Co-Composing a Village History in the Archipelago of South-Western Finland," in *The Relational Dynamics of Disenchantment and Sacralization: Changing the Terms of the Religion versus Secularity Debate*, ed. Peik Ingman, The Study of Religion in a Global Context (Bristol: Equinox Publishing Ltd, 2016), 236; Eileen Crist, "Against the Social Construction of Nature and Wilderness," in *The Wilderness Debate Rages on: Continuing the Great New Wilderness Debate*, ed. Michael P. Nelson and J. Baird Callicott (Athens: University of Georgia Press, 2008), 507–8; Borella, *Crisis*, 389; Keith H. Basso, *Wisdom Sits in Places: Landscape and Language among the Western Apache* (Albuquerque: University of New Mexico Press, 1996), 108; David Lawlor, "Returning to Wirikuta," *European Journal of Ecopsychology* 4 (2013): 22, with case examples from the Huichol Indians.
[14] Hall and Cole, "Immediate Conscious Experience in Wilderness," 40–41, 44.
[15] Edward Abbey, *Desert Solitaire: A Season in the Wilderness* (London: Clark, 1992), 241–42; Kerry S. Walters, *Soul Wilderness: A Desert Spirituality* (New York: Paulist Press, 2001), 1; see Andre Miquel, "Le Désert dans la Poésie arabe preislamique," in *Les Mystiques Du Désert dans l'Islam, le Judaïsme et le Christianisme* (Gordes: Association des Amis de Sénanque, 1975), 78–81 on how these feature in pre-Islamic Arabic poetry.

thorny, stunted and twisted as they are tenacious."[16] They knew the desert was harsh, dangerous, and uncompromising (Ps 107). Research shows the unknown danger of the wilderness is one of the most significant experiential aspects people undergo.[17] For biblical writers, the desert was unknown, unmapped (Jer 51), much of it unnamed, evoking "an elusive hint of something unknown, unknowable, about to be revealed."[18] The desert is immense, immeasurable.

On the other hand, the deserts of Midian, Edom, and the Negev are *bādia*, not *ṣaḥrā*, not all sand, and capable of growing vegetation and even of cultivation when winter rains send torrents streaming down the wadis (Ps 113).[19] Perennial plants also grow wherever ground water is available in cracks in the hard rock.[20] Fauna, too, abound: the habitat diversity of small mammals is very high compared to other deserts.[21] Thus, Muslim tradition says Rabbi Ka'ab al-Aḥbar told Caliph Umar, "When God created

---

16 Abbey, *Desert*, 241–42.

17 Michael E. Patterson et al., "An Hermeneutic Approach to Studying the Nature of Wilderness Experience," *Journal of Leisure Research* 30 (1998): 440–41.

18 Abbey, *Desert*, 241.

19 Jibrā'īl Sulaymān Jabbūr, *The Bedouins and the Desert: Aspects of Nomadic Life in the Arab East*, SUNY Series in Near Eastern Studies (Albany: State University of New York Press, 1995), 44–46; Avinoam Danin, *Plants of Desert Dunes*, Adaptations of Desert Organisms (Berlin ; New York: Springer, 1996), 88; Gisbert Greshake, *Die Wüste bestehen: Erlebnis und geistliche Erfahrung* (Kevelaer: Verlagsgemeinschaft Topos plus, 2004), 65; Mohamed Tawfic Ahmed, ed., *Ecosystems and Human Well-Being: El Maghara, Northern Sinai, Egypt* (Nairobi: UNEP ; Ford Foundation, 2010), 78–79.

20 Sharif Harir, "Adaptive Forms and Process among the Hadendowa," in *Survival on Meagre Resources: Hadendowa Pastoralism in the Red Sea Hills*, ed. Leif O. Manger (Uppsala: Nordiska Afrikainstitutet, 1996), 42.

21 J. Filser and R. Prasse, "A Glance on the Fauna of Nizzana," in *Arid Dune Ecosystems: The Nizzana Sands in the Negev Desert*, ed. Siegmar W. Breckle, Aaron Yā'ir, and Maik Veste, Ecological Studies 200 (Berlin: Springer, 2008), 125.

things, he made for each a partner...Hardship said, 'I am setting out for the desert,' and Salubrity said, 'And I go with you.'"[22]

Since cognitive science implicates the individual, their body and senses, let me follow anthropologists in using *participant observation*,[23] here providing some statements of those who have reflectively written on desert experiences.

Edward Abbey's first observations as a ranger for the National Park Service near Moab, Utah, in his 1968 memoire *Desert Solitaire* was "the immense silence in which I am lost"[24]-- something highlighted by many. Thus, Aldous Huxley: the "Silence of the desert is such that casual sounds...cannot abolish it. They co-exist with it."[25] Jean Baudrillard extends this to the realm of sight: "The silence of the desert is a visual thing, too. A product of the gaze that stares out and finds nothing to reflect it."[26]

Naturalist Joseph Wood Krutch, who lived in the Arizona desert for 20 years, notes, "Under the open sky the sun's rays strike with an almost physical force."[27] Yet Krutch also speaks of the desert as filled with life: "The desert is sprinkled with hundreds, probably thousands, of evenly placed shrubs, varied now and then by a small tree," including the acacia abundant in the deserts of Edom and

---

22 Jabbūr, *Bedouins*, 48.
23 Kouri, "Co-Composing a Village History in the Archipelago of South-Western Finland," 232, 237–38; Lane, *The Solace of Fierce Landscapes*, 19; Basso, *Wisdom Sits in Places*, 68–69.
24 Abbey, *Desert*, 11.
25 Aldous Huxley, "The Desert," in *Adonis and the Alphabet* (London: Chatto & Windus, 1956), 77.
26 Jean Baudrillard, *America* (London ; New York: Verso, 2010), 6.
27 Joseph W. Krutch, *The Voice of the Desert: A Naturalist's Interpretation* (New York: William Sloane, 1966), 13.

Midian.²⁸ As in Edom and Midian, "All the little annual flowers and weeds which spring up after the winter rains and rush from seed to seed again in six weeks gave up the ghost at the end of their short lives."²⁹ Yet as Krutch—like Israel—notes, the flora and fauna adapted to the desert's climate are twisted and outlandish.³⁰

God is not merely the desert, but in Zechariah 9 a desert storm, the unforgettable desert *Khamsin* with its accompanying sandstorms.³¹ The south wind is feared in the Levant (Jer 13; Job 37). Jeremiah 4:11 says, "A searing wind blows from the barren heights in the wilderness." Isa 21:1 speaks of "the whirlwinds of the Negev". In the Talmud, Abba Arikha claims four winds blow each day and the South is the harshest of them all: were not for the angel who blocks it, it would destroy the entire world (*b. Gittin* 31b, based on Job 39:26).

The Khamsin originates in Arabia and reaches Palestine dry and with high-speed winds, lasting up to seven days.³² Barometric pressure plummets, visibility is impaired, and the sky turns yellow or red.³³ The winds "desiccate the landscape, wither leaves and fruit on trees, render the brush vegetation susceptible to fires."³⁴

---

28 Krutch, *Voice*, 13.

29 Krutch, *Voice*, 14.

30 Krutch, *Voice,* 17.

31 Karl-Heinz Fleckenstein, *Botschaft der Wüste* (Innsbruck: Tyrolia-Verlag, 2016), 89; Walters, *Soul Wilderness*, 85 speaks of "Holy Sirocco."

32 P. Brydone, William Beckford, and Johann Friedrich Junius, *P. Brydone's Reise durch Sicilien und Malta, in Briefen an William Beckford. Esq. zu Somerly in Suffolk : nebst einer Charte von Sicilien und Malta.* (Leipzig: Bey Johann Friedrich Junius, 1777), 345; Tage Sivall, "Sirocco in the Levant," *Geografiska Annaler* 39 (1957): 121; J. Gregoire, "Du Khamsin et des ses Effets," *Mémoires Ou Travaux Originaux Présentes et Lus à l'Institut Égyptien* 1 (1862): 369.

33 Sivall, "Sirocco in the Levant," 122; Gregoire, "Du Khamsin et des ses Effets," 369, 372.

34 Colbert C. Held, *Middle East Patterns: Places, Peoples, and Politics*, 3rd ed (Boulder: Westview Press, 2000), 1.63; Gregoire, "Du Khamsin et des ses Effets," 370.

Breathing becomes difficult, like a high altitude.[35] Sandstorms stir up, whirlwinds of tremendous height engulfing foliage and scouring up the soil.[36]

As T. E. Lawrence described:

> The sun disappeared, blotted out by thick rags of yellow air over our heads. We stood in a horrible light, ochreous and fitful. The brown wall of cloud from the hills was now very near, rushing changelessly upon us with a loud grinding sound. Three minutes later it struck, wrapping us in a blanket of dust and stinging grains of sand, twisting and turning in violent eddies, and yet advancing eastward at the speed of a strong gale. …these internal whirling winds tore our tightly-held cloaks from our hands, filled our eyes, and robbed us of all sense of direction.[37]

Let us return to the Bible's literary desert in the literary South, to see how biblical language speaks of the desert South to evoke that place in a particular way.

Of the three words for "South," *Teman* can be a proper place name, can mean "south," or it can be translated "South Wind." *Teman* South Wind is not always negative: in Song of Songs 4, it blows on the beloved's garden spreading fragrance. *Darom*, likewise, has both a directional sense and the meaning "South Wind," which in Job 37 brings dreadful heat on the land. *Negeb* derives from a verbal meaning of "to cleanse" or "to wipe."

The same terms are variously translated "desert" or "wilderness" by English versions. *Midbar* derives from the root *DBR* in the

---

35 Gregoire, "Du Khamsin et des ses Effets," 370, 376; Brydone, Beckford, and Junius, *P. Brydone's Reise durch Sicilien und Malta*, 345.
36 Jabbūr, *Bedouins*, 50.
37 T. E. Lawrence, *Seven Pillars of Wisdom* (London: Jonathan Cape, 1935), 206.

meaning of "back, remote"[38] and is used for the Exodus and subsequent testing, secondarily in prophetic passages anticipating redemption through the wilderness. A number of passages describe the *midbar* as arid, uninhabited, without plant life, inhabited by snakes, scorpions, and owls. Figuratively, *midbar* is "barren, howling" and "great and terrible," noted for its wind.

The postexilic term *Tsiyya* is used for the testing in the wilderness. *Jeshimon*, from the root YŠM, "to be desolate,"[39] appears for both the wilderness testing and for predictions of future redemption through the wilderness. *Arabah*, often a proper name for the Rift Valley south of the Dead Sea, also translates as "desert" or "wilderness," particularly in predictions of redemption through it. In Jeremiah 5, it is the domain of the wolf, in 51 "arid…land where no one lives, where no human being even passes through"—exactly as Baudrillard claims: "The grandeur of the desert derives from their being, in their aridity, the negative of the earth's surface and of our civilized humors."[40] *Arabah* lacks any of the positive associations that can accompany *midbar*.

The desert/wilderness is used multiple ways in the Old Testament. The first is resoundingly negative, the desert as a sort of hell, as in Ugaritic texts it is Mot's abode. This underlies the

---

38 James Barr, "Migraš in the Old Testament," *Journal of Semitic Studies* 29 (1984): 24–25; Paul Nadim Tarazi, *The Rise of Scripture* (St. Paul: OCABS Press, 2017), 92–94 argues it is the same root as *dabar*, "word," citing as evidence Song 4:3, where *midbarim* clearly means "words" (of the "mouth")—as the LXX knows—but in the context of terms pertaining to oasis life; also Isa 5:17 and Mic 2:12, where *dober* clearly means "wilderness." But he also notes Pss 18:48; 47:4, where the hiphil *hidbir* means "drive back," allowing "back" as the base meaning.
39 Narelle J. Coetzee, "Wild God in the Wilderness: Why Does Yahweh Choose to Appear in the Wilderness in the Book of Exodus?" (Diss., University of Birmingham, 2016), 327; Albert De Pury, "L'image du Désert dans l'Ancien Testament," in *Le Désert: Image et Réalité: Actes Du Colloque de Cartigny 1983, Centre d'étude du Proche-Orient Ancien (CEPOA), Université de Genève*, ed. Yves Christe, Les Cahiers du CEPOA 3 (Leuven: Peeters, 1989), 117.
40 Baudrillard, *America*, 6.

sending of the Azazel goat covered in sins into the desert. The demonic denizens of the desert are the שָׂעִיר of Leviticus 17; Isaiah 13 and 34 and the Lilith of Isaiah 34.

A similar view is found in cuneiform literature, where the same words are used for the desert as for the netherworld: *ki-erṣetu* and *kur-šadu*.[41] In the interrelated Old Babylonian myths of Inanna, Ninurta, Lugalbanda, and Gilgamesh, the wilderness is a fearsome land of terrors (*Inanna and Ebih*, 116-20, 127-30; *Lugalbanda in the Mountain Wilderness*, 151-70; *Lugalbanda and Anzu*, 1-5) that nevertheless by the actions of heroes can be transformed and organized into a source of plenty (*Lugal-E*, 347-67; *Inanna and Ebih*, 121-26; *Lugalbanda in the Mountain Wilderness*, 265-325).[42] Outside the narrative genre, the tenor is far more negative: in magic texts, the steppe is the domain of demons, and exorcists address the desert demons oppressing their patients.[43] *Madbaru* is a "place of hunger and thirst", "where there are no wild animals" (Assurbanipal).[44] *Ḫuribtu* is "uninhabited" (Ashurnirari VI), a place of ghosts (*eṭemmu*; KAR 184).[45]

A second sense in the Bible is Wilderness as a place of trial, in particular the testing during the Wilderness Wanderings. This draws on the negative connotations of the desert, but another tradition sees that same period as a time of closeness to God (Deut

---

41 Alfred Haldar, "The Notion of the Desert in Sumero-Accadian and West-Semitic Religions," *Uppsala Universitets Arsskrif* 3 (1950): 13; Laura Feldt, "Religion, Nature, and Ambiguous Space in Ancient Mesopotamia: The Mountain Wilderness in Old Babylonian Religious Narratives," *Numen* 63 (2016): 357.

42 Feldt, "Religion," 363–71.

43 Sylvie Lackenbacher, "L'Image du Désert d'après les Textes littéraires assyro-babyloniens," in *Le Désert: Image et Réalité: Actes du Colloque de Cartigny 1983, Centre d'étude du Proche-Orient ancien (CEPOA), Université de Genève*, ed. Yves Christe, Les Cahiers du CEPOA 3 (Leuven: Peeters, 1989), 72, 75.

44 *CAD* 10.1.12.

45 *CAD* 6.251.

32; 1 Kgs 19; Jer 2; Hos 2; Ps 55). The Wilderness is where the Law, the covenant, the sanctuary, and the festivals originated. This positive sense is not at odds with its "testing" connotation, nor independent of being an actual desert. Desert environment serves as a contrast to the "fleshpots of Egypt", and to the rains, fertility, and agriculture of Baal in Hosea. The use of the desert as a particular form of punishment for sin is dependent on it being a place of closeness to God and of testing.

Finally, another usage of the desert is the association we have seen in a set of poetic fragments of God himself with the desert, of the desert being the domain of the divine, the source of Yahweh's horizontal theophany.

The desert archetype, although by no means a central image in mystic reflection, has served several distinct but non-exclusive functions in the history of Christian spirituality. The most familiar is the desert as a place to which ascetics have fled and where they encounter God, a usage that goes back to the Jewish Essenes (1QS [Community Rule] 9.19-20;[46] 1QS 8.12-14; cf. Philo, *De Decalogo*, 10-11), and Therapeutae (Philo, *De Vita Contemplativa* 2.18-20). It may explain Paul's sojourn in Arabia after his conversion mentioned in Gal 1:17. Christian reflection on this Anthonian sense of desert, exemplified in the Desert Fathers (e.g., Athanasius, *Vita Antonii*), extends from the works of Origen[47] to Francis of Assisi on La Verna and Ignatius of Loyola's Manresa.[48] It appears in slave songs of 19th-century America, where lyrics like "If you want to see Jesus, go in the

---

[46] Building on the understanding of the desert as a place where the Torah can be rightly followed in *CD* 6.11, 18-20.

[47] Uwe Lindemann, *Die Wüste: Terra Incognita, Erlebnis, Symbol: Eine Genealogie Der Abendländischen Wüstenvorstellungen in Der Literatur von Der Antike Bis Zur Gegenwart*, Beiträge Zur Neueren Literaturgeschichte 3.175 (Heidelberg: C. Winter, 2000), 70.

[48] Markus Hofer, *Francis for Men: Otherwise We Need Weapons* (Cincinnati: St. Anthony Messenger Press, 2003), 75–76; Greshake, *Die Wüste bestehen*, 40.

wilderness," "Jesus a'waitin' to meet you in the wilderness," and "I seek my Lord in the wilderness" had the double meaning of the wildernesses of southern states where clandestine religious gatherings met.[49]

A second sense in Christian spirituality is the image of an interior desert, a state of solitude and detachment where the Christian mentally communes with God. Appearing first in Eucherius of Lyon's 5th-century *De laude heremi* (23, 39), this is exemplified in the West in Richard of St. Victor (12th century) and Mechthild of Magdeburg (13th century)'s *Wüstunge*.[50] It reappears with the Spanish Carmelites, although they also use the desert as an image for the Dark Night of the Soul, and it is a part of some contemporary spiritual direction.[51] In Judaism, it is suggested by the Midrash in *Numbers Rabbah* 1.7: "If one cannot make oneself open and ownerless like the desert, one can acquire neither wisdom nor Torah."

Yet the connotation of desert in Christian spirituality that comes closest to the desert God, the Yahweh of Teman, is not prominent until the Middle Ages, especially with the Rhineland Mystics, a largely Dominican movement of speculative, apophatic spirituality. Meister Eckhart (d. 1327) popularized the desert as

---

[49] Miles M. Fisher, *Negro Slave Songs* (Ithaca: Cornell University Press, 1953), 68–69; Erik Nielson, "'Go in de Wilderness': Evading the 'Eyes of Others' in Slave Songs," *The Western Journal of Black Studies* 35 (2011): 106–7, 111–14.

[50] George H. Williams, *Wilderness and Paradise in Christian Thought*, Menno Simons Lectures (New York: Harper & Brothers, 1962), 50–52; Michael Egerding, *Die Metaphorik der Spätmittelalterlichen Mystik /: Michael Egerding*, vol. 2 (Paderborn: Schöningh, 1997), 722; also William of Saint-Thierry, David of Augsburg, Conrad of Eberbach, Gilbert of Hoyland, and Isaac of Stella; Bernard McGinn, "Ocean and Desert as Symbols of Mystical Absorption in the Christian Tradition," *The Journal of Religion* 74 (1994): 164–65.

[51] Martha Robbins, "The Desert-Mountain Experience," *Journal of Pastoral Care* 35 (1981): 21; Greshake, *Die Wüste bestehen*, 110 cites examples in the writings of Nietzsche.

an image for God, using it more than a dozen times.[52] "God's desert is God's simple nature," he writes (*Tractate* 11[53]). For him, God is *Stille Wüste* (e.g., *Predigt* 10). The desert is God, or God is the desert, because of the desert's solitude (*Einöde*) (*Predigt* 10).

This sense of the mythic desert imaging God is picked up by Eckhart's disciple, Johannes Tauler (d. 1361) and Jan van Ruysbroeck (d. 1381). Tauler, for example, says God is "simple hidden desert (*Wüste*) beyond being" (*Sermon* 60). He highlights both the unknowability of God (*Predigt* 11; 55.5-7) and also God's "silent desert divinity" (*stille wüste Gottheit*, 278.3). Another of Eckhart's disciples, Henry Suso (d. 1366) speaks of the "*Weiselosigkeit*" of "desert deity" (*Wüste gotheit*).

The background of this understanding is twofold and Eastern Christian. The first is a strand that begins with Neo-Platonism. In the 3rd century, Plotinus borrowed the term used for the recess within the Delphic temple where the Pythia gave her oracles, called the αδυτον "not to slip in" or "beyond the image," to speak of the absolute spiritual beyond, surpassing visible reality (*Enneads* VI.9.11).[54] By the end of the 5th century, αδυτον was for Simplicius of Cilicia, "the cloud of unknowing that the mystic encounters before the Ineffable One," and Damascius explained that its inaccessible character symbolized the transcendent ultimate, ineffable principle (*Difficulties and Solutions of First Principles* I.8.6-20). This usage had already found its way into Christian thought when Gregory of Nyssa used αδυτον to express the unknowability of God (*Life of Moses* 2.163-64).[55] Pseudo-

---

52 E.g., in his authentic works, Sermon *Of the Nobleman*; *Predigt* 10; *Predigt* 12; *Predigt* 48; *Predigt* 60; *Predigt* 81.
53 Perhaps pseudepigraphal but from his circle.
54 Walter Burkert, "The Temple in Classical Greece," in *Temple in Society*, ed. Michael V. Fox (Winona Lake: Eisenbrauns, 1988), 36.
55 Barry D. Smith, *The Indescribable God: Divine Otherness in Christian Theology* (Eugene: Pickwick Publications, 2012), 40.

Dionysius (c. 500) borrows directly from Neoplatonism, and αδυτον becomes in Latin *vastitas*, "wasteland."[56]

In the 9th century West, John Scotus Eriugena read Pseudo-Dionysius and made the desert wasteland the image of the divine.[57] In his commentary on the Gospel of John (1.27.80), Eriugena says, "The desert is the ineffability of the divine nature." When he goes on to say that the Greek word ερημια conveys the divine nature (*quod omnino diuinae coneunit naturae*; 1.27.85), he is echoing Pseudo-Dionysius (*Ecclesiastical Hierarchy* 3.7; *Divine Names* 4.24).[58] Eckhart and his school were reading Eriugena and perhaps Pseudo-Dionysius, as well, as when Van Ruysbroeck says, "We must all found our lives upon a fathomless abyss" (*Sparkling Stone*).[59]

On the other hand, the Eckhartian divine desert is a development from earlier Rhineland mystics who used the "Anthonian" understanding. Thus, van Rusybroeck draws on Pseudo-Hadewijch of Brabant (*Mengeldichten* 25-29), which draws on the authentic Hadewijch (*Mengeldichten* 1-16), both of which see the desert as a place to meet God, when he writes of "A wild, waste desert where God who lives us, lives" (van Ruysbroeck,

---

56 Lindemann, *Die Wüste*, 88; Jean-Yves Leloup, *Désert, déserts* (Paris: Albin Michel, 2000), 68–69; McGinn, "Ocean and Desert," 161–62, 166; Williams, *Wilderness and Paradise in Christian Thought*, 52; Sarah Coakley, "Re-Thinking Dionysius the Areopagite," *Modern Theology* 24 (2008): 531–32.

57 McGinn, "Ocean and Desert," 162; Eriugena was the first to translate Pseudo-Dionysius into Latin, and Eckhart depended on him (and Dionysius) in many other areas, as well; Mary Brennan, *Guide des Études érigéniennes: Bibliographie Commentée des Publications 1930-1987 = A Guide to Eriugenian Studies*, Vestigia Études et Documents de Philosophie Antique et Médiévale 5 (Fribourg: Fribourg University Press, 1989), 132, 294.

58 Jean Scot, *Commentaire Sur l'Evangile de Jean*, trans. Edouard Jeauneau, Sources Chretiennes 180 (Paris: Cerf, 1972), 140–42 n.18.

59 Kevin A. Gordon, "Traces in the Desert: The Poetics of Sand, Dust, and Ash in German Literature" (Diss., University of California, Berkeley, 2014), 9.

Werken 3.217).⁶⁰ Van Ruysbroeck has taken the Anthonian desert and made it God's abode. But he also understands the desert and its "unconditioned dark" to be God (*Seven Degrees of Love*, chap. 14).

What all of this shows is that if Yahweh is the desert God, he is strange, unfamiliar and fantastic. Yahweh is dangerous, as uncompromising as the desert, and this is especially true of how God appears in stories set in the desert. Yahweh is unknown, unknowable, but on the verge of being revealed. The desert God is formless and incorporeal as the desert is--immeasurable, inestimable. As Aldous Huxley wrote, "Boundless and emptiness—these are the two most expressive symbols of that attributeless Godhead." All the same, Yahweh is not malevolent, he is "salubrious."⁶¹ Desert silence, too, is a symbol of the divine, not a silent God, but a powerful, thick silence that Martha Robbins calls desert's "peace deeper than terror."⁶²

The desert God is an image that expresses a paradox: Israel suggests Yahweh is wild, enigmatic to the point of alien. Where Yahweh is not surreal, he is dangerous, the awful wind, soaring, surging, and looming. Paradoxically, the same God is both "twisting and turning in violent eddies" and the "peace deeper than terror," tranquil and still as the motionless desert, dreadfully benevolent." Yahweh "engulfs you and plunges you into a dark cloud" and also allows you to hear your own breath in the uttermost silence.

---

60 Paul A. Dietrick, "The Wilderness of God in Hadewijch II and Meister Eckhart and His Circle," in *Meister Eckhart and the Beguine Mystics: Hadewijch of Brabant, Mechthild of Magdeburg, and Marguerite Porete*, ed. Bernard McGinn (New York: Continuum, 1994), 33, 35–36, 38–39; John of Ruysbroeck, *Les noces spirituelles*, trans. André Louf (Bégrolles-en-Mauges: Abbaye de Bellefontaine, 1993), 221; Lane, *The Solace of Fierce Landscapes*, 49.

61 Huxley, "Desert," 73.

62 Robbins, "Desert-Mountain," 23.

Carl Jung said, "We constantly use symbolic terms to represent concepts that we cannot define or fully comprehend."[63] They enable authors to communicate concepts that cannot be communicated by other means.[64] Archetypes possess us, overwhelm us, because the experience of their encounter is vivid and momentous.[65] The staunchly anti-Jungian Jean Borella agrees: "Awareness of the sacred symbol is a disruptive and dazzling experience from which springs a consciousness of reality…experience of the Transcendent within the experience of its sign's presence."[66]

The desert, he continues: "is the archetype…of which signifier, meaning and particular referent are only distinct manifestations,"[67] meaning, as we have said, biblical authors did not choose the image of the desert out of the blue, but because it supported theology that was already there. As Ernst Cassirer wrote, the symbol or archetype presupposes that the ideas "are already given."[68] Father Tarazi shows that from the biblical perspective, the divine world is a projection of the human mind. To grasp at a God who is "solitary," "silent," "fierce," "beautiful," "unending," and "strange," we must go to the desert.

---

63 Carl G. Jung, "Approaching the Unconscious," in *Man and His Symbols*, ed. Carl G Jung and Marie-Luise von Franz (Garden City, N.Y.: Doubleday, 1964), 21.
64 René Guénon, *Fundamental Symbols* (Oxford: Alden, 1962), 14 (1925).
65 Murray Stein, *Jung's Map of the Soul: An Introduction* (Chicago: Open Court, 1998), 100.
66 Borella, *Crisis*, 3.
67 Borella, *Crisis*, 3.
68 Cassirer, *Language*, 87.

Deut 33:2:
He said, "Yahweh came from Sinai
 And dawned on him from Seir
He shone forth from Mount Paran
 And went from his peak sanctuary
From his southland mountain slopes for them"

Judg 5:4-5:
Yahweh, when you went out from Seir
 When you marched from the territory of Edom
The earth shook, and also the heavens, they dripped
 The clouds dripped water
The mountains trembled
 Before Yahweh, the One of Sinai
 Before Yahweh, the God of Israel.

Hab 3:3-7:
God came from Teman
 The Holy One from Mount Paran…
His brightness was like the light
 rays flashed from his hand; there he veiled his power…
 The eternal mountains were shattered;
  along his ancient pathways
  the everlasting hills sank low.
I saw the tents of Cushan tremble
 the curtains of Midian.

Ps 68:8-9:
God, when you went forth before your people,
 When you marched from the desert, (Selah)
The earth quaked, the heavens poured
 Before God, the One of Sinai
 Before God, the God of Israel.

Zech 9:14:
And Yahweh will appear over them
 And his arrow will go out as lightning
The Lord Yahweh will sound the shofar
 And he will come in the storms of Teman [or "of the South"].

Figure 1

The Parable of the Wicked Servant (Matthew 18:21:-35) and its Implications for the Understanding of Salvation

Rev. Fr. Ron Poworoznik

A couple of years ago, I was enjoying a light conversation with a friend, who was a guest at our home. She was a Protestant who was attending an Antiochian Orthodox Church, by way of a boyfriend. She had attended for some time, singing in the choir and even chanting some services.

After a while, I discovered that despite her attending our local Antiochian parish, her theological views and understanding remained rather solidly Protestant. No surprise really. She was never formally catechized in our Faith, and she had spent many years as an active member of an Evangelical church.

Specifically, what caught my attention to her leanings was a short conversation about salvation. Protestants in general are very, very well versed on this topic, and I would argue, and perhaps you would agree, that we Orthodox are not. So, this presentation I am making today will examine this disparity.

When we discussed salvation, I quipped that salvation was a journey; an ongoing process. We have all heard and even perhaps used the line we Orthodox like to use: "I am saved, I am being saved, and I will be saved." No pushback from her, until I suggested that salvation was *provisional*. After suggesting this provisional element, there was pushback...fearful pushback! We quickly moved on to other topics, after I sort of assured her and comforted her, because I admittedly felt a little uneasy at that moment.

But then I got thinking about this later. Not so much about her theological understanding, but about her fear. So, I decided to do some sleuthing. YouTube is great for this, by the way.

What I discovered after this encounter is that people are generally very nervous about their salvation. Several Protestant churches have and do maintain that it is God who saves, and it is not dependent on us. There are churches who teach that "once saved, always saved," or that one is "eternally secure." Of course, the most, for me, enigmatic Protestants, the Christians of the Calvinistic Reformed tradition go all the way: if you are elected, you will persevere to the end. Naturally, they have the Bible verses to back this up. For those who trust their interpretation, they are assured, and they rest in this assurance.

However, there are those who read their Bibles, and see all the verses that seem to contradict this. I remember watching a Christian talk show on YouTube where the hosts were fielding questions about their caller's concerns that their salvation was not as certain as they were led to believe. I too wondered how they handled this challenge. There is no shortage of texts where we are warned, and the one parable I believe really hits this home is the parable of the wicked servant.

What I discovered, through reading numerous commentaries and listening to several sermons, mostly from Protestants, but not exclusively, is that this parable really causes them to react in generally two ways: either they ignore the implications, or they dismiss this parable as not pertaining to the already saved. They either focus on forgiveness, or they will simply say that the wicked servant was never saved in the first place. Practically no one will address head on the consequences, that one can be saved, but then lose their salvation.

The parable of the wicked servant is a direct hit on any notion of eternal security. It does not mince words. It is very easy to understand. It is nearly impossible to misinterpret. The King sums it up forcefully and unambiguously: "I showed you mercy. Should you not have shown your fellow servant mercy?" And should anyone even think of trying to read into this anything other than the obvious, Matthew doubles down and ends it by saying that, "so too will your Heavenly Father treat each of you if you do not forgive your brother from the heart." Notice he says, "each of you." To quote the apostle Thomas: "My Lord and my God!" is my gut reaction.

Since this parable is so obvious, one must really dig to extract further conclusions, which are pastorally meaningful for us, and this is what I offer to you. A few things to note for our consideration:

First, the King wanted to settle accounts; no warning. Nassim Nicholas Taleb compares this to a turkey, who for weeks lives a carefree life, and then suddenly, it's Thanksgiving!

Second, the King orders the slave to be sold with his wife and children, and all his possessions, to settle the account. What a friend we have in Jesus, right?

Third, and perhaps surprisingly (and many miss this), the King does not give the servant what he asked for. The King went way beyond this. The servant asked for patience, and the King forgave the enormous debt.

Fourth, the servant, with his new-found freedom, becomes rather cocky, wouldn't you say?

Fifth, the King forgave out of his gut (from the Greek word *splanchna*), but only asked that the servant show mercy. However, in so doing, he defines mercy. It is a bit of a chiasm: gut-mercy-

mercy-heart. So, what does this parable teach us, other than the obvious?

First, regarding the settling of accounts. We don't come to God, he comes to us and puts us in front of him and redefines our lives from that moment on, merely by his call, which represents for the hearer, his presence. It's Thanksgiving Day! We cannot escape our destiny. We owe too much, and we cannot pay.

Second, what we have to offer in exchange is insufficient to say the least. What we are faced with is a King who is like lady justice: blindfolded and holding a scale. There is no chumming up to this King, who only considers what he is owed. This is a far cry from a Jesus who carries us while leaving only his footprints. Note also that there is no dichotomy here, which we hear and use so often: we must love the sinner and hate the sin. At this point, sinner and sin are one and the same.

Third, the King, after hearing the pleas of the servant, does a bait and switch. He acts independently of the servant. Remember the prodigal son, who asked his father to treat him as one of his servants, and his father ordered a feast for him? We find this in the Gospel of John frequently. Jesus never seems to answer the question he is asked. In a kind of bait and switch, the King made it much worse for the servant. He owed 10 thousand talents, which is a finite amount. Instead of more time, the servant got in response, not an explicit command, but worse, the voice inside his head, to forgive an infinite amount. Notice the King didn't command anything, but it was implied. This is evident in this text and other texts in Matthew, where the command is to do unto others from the heart. You cannot just do good, but you must do good with the right attitude, lest one does good to impress others. And, to put more pressure on the hearer, there is no expressed command by the King, but the expectation remains. This is reminiscent of Paul in Romans, where in the absence of the written law, one's conscience is enough to either accuse or acquit.

Fourth, freedom is never free, because if it was free it would be cheap. I believe this is exactly why it is so easy to be saved and be proud of it. The obvious danger is a "we" versus "they" approach by the "saved" toward the "unsaved." Out of compassion, the King removes any possibility that the servant could legitimately adopt this attitude.

Fifth, the interesting choice of words used by Matthew. This King, despite his rather unfeeling demeanour, can be entreated, and responds with compassion from his gut. This servant was doomed, but he begged the King for patience, and received a response. This rather flies in the face of the Calvinistic doctrine of total depravity, which teaches that we cannot even will to do good, which is why one's election is "unconditional." Nowhere at this point in this parable is there any indication of anyone whispering into the servant's ear what to say next, or that the King decides in an about face move to forgive the debt willy-nilly. No, he responds to the servant's begging. He says this explicitly later in parable when he says, "Because you begged me, I canceled all your debt." In return, the King only asks for mercy from the heart. Perhaps this reflects the differences in the amount owed. Only compassion from the gut could wipe away such an enormous debt, which no human is really in a comparative position to do. However, for smaller, manageable debts, mercy from the heart is not unreasonable.

This parable has a certain functionality to it. The first time you either read or hear the parable, it functions as your "personal" moment of being brought before the King to settle accounts. At that moment, if you entreat the King, he will forgive you everything. That is what this parable assures us of. We want assurance? We got it! We can take comfort that we cannot save ourselves, so there is only one thing to do. And that is, to call upon his name. And he will and does respond favourably from his gut! If only the parable ended at this point. However, as Father Paul Tarazi always reminds us, "Keep reading!"

By obeying Fr. Paul's directive to keep reading, we discover that this salvation which we do not deserve, is given as a gift, not because we repent, but *at the moment* we repent. So it is not so much a cause and effect, where our repentance compels God to forgive us, but more akin to the prodigal son, who came to his senses and returned to his Father's house. We are not saved by works, but we must at least show up. However, though salvation is not earned, it nevertheless must be maintained, and this unfortunately is misunderstood by our Protestant brethren as saying that this is salvation by works. This is the "provisional" aspect of our salvation, and it absolutely stuns me that so many Christian's conflate these two aspects and end up teaching the most ridiculous things. And they know this. Google it and you will discover numerous articles and blogs about the crisis in the church regarding backsliding and how to appropriately respond.

To conclude, this parable is frightening because, I believe, it is so straight forward. One cannot wiggle one's way out of the meaning. I know that this presentation has stated the obvious, but I would like to add one more thing for our consideration.

Since this parable is directed towards us, how do we handle the evident and uncomfortable conclusion that none of us can forgive each other from the heart (especially those who have hurt or harmed us or those we love)? We know that this is almost impossible, or at least unrealistic. Is there anyone here who can admit that they can do it? One at a time, please! If that's the case, are we all then doomed because of explicit directives and consequences in this parable?

I would like to submit that the meaning of this parable is not only to command us to forgive, lest anyone who *can* forgive everyone from the heart become arrogant, but to rely solely on God who alone decides. This is reminiscent of something that "Boulos and Benton" taught on their podcast. We cannot forgive, we cannot follow the law, and we cannot obey the commandments, but we must! We are thus pressed on either side.

Instead of the inaccurate dichotomy between either ignoring the directive's consequences, or to simply say that this does not apply to the saved, perhaps the accurate dichotomy should be: we must obey the law, but if we do we are really setting ourselves up for a fall, because even by taking note of our forgiveness from the heart, we stand condemned as the Pharisee toward the publican. I dare to say that if we even came close to accomplishing what this parable is directing us to do, God would simply up the ante until we failed.

I said earlier that this parable has functionality. But in saying this, it must have functionality for *everyone*. In other words, if it only has a message for the unforgiving sinners, then what does it say to the ones who are forgiving, except to point out to those who are forgiving how terrible the unforgiving are, and this can lead to self-righteousness.

This parable does not merely outline our propensity to cockiness, but, I would submit, it *provokes* it. Take note of the rather seemingly benign servants, who merely act as messengers to the King after they witnessed the wickedness of the servant. Have we perhaps considered their plight? Namely, are they not stand ins for us hearers, who by their actions of recognizing and reporting to wickedness, are also put under the same pressure to perform, and who are now without excuse if they act the same way? This is reminiscent of the bait and switch that Jesus did to the Pharisees in the parable of the vinedressers, when he drew them into rage and judgment and then summarily condemned them when they showed their agreement. When we hear the parable and are appalled at how stupid the wicked servant was, and how he could miss something so obvious, then I submit we as hearers have been, "triggered!" One cannot hear this parable without escaping condemnation, one way or another. We are either not ourselves forgiving, or we are condemning the unforgiving.

Though it is frightening, it is also quite remarkable. How can a single parable put everyone, from the most rebellious and dismissive to the most obedient and willing, into the same position before God? This parable teaches that no matter where we find ourselves on this spectrum, we have nothing other than to do good, and live in hope that God will ***again*** be compassionate. ***God*** saves us, as St. Paul reminds us, that even though we may have a clear conscience, we are not yet acquitted.

To paraphrase St. Peter who rightly asks, "Who then can be saved?" For man, this is impossible. With God, all things are possible. Let us take comfort these words.

The Seleucid Period in Light of *The Rise of Scripture*

Dr. Nicolae Roddy

Those who have not been following Fr. Paul Nadim Tarazi's career in recent years, most notably the publication of his recent monograph *The Rise of Scripture*, might be taken aback by his audacious thesis that the Bible was produced as an antihellenistic epic specifically aimed at trumping the philosophical and epic literature of the Greeks—in other words, a literary act of defiance aimed at Hellenistic cultural and political hegemony. Tarazi's own literary-critical approach undermines the well-worn default modes of biblical literalist and historicizing trends that began among European (most notably German) Protestant scholars in the mid-nineteenth century. Instead, he presents the Hebrew epic as an edifying story, or *mashal*, that conveys a body of essential teaching appropriate for Jews, Christians, or Muslims. Consequently, Tarazi disdains archaeology almost as much as he eschews theology; however, by situating the Bible's origin and function in a specific location, namely Coele Syria,[1] at a particular time, circa the third century BCE, he makes of it an artifact, and thus fair game for exposure to the rigors of scientific method.

It is important to realize that the type of archaeology Fr. Paul is opposed to is modern biblical archaeology, a pseudo-science founded in the early twentieth century by William Foxworth Albright (1891–1971), whose extensive surveys and excavations throughout Palestine were influenced and guided by the methodologically flawed conviction that archaeology reveals and supports an actual history for a dubious land called biblical Israel. Albright's many valuable methodological contributions to Syro-

---

1 The name, which from the Seleucid era means "all Syria," generally refers to the region between the Euphrates river and the Mediterranean sea.

Palestinian archaeology notwithstanding, the generations of American, British, and Israeli archaeologists Albright influenced continue to bewitch Jewish and Christian religious conservatives with the illusory spell of biblical historicity, so that each new material discovery—authentic or not—rekindles the fires of conviction that the biblical story is historically reliable to a high degree. My own twenty-year long career in Syro-Palestinian archaeology has led me to the conclusion that the remembrance of actual toponyms incorporated with plausible details in the weaving together of a grand narrative does not support the historicity of the Bible, which raises the need for producing other interpretational possibilities. The purpose here will be to explore and possibly expand the sociohistorical and archaeological underpinnings of Fr. Paul's hypothesis regarding the Bible as an anti-hellenistic, anti-urban manifesto.

It has not gone unnoticed that of all the pages devoted to hellenistic cultural and political hegemony in the ancient Near East in *The Rise of Scripture*, no supporting scholarly citations are found other than the occasional self-referencing of the author's previous works.[2] This is not a deficiency, but simply an observation that Tarazi is above all a pastor—that is, a shepherd—who with staff in hand herds people through the process of careful reading to a proper understanding of Scripture. Given his nearly seven decades of faithfully proclaiming the Word, perhaps Tarazi is more than a pastor; rather, something akin to a prophet, who has no need to cite his Source. At any rate, those of us who labor in academia's ivory city tower are not so privileged. Thus, I will be addressing the anti-hellenism thesis in *The Rise of Scripture* in scholarly historical and archaeological terms, with special attention devoted to the biblical symbols of Aram and Aramean,

---

2 See, for example, Daniel Ayuch's review of *The Rise of Scripture* in Theological Review 39.1 (2018): 53-56.

offering documentation and nuance to strengthen the connection between parish and classroom in line with the work and mission of OCABS. The aim here is merely to investigate, assess, and in the end provide support for Tarazi's seemingly audacious and extraordinarily unconventional claims.

The Semitic view of man

One of the pillars of the book's argument for the "rise" of Scripture concerns the difference in anthropological perspective between the Macedonian Greeks and other peoples of the ancient Near East. Mesopotamian cosmogonies assert that human beings are basically blood-filled dirt pods that emerge from the ground and return to it when their breath departs. In the Sumerian *Song of the Hoe*, Enlil, with the help of Ninmena the birthgiver, cultivates humans like seedlings from the soil.[3] In the Akkadian story of *Atrahasis*, Enki commands that the blood of a slain god be mixed with clay, thus forming humans. In the *Enuma Eliš*, Marduk slays Tiamat's champion avenger Qingu, causing his blood to fall upon the dust of the ground and sprout into human beings. Finally, in the book of Genesis, God fashions *haʾadam*, the first man, from *haʾadamah*, the ground, the latter a feminine noun. (2:7) In light of this shared worldview, Fr. Paul Tarazi asserts that Mesopotamian sources not only regard human beings as inextricably tied to the ground, but they make no essential distinction among other ancient Near Eastern peoples. Thus, even the priests of Babylon are able to welcome Cyrus the Great, leader of the Persians and the Medes, as a deliverer and less a foreign conqueror.

By contrast, the Macedonian Greek leaders brought with them a variety of strange new ideas, institutions, and attitudes, all

---

3 Black, J.A., Cunningham, G., Fluckiger-Hawker, E, Robson, E., and Zólyomi, G., *The Electronic Text Corpus of Sumerian Literature* (http://www-etcsl.orient.ox.ac.uk/), Oxford, 1998–2018.

summed up in the *polis hellenis*, a term used by Strabo, Josephus, Plutarch, and others, referring to a sui generis urban phenomenon by which Macedonian hegemony was maintained over the broad expanse of Mesopotamia and its many urban settlements.[4]

It is archaeology, not literature, that attests to the fact that Alexander was not the first to bring Greek culture to Syria,[5] for such is already evident from the 7th century BCE onward. What Alexander brought to the region was bureaucracy in the founding of the Greek city, accompanied by the establishment of a political elite, military garrisons (*choria*) to protect them, and colonies (*katokiai*) of relocated citizens from the Greek mainland that would ostensibly support hellenist ideals, values, customs, and way of life. Its institutions included Hellenistic educational facilities such as the *gymnasion* and *ephebion*, Greek theater, and other public fora, moving the heart of city life from the city gate to the city center, and the most offensive cultural imposition of all, imposition of the Greek cult.[6] Resistance to these institutional impositions is especially evident roughly a century later in the books of the Maccabees, where Judean taboos against nudity, disguised play-acting, an occupier's military garrison, and the installment of pagan shrines become reasons for resistance. Another factor—also evident in 1 Maccabees, but often overlooked—is the complicity of native collaborators who support the occupier for personal advantage.

---

4 Getzel M. Cohen, *The Hellenistic Settlements in the East from Armenia and Mesopotamia to Bactria and India* (Berkeley: University of California Press, 2013), 360.

5 Herodotus records that the biblical Aram was designated "Syria" by the Greeks, in reference to the Assyrians (VII.63).

6 Unfortunately, Seleukeia on the Tigris remains the only hellenistic site that has been systematically excavated, and excavations at the hellenistic level remain incomplete. Cohen, *Hellenistic*, 1-2.

Mesopotamian urbanism and the advent of Macedonian hegemony

The way of life established by Alexander and his immediate successors in Mesopotamia only grew and intensified with the establishment of Seleucid rule. Sometime after the untimely death of Alexander, Seleucus, who was a junior officer and protégé of Perdiccas, Alexander's regent in Babylon, led a mutiny against his patron and murdered him in his tent, thus acquiring the satrapy of Babylon. For the next several years the young warrior was involved in wars among his fellow *diadochi* and eventually fled Babylon for protection in Egypt. In 312 BCE, Seleucus returned to Babylon and with Ptolemaic support proclaims the Anno Græcorum, ushering in the Seleucid era. Upon killing Antigonus "the One-Eyed" at the Battle of Ipsus (301 BCE), Seleucus becomes ruler of all the land stretching from the Mediterranean Sea to modern day Afghanistan, and founds a number of cities, most notably Seleukeia on the Tigris, and Antioch on the Orontes, a Syrian city located today in south-central Turkey. Seleukeia replaces Babylon as the key administrative and commercial center of the region, and, with the founding of Antioch, Seleucus has a new capital city in Syria.

Unlike the polis, for which abundant documentation in Greek sources exists,[7] only a paucity of primary texts witness to Mesopotamian urbanism before the advent of Alexander. Under the Achaemenid Persians, Mesopotamia was divided into four distinct areas comprising roughly twenty satrapies with several relatively autonomous cities. Again, archaeological research supplements the picture. The Mesopotamian city (u r u, *ālu*, in

---

7 Greek and Latin sources include Diodorus Siculus, Strabo, Pliny the Elder, Plutarch, and others.

Akkadian)[8] was a unique institution that resulted from a process of conglomeration beginning with the sharing of social and economic power between a growing centralized administration and the temple, leading to integration among city-dwellers, agriculturalists, and pastoralists.[9] It is important to note that anti-urban movements existed,[10] such as the kind we find in *The Rise of Scripture*, but mostly in the form of a symbiotic tension between urban society and the farmers and pastoralists that interacted with them. It is the case that farmers and shepherds had no intrinsic need for the city and could survive just fine without it; but this need was not reciprocal.

With the coming of the Macedonians, things changed, but some things remained the same. One of the things that changed was the sizeable increase in the number and types of cities, especially with the founding of several Greek cities in northern Syria. Alexander the Great, Antiochus I, and Seleucus all founded cities across the Macedonian empire. Appian lists several Greek and Macedonian cities that were named in honor of the Greek kings or their achievements, or after places in Macedonia (Syr 57).[11] The colonization of Syria, Mesopotamia, and western Iran was, in effect, an effort to establish a new Macedonia in the Land between

---

[8] According to Oppenheim, these terms are not indicative of the size of the settlement. The term applies to any permanent settlement constructed of mud brick or huts, including a structure serving an administrative function. These settlements were usually walled, situated along a river or water channel, and in proximity to its own shrine (*bīt akītu*). A. Leo Oppenheim, *Ancient Mesopotamia: Portrait of a Dead Civilization* (Chicago: University of Chicago Press, 1964, 1976), 114.

[9] The larger cities themselves consisted of distinct parts. There is the city proper, which included the temple-palace complex along with residences for administrative personnel; the city gate (*babtu*), where the affairs of the city were conducted, serving judicial, storage, military, and cultic purposes. Surrounding this was an outer city, consisting of domiciles, agricultural plots, and pastures for sheep and cattle. There was probably also a dock on the water channel. See Oppenheim, *Ancient*, 113.

[10] Oppenheim, *Ancient*, 110.

[11] Cohen, *Hellenistic*, 305.

Rivers.[12] Seleucus alone founded at least twenty of these cities, of which the most famous are those of the Syrian tetrapolis: Seleukeia-in-Pieria, Laodikeia, by the sea; and Antiocheia and Apameia, both along the Orontes river, and all of which situated roughly thirty miles from the Mediterranean.[13] By contrast, pre-established Mesopotamian cities remained structurally unaltered and Hellenization policies were only moderately enforced as efforts were made to accommodate native religion, culture, and civic administration. Also, sources indicate that the Seleucids respected the native priesthoods outside Judea there appears to be no record of suppression. As a result, Greek ideas influenced had a great deal of influence among the educated class, to the point that many learned Greek and opted into the Greek bureaucracy.

It is here that the line between Greeks and Arameans begins to blur. The situation is complicated, and it is important not to force too great a distinction between them. As indicated earlier, Arameans were already well acquainted with Hellenistic culture. Greek political hegemony was established by the imposition of the polis, but for those western Mesopotamians who knew Greek and were amenable to the presence of Greek culture, ethnicity was something that was apparently mutable. In other words, one could join the occupation as a collaborator and be viewed by outsiders, including members of one's own family, as a Hellene. Writing about the inhabitants of Seleukeia on the Tigris, Josephus observes that the population consisted of many Macedonians, -- a majority of Greeks and not a few Syrians.[14] He adds that there had been civil unrest between Greeks and Syrians, but when the Jewish community increased the citizens turned their attention toward them. Writing about the Hellenistic Levant, Herodotus asserts

---

12 Cohen, *Hellenistic*, 14-15.
13 Graham Shipley, *The Greek World after Alexander 323-30 BCE* (New York: Routledge, 2000), 305.
14 Josephus, *Jewish Antiquities* 18.372-74.

"the kinship of all the Greeks in blood and speech, and the shrines of gods, and the sacrifices we all have in common, and the likeness of our way of life,"[15] again suggesting that being a Hellene was not necessarily an ethnic distinction but a cultural one. Elsewhere, Josephus observes that Jews were permitted to refer to themselves as Macedonians.[16] In 1 Maccabees, the priestly Oniads, Jason (born Yeshua) and his brother Menelaus serve as regents of Jerusalem. Furthermore, young Judean men are reported to have had their circumcisions surgically altered (*epispasmos*), ostensibly in an effort to reduce or altogether remove the embarrassment of provincialism and become cosmopolitan—literally, citizens of the world.[17] Finally, Josephus records an account by the Peripatetic philosopher, Clearchus of Soli, which describes Aristotle's encounter with a Jew from Jerusalem named Hyperochides, who Aristotle refers to as Greek not only in language, but also in his soul.[18] It thus appears that the designation Hellene could apply to hellenized natives, even if ethnic Greeks themselves did not accept them as such.[19] One did not have to be Greek ethnically to be considered a Greek functionally. All one would have to do is participate in what Oppenheim calls the "deeply agonistic mood of the Greek city where an ever-enlarging arsenal of complex and elaborate practices was needed to keep the city government functioning in the face of the ambition of certain individuals, who wished to assume control and to exercise power over their fellow citizens."[20]

---

15 Cohen, *Hellenistic*, 361.
16 Josephus, *Jewish War* 2.488.
17 1 Macc 1:11-15; Jub 15:33-34.
18 *Against Apion* 1.21.
19 Cohen, *Hellenistic*, 368, fn 28.
20 Oppenheim, *Ancient*, 114.

Chariots of fire

In addition to Scripture's obvious anti-urban and anti-king agenda, one finds also a critique of Israel's dependence on its military weaponry, most noticeably the chariot.[21] For biblical Israel, these military tanks of the ancient world are all but missing from Scripture. Apart from Solomon's exorbitant number of chariots (40,000 stalls, 1 Kgs 4:26; but 2 Chr 9:25 records 4,000 stalls), only Israel's enemy neighbors have chariots—and quite a lot of them. But according to Scripture, Israel's highest and best line of defense is not represented by chariots constructed of wood and metal, but by chariots of fire and horses of fire (2 Kgs 2). In 2 Kings 6, the fiery horses and chariots that passed between Elisha and Elijah show up again when Elisha and his disciple find themselves surrounded by Aram's massive army of horse-drawn chariots. Elisha's disciple is filled with fear, but the prophet admonishes him, saying they are not outnumbered, but that they outnumber them. The disciple's eyes are then opened, and he beholds the mountains all around him gleaming with chariots and horses of fire (2 Kgs 6:17).

The fact that biblical Israelites lack chariots when all the surrounding nations have many is significant. The fact that Aram and the Philistines have the most chariots to bring into battle against biblical Israel is also significant. The Greeks had hundreds of dreaded scythed chariots, many of which they took from the Persians. According to Greek historians, Seleucus had no less than 120 scythed chariots at his disposal at the battle of Ipsus (301

---

21 Nicolae Roddy, "Chariots of Fire, Unassailable Cities, and the One True King: The Prophetically Influenced Scribal Perspective on War." Perry T. Hamalis and Valerie A. Karras, eds.; *Orthodox Christian Perspectives on War* (Notre Dame: University of Notre Dame Press, 2017), 61-84.

BCE),[22] and he and his successors continued using them, with varying degrees of success, in his wars with the Ptolemies as well.

This ties in well with Fr. Paul's thesis regarding the nations. How so? The interchange of symbols between Aram and Aramean creates an ambiguity between the fixed permanence of the former, and the fluidity of "Who or What is an Aramean?"—a wandering inhabitant of the earth, according to Fr. Paul.[23] Geographically, Aram (called Syria in the LXX) overlaps the Syrian Wilderness, a symbolic region that figures so prominently in *The Rise of Scripture*. The Scriptural Arameans are descendants of Aram, a son of Shem, a son of Noah (Gen 10:22), of the significant Sethite lineage. Throughout the book of Genesis, the biblical ancestors are described as Aramean, and in the book of Deuteronomy it is part of the memorializing confession: "A wandering Aramean was my father" (Deut 26:5). In the Former Prophets, Israel battles the Arameans. They fatally wound King Joram, and the Yahweh sends them with the Babylonians, Edomites, and Moabites to destroy Jerusalem. Thus, there is an interesting kinship between the biblical ancestors and their later antagonists, so that being Aramean appears less an ethnic designation, than a geographical one. *The Rise of Scripture* situates them among the nations, but tying together everything we have covered, I would suggest that while the Philistines are stand-ins for the Greeks (and Goliath as Alexander), the Arameans are stand-ins for Greeks and natives together as people who inhabit Aram, some of which wander about the region, while others dwell in cities. It is the latter of these that desire to seize and wield control over the Syrian Wilderness.

---

22 Bezalel Bar-Kochva, *The Seleucid Army: Organization and Tactics in the Great Campaign* (Cambridge: Cambridge University Press, 2012), 83-84.

23 Paul Nadim Tarazi, *The Rise of Scripture* (St. Paul: OCABS Press), 297 ff.

In Scripture, Aram is also an arena for antagonism against Israel's kings and the wars of conquest against them, as in the Aramean-Israel alliance formed by kings Rezin and Pekah respectively against King Ahaz of Judah. In addition to being a battleground for iron chariots (*rekeb barzel*), Aram is linked to significant prophetic activity, most notably that of Elijah and Elisha, whose divinely endowed power is represented by fiery chariots and horses.[24]

In sum, there seems to be a clear a distinction between Aram's overlap with the Syrian wilderness and the biblically ambiguous Arameans themselves. The literary ambiguity of being Aramean vis-à-vis a fixed Aramean nation brings enemies together on a level playing field. Ethnicity is malleable; just as for Paul there is no Jew nor Greek, neither is there Syrian or Macedonian. All are accountable to the God of Scripture. As Fr. Paul Tarazi points out, the God of Scripture grants victory and healing to this leprous enemy king, Naaman the Aramean, whom Elisha heals without condition so that the enemy king goes his way acknowledging the scriptural Deity.[25] Conversely, Elisha's servant is punished with leprosy for his greed in running after Naaman and shaking him down for payment. By leveling the playing field in this way, one sees that no inhabitant of the earth is privileged.

Conclusion

The task here has been to explore further the real world out of which the Bible is purported to have emerged according to Tarazi's *The Rise of Scripture*. The book's general assertions about the Greek presence in Mesopotamia are reliably sound but benefit from a few significant nuances. First, the putative scribal community that produced the Bible was ostensibly one of many

---

24 See 2 Kgs 2; 6:8-23; 13:14-16.
25 Tarazi, *Rise*, 302-303.

other anti-urban groups, but the fact that it is the only one known to have provided a cryptic account of its own unique story makes it difficult to elevate the hypothesis to the level of theory. To be sure, the hypothesis is supported by a persuasive literary analysis out of which the Bible seems to function as a scathing, self-effacing epic that criticizes its own institutions, which I have identified elsewhere to include the city, the monarchy, the military, and the cult. The question is whether this overall critique is rooted in an anti-hellenistic literary campaign, as Tarazi asserts, or is a concerted Persian-era response to the destruction of the Jerusalem temple. Such a critique of institutions would be appropriate in either case.

Finally, while Greek ethnocentricity was strong and immutable, elements of hellenistic ethnicity were fluid, which is to say that hellenism was a concept that non-Greeks could ostensibly buy into whether the ethnocentric Macedonian Greeks actually accepted them or not; thus, the antithetical stereotyping of Greek and Mesopotamian urbanism can be misleading. For example, scholars generally agree that the political organization of Mesopotamian cities was not significantly affected by the arrival of the Greeks,[26] even though the idea of having individual citizenship was foreign to Mesopotamian urban society. Even under Greek hegemony, Mesopotamian cites continued to be made up of a conglomeration of social configurations—familial, ethnic, residential, etc.—in contrast to Greek cities, where free citizens are primarily regarded as individuals, albeit drawn together by public places like the agora, fora, or baths, and in institutions such as the assembly. In sum, there remained more similarities than differences between Greek and Mesopotamian

---

[26] Marc van de Mieroop, *The Ancient Mesopotamian City* (Oxford: Oxford University Press, 1999), 253.

cities.²⁷ Thus, while the biblical Philistines may be stand-ins for the Greeks, as Tarazi asserts,²⁸ the ambiguous Arameans may well represent both urban Macedonian invaders and Mesopotamian pastoral wanderers interacting in the (historical) Aram overlapping the (literary) Syrian Wilderness, offering a scathing comprehensive critique of all human beings on a level playing field.²⁹ Such would accord quite well with Tarazi's hypothesis. Although actual literary connections to the sociohistorical milieu remain tentative, the Scriptural effect is not dependent upon the putative sociohistorical cause.

---

27 Van de Mieroop, *Ancient*, 258.
28 Tarazi, *Rise*, 265 ff.
29 This might explain the assertion expressed in 1 Macc 12:20-23, echoed by Josephus in *Ant.* 12:4:10, that Jews and Lacedemonians (i.e., Spartans) stem from a common ancestor.

The Bible in Miniature: The Blasphemer and the Law in Leviticus 24:10–23

Harrison Russin

"Just give me fifty-one percent," was the beginning of Fr Paul Tarazi's "Introduction to Old Testament" class. While the course was a notorious stumbling block and bugbear for first-year seminarians at St Vladimir's Seminary, those who paid attention received an incomparable gift from our professor—the capability to read the Bible as a whole.

This gift is indeed rare among teachers of scripture. In an age of academic specializations with increasingly narrow focuses and sub-fields, Tarazi has shown his students that this text—these writings which tell us who God is—needs to be read as a whole. It is one story, the same story, told over and over and over again, through different narrators and different voices.

I remain a layman in several senses of the word. I am not ordained to the major orders of our church's tradition (i.e., the presbyterate and the diaconate), and I am not an academic who focuses on scripture. I have, on the other hand, received a seminary degree and I have graduate degrees in music history. While my education discloses a certain status regarding understanding scripture, the Church, and its traditions, I still consider myself a layman and neophyte in these matters. But I am, at least, a layman who cares, who struggles with scripture, who has attempted to learn Hebrew and Greek. I read the Bible with Tarazi's questions in mind—"why?", but more importantly, "what for?"

As Orthodox Christians, we are most accustomed to encountering scripture in short pericopes and readings. Our readings at liturgy rarely exceed a dozen verses from the epistles and the gospels, and those who peruse the scriptures daily do not often read entire books at a time. Indeed, these short pericopes give us a narrow and focused window into scripture, but that window needs to be opened regularly to show us the panorama of God's law.

These open windows point out the oddities of scripture. Leviticus—the middle of the Torah, the centerpiece of the Law—contains very little narrative. Thus, when we encounter stories within this text, we should pay extra attention. In the midst of innumerable paragraphs beginning with "The Lord said to Moses," we find this story:

> Now an Israelite woman's son, whose father was an Egyptian, went out among the people of Israel; and the Israelite woman's son and a man of Israel quarreled in the camp, and the Israelite woman's son blasphemed the Name, and cursed. And they brought him to Moses. His mother's name was Shelomith, the daughter of Dibri, of the tribe of Dan. And they put him in custody, till the will of the Lord should be declared to them.
>
> And the Lord said to Moses, "Bring out of the camp him who cursed; and let all who heard him lay their hands upon his head, and let all the congregation stone him. And say to the people of Israel, "Whoever curses his God shall bear his sin. He who blasphemes the name of the Lord shall be put to death; and all the congregation shall stone him; the sojourner as well as the native, when he blasphemes the Name, shall be put to death. He who kills a man shall be put to death. He who kills a beast shall make good, life for life. When a man causes a disfigurement in his neighbor, as he has done it shall be done to him, fracture for fracture, eye for eye, tooth for tooth; as he has disfigured a man, he shall be disfigured. He who kills a beast shall make it good; and he who kills a man shall be put to death. You shall have one law for the sojourner and for the native; for I am the Lord your God." So Moses spoke to

the people of Israel; and they brought him who had cursed out of the camp, and stoned him with stones. Thus the people of Israel did as the Lord commanded Moses. (Lev 24:10–23 RSV)

Narrative is rare in Leviticus, as well as within the legal chapters of the Pentateuch as a whole. There is only one other narrative portion of Leviticus—the story of Nadab and Abihu (Lev 10:1–11), the sons of Aaron who offered unholy fire to the Lord and were devoured by fire from the Lord.[1] The book of Numbers contains three further narratives which act in a similar manner to the Levitical narratives. Numbers 9:6–14 presents the story of "certain men" who defiled themselves by touching a dead body on the passover; Numbers 15:32–36 is the story of a "a man gathering sticks on the sabbath day"; and Numbers 27:1–11 shows the daughters of the deceased Zelophehad requesting an inheritance among their father's brethren.[2]

Scholars and attentive readers of scripture have long been perplexed by these short stories, and particularly by the story of the blasphemer in Leviticus 24. Some writers have gone to great lengths to explore the background of this nameless blasphemer, postulating, for instance, that Shelomith was given in marriage to the son of the Egyptian slain by Moses (Exod 2:11); or, that Shelomith was raped by an Egyptian, who was killed by Moses in Exodus 2 as the Egyptian was quarrelling with Shelomith's Israelite husband; or that the blasphemer, having been denied a paternal inheritance in court, curses the Name out of anger and alienation.[3]

---

[1] Many commentators note the structural similarity of Lev 24:10–23 and 10:1–11. Cf. Milgrom, *Leviticus*, Anchor Bible 3B (New York: Doubleday, 2000), 2102.

[2] Jonathan Vroom, "Recasting *Mispatim*: Legal Innovation in Leviticus 24:10–23," *JBL* 131 (2012):27–44, at 27, n.1.

[3] H. Mittwoch, "The Story of the Blasphemer Seen in a Wider Context," *Vetus Testamentum* 15 (1965), 386–389; Ephraim Radner, *Leviticus* (Grand Rapids: Brazos,

Tarazi reads Leviticus as central to the entire biblical story—but already dealing with the eschatological city of Ezekiel.[4] The laws of the atonement, the jubilee year and the sabbath (in Deuteronomy) assert the priority of the land over the people— these laws "protect the earth from the children of Israel."[5] It is furthermore necessary to hear not only the laws but the narratives of the Pentateuch as eschatological in that same sense—asserting the given-ness and contingency of Israel's "election."

Thus, we are immediately attentive to one of the startling features of this story—the main character has no given name. Instead, we encounter a genealogy providing his lack of bona fides. But the lack of a name highlights the salience of names when the do appear. The blasphemer, in other words, cannot be spoken of directly; yet, he is in a similar position to "named" characters throughout the scriptures whose names are divine jokes. Adam, for example, barely owns his own name, as it applies to all men; Isaac's name is imposed as a pun, and the sons of Elimelech and Naomi have no identity outside of their premature illnesses and deaths. The lack of a name is as functional as the specification of one.

The blasphemer's genealogy implies he is impure in his ethnicity—"an Israelite woman's son, whose father was an Egyptian." Despite the attempts cited above to discern more about this son's identity and history, we only know that his father was an Egyptian. But the grave challenge of his ethnicity is that the

---

2008), 258–264; Yossi Feintuch, "Life and Death in the Power of One's Tongue: The Case of Shelomith Bat-Dibri," *JBL* 34 (2006), 16–19.

4 Paul Nadim Tarazi, *The Old Testament Introduction, vol 1 – Historical Traditions, new revised edition* (Crestwood: St Vladimir's Seminary Press, 2003), 120.

5 Paul Nadim Tarazi, *Land and Covenant* (St Paul: OCABS Press, 2009), 107.

father of sinful Israel is Egypt. Ezekiel provokes his listeners by asserting their mixed ethnic identity:

> Thus says the Lord God to Jerusalem: Your origin and your birth are of the land of the Canaanites; your father was an Amorite, and your mother a Hittite. And as for your birth, on the day you were born your navel string was not cut, nor were you washed with water to cleanse you, nor rubbed with salt, nor swathed with bands. (Ezek 16:3-4)

The blasphemer's upbringing, however, affords him every chance to honor, rather than to blaspheme, the Name. That he "went out" among the sons of Israel might necessitate that he came from among them to begin with—especially when considering his Israelite ancestry. The quarrelling recalls Moses's intervention of the quarrelling of two Hebrews (Ex 2:13), the first instance of the verb *n-ts-h*. In addition to quarrelling, the unnamed one blasphemes (*naqab*) the Name and curses (*qalal*). It is not obvious that the three actions—quarrelling, blaspheming, and cursing—are related. But after the impropriety of his deeds is brought to Moses, his genealogy is clarified, as if pointing out that he should have known better.

The blasphemer's mother is Shelomith—from the triliteral *sh-l-m*, "peaceful." Shelomith is the daughter of Dibri, from the triliteral *d-b-r*, "word." And Dibri is of the tribe of Dan, whose name derives from *d-y-n*, "judge." In Leviticus 26:6, God promises "peace in the land, and you shall lie down, and none shall make you afraid." Indeed, the verb of *sh-l-m*, which can also mean to make good or to make restitution, clarifies that peacefulness is the order of God's land.[6] Furthermore, peace comes from (or is in this instance the daughter of) the Word. The Word of God is the source of life throughout scripture. "By the word of the Lord the

---

[6] The verb is extensively used in the restitution laws of Exod 21–22, and later on in this very pericope (Lev 24:18).

heavens were made, and all their host by the breath of his mouth" (Ps 33:6); heeding his word is equivalent to heeding his law (Isa 2:3), the law being received throughout the book of Leviticus. The patrimony of the blasphemer leads to Dan, the judge. The judgment of Dan—petulantly wrong, most famously in the idolatry of Judges 17–18—is in stark contrast to the judgment of God:

> For the Lord will judge His people and have compassion on His servants, when He sees that their power is gone, and there is no one remaining, bond or free. (Deut 32:36, NKJV)

Perhaps the ultimate irony of this passage is that the nameless blasphemer—a descendent of Shem (Gen 11)—defiles the Name (*ha shem*). His sin is abusing something he cannot even afford in the narrative.[7]

The blasphemer, in other words, is Israel, given the peace, word, and judgment of God through his law, yet remaining in quarrelling, blasphemy, and cursing. The punishment for this behavior applies to the sojourner as well as to the native—"you shall have one law for the sojourner and for the native." The universality of this law highlights its eschatological setting, but also demands identification of the native with the foreign-born.

> You shall not oppress a stranger (*ger*); you know the heart of a stranger (*ger*), for you were strangers (*ger*) in the land of Egypt. (Exod 23:9)

---

[7] The meanings of these names within the narrative have been recognized and parsed by other writers. See Trevaskis, "The Purpose of Leviticus 24 within its Literary Context," *Vetus Testamentum* 59 (2009):295–312, at 309; Mark Leuchter, "The Ambiguous Details in the Blasphemer Narrative: Sources and Redaction in Leviticus 24:10–23," *JBL* 130 (2011): 431–450, at 438; Erhard Gerstenberger, *Leviticus*, trans. Douglas W. Stott (Louisville: Westminster John Knox, 1996 [1993]), 361; Mary Douglas, *Leviticus as Literature* (Oxford: Oxford University Press, 1999), 211–215.

The *lex talionis* which follows is, then, the instantiation of God's law in the eschatological Israel. Mary Douglas brilliantly observes how, throughout the legal cases of sin in Leviticus, Numbers, and even Daniel (in Greek), the type of punishment accords to the crime by means of a subtle word play. *N-q-b*, to dishonor, "has the same stem as 'to bore a hole', or 'to pierce', and by extension, to specify, to pronounce explicitly, to identify."[8] Fittingly, then, the punishment for such dishonor is hurling or pelting. Thus, as Douglas states, "the blasphemer has hurled insults at the name of God, let him die by stones hurled at him. … [H]e has slung mud, let him die by mud slung at him."[9] In other words, the *lex talionis*— "as he has done it shall be done to him, fracture for fracture, eye for eye, tooth for tooth"—is not some mindless retribution system, but rather the eschatological statement that the sins of Israel create their own reality, always falling short of God's law and commandments. This retribution is a literary reality, made possible through text and wordplay, and not a system of revenge. Heard in this way, then, Jesus's words in Matthew 5 are clarifying, not abrogating.

> You have heard that it was said, 'An eye for an eye and a tooth for a tooth.' But I say to you, Do not resist one who is evil. But if any one strikes you on the cheek, turn to him the other also. (Matt 5:38-39)

Despite the tendency of some commentators to view Jesus's words as nullifying the law of Leviticus, Jesus is highlighting the law's end. Jesus offers that same law, with that same eschatological promise.

Furthermore, when that law is followed, those who do it are perfect. "You, therefore, must be perfect, as your heavenly Father

---

8 Mary Douglas, *Leviticus*, 206, citing Baruch Levine, *The JPS Commentary, Leviticus* (New York: Jewish Publication Society, 1989), 166.

9 Douglas, *Leviticus*, 207.

is perfect" (Matt 5:48). The commandment here again mirrors Leviticus: "You shall be holy; for I the Lord your God am holy" (Lev 19:2b). Perfection and holiness are the states of those who follow this eschatological law.

The story of the blasphemer in Leviticus 24, then, is a reduction of the scriptural story to its most fundamental parts. As Tarazi is fond of saying, scripture is boring because it is the same story over and over. The blasphemer narrative is the same story as Genesis 1–4, and the same story as Ezekiel—God's people are given his law and do not keep it, but he will provide for them until they learn to keep it.

The Mary and Martha Paradigm (Luke 10:38-42): A Call to Training for Mission and Contemplation of the Word of God. A Roumanian Orthodox Point of View

Rev. Cătălin Varga

Preliminaries

The theme of this research aims to highlight a new perspective of the well-known story of Martha and Mary. I try to go beyond the literary sense of the Greek text, passing it through a new optic: both Mary and Martha can be seen as missionary models, but only when both are considered together, as any attempt to individualize results in bankrupting the mission. The true mission, or "the good part that will not be taken" (Luke 10:42a) must first pass through the spiritual exercise of contemplation of the Word and prayer through the benevolent ascetic of the wilderness (Matt 4:2), and only then move to action, to the mission itself. These two coordinates - knowing and living - cannot be separated. They must be practiced synchronously, because you cannot achieve a fruitful mission without knowing and living the Word of the Gospel. At the same time, the sole contemplation of the Word is not sufficient without genuine praxis.

The Martha model is insufficient, because it calls for action only, while the Mary model is a hard one to understand in the strict terms of our questioning, because Christ shows proof of his behavior to her. At first reading, I was inclined to say that Mary ignores the ministry, putting the hardship of the mission on her sister's shoulders. The Martha mission model is wrong also from another point of view. Martha was anxious to handle the peripheral details[1]. Christ only wanted a simple meal in the company of good friends.[2] The verb περιεσπᾶτο (Luke 10:40) means "to be distracted" or "to divide in all directions"[3], that is, to dispel yourself unnecessarily by cultivating incoherent actions. The imperfect of the verb κατέλιπεν also expresses the state of continuity of neglect by Mary. This Greek word does not assume that there was a time when Mary would have helped Martha and then abandoned her in favor of contemplation; but simply that Martha was overlooked[4] from the beginning.

The Romanian Bible[5] translations lose sight of this nuance by translating the verb περιεσπᾶτο into the "to urge" variant, which can give rise to confusion. According to this perspective, we would be tempted to believe that Martha "was urging herself " in the fulfillment of a dynamic ministry, full of abnegation and

---

[1] John MacArthur, *Comentariul Biblic MacArthur*. Noul Testament (Făgăraș: Agape, 2009), 221-222.

[2] Don Fleming, *Bridgeway Bible Commentary* (Brisbane: Bridgeway Publications, 2005), 461.

[3] Barbara Friberg, Timothy Friberg, and Neva F. Miller, *Analytical Lexicon of the Greek New Testament* (Grand Rapids: Baker Books, 2000); F. Wilbur Gingrich, *Shorter Lexicon of the Greek New Testament* (Chicago: The University of Chicago Press, 1979), 157.

[4] Alfred Plummer, *A Critical and Exegetical Commentary on the Gospel According to St. Luke* (New York: Charles Scribner's Sons, 1903), 291.

[5] †Bartolomeu Valeriu Anania, *Biblia sau Sfânta Scriptură* (Cluj-Napoca: Editura Renașterea, 2009), 1535; *Biblia sau Sfânta Scriptură* (București: Editura Institutului Biblic și de Misiune al Bisericii Ortodoxe Române, 2005), 1181. The Catholic and Protestant translations of contemporary Romanian Bible are much more faithful to the sacred text, by using the variants "she was busy with many chores" or "she was divided with much service". See in respect Emil PASCAL, *Noul Testament* (Paris: Éditions du Dialogue, 1992), 284; The same reasoning surrounds the SBIR interconfessional translation through the formula "she was busy with many chores". See in respect *Noul Testament. Traducere după textele originale grecești* (București: Societatea Biblică Interconfesională din România, 2014), 140.

harmony, but this is not what St. Apostle Luke⁶ writes. It is precisely for this that Christ intervenes.

Scholar B. Witherington expresses surprise by the behavior of Christ the Savior, which becomes for him atypical to the Jewish world, because a rabbi was forbidden to go to a single woman's house. Moreover, this biblical scholar says the gesture seems to be out of the ordinary. It would have been unusual for Christ to speak alone in the same room with two women who were not his close relatives.[7] What this scholar seems to omit is the very construction of the prologue of this pericope: Ἐν δὲ τῷ πορεύεσθαι αὐτοὺς "While they were going," in which this personal pronoun αὐτοὺς plays an essential role in this problem. It shows that the Savior was not alone with Martha and Mary; thus not breaking any Jewish custom, but with his disciples and apostles.

Martha was a woman much appreciated by Jesus (Luke 8:11) because she was an active and trustworthy[8] disciple. Along with her practical spirit, Martha believed with sincerity in Jesus the Messiah. Her confession in this respect, counting among the most

---

[6] It is timely to follow the parallel Martha/non prodigal Son in the logic of their ministry, both cases encompassing correspondents in St. Luke the Evangelist. Martha is characterized by the verbal description περιεσπᾶτο of the adult son of Luke 15:29, and the following pattern is being constructed: ἰδοὺ τοσαῦτα ἔτη δουλεύω σοι ("I have been serving you for so many years"). Both cases are examples of missions who miss their target due to their subjective implications, the former betrayed a cunning zeal, and the second purely contractual interests. The Lord does not remain indifferent to these instances of erroneous understanding of the mission, but He cares for both of them, seeking to correct them.

[7] BenWitherington III, *Women in the Ministry of Jesus* (Cambridge: Cambridge University Press, 1984), 101: "Not just Mary's assumed role but Christ's behavior itself in this scene comes to contrast with what was normally expected from a woman and a Jewish man."

[8] Gerhard Maier, *Evanghelia după Luca*, (Sibiu: Lumina Lumii, 2013), 480; Roswell D. Hitchcock, *Hitchcock's Bible Names Dictionary* (Grand Rapids: Christian Classics Ethereal Library), 92.

impressive evocations[9] (John 11:27). But only Mary's example is praised by Him.[10] She sat at the feet of the Lord[11] listening to His Word. For the Jews, this was the position of the disciple who thus forms, with all the condescension of the conjuncture, his new doctrinal and moral convictions, as St. Apostle Paul at the feet of the erudite Gamaliel (Acts 22:3).[12] Here, St. Luke does not relay the substance of the conversation, but its significance can be understood from 10:42b, where Jesus praises Mary's attention. The Lord probably interpreted the Scriptures, especially the Messianic prophecies. Just as in the Lucan narrative (1:1-4; 2:30-32; 3:4-6; 4:16-30; 24:25-27, 44-47) there is a tendency to show that the references of the prophets to the person of Messiah are fulfilled in Christ and in His soteriological work begun in the people of Israel.[13]

The contemplation of the Word, the premise of an authentic mission

From the happy example of Mary, we observe the necessity of contemplation and prayer; imperatives that become *sine qua non*

---

[9] Richard R. Losch, *Dicționar enciclopedic de personaje biblice* (Oradea: Editura Casa Cărții, 2014), 328.

[10] But Martha's image will be indirectly rehabilitated when she serves in Bethany a few days before the Jewish Passover, this time meditating at the same time on the Word of God (John 12:2). It seems that the advice he received in her house from Jesus (Luke 10:42: "One thing is necessary") was not indifferent to her.

[11] Even this unhumble attitude of Mary raises doubts for the negative criticism, saying, contrary to the Lucan text, that she did not stand at her Teacher's feet because the meal was not yet served. See in respect Plummer, *Critical and Exegetical Commentary*, 290-291. Others, like R. Schnackenburg, strengthen the words of praise by Mary's gesture to sit at the feet of Jesus to listen to Him in faith, thus assuring her, contrary to her sister, the good part, the perseverance of her faith. See Rudolf Schnackenburg, *Die Person Jesu Christi im Spiegel der Vier Evangelien* (Freiburg: Verlag Herder, 1993), 230.

[12] Eugène Jacquier, *Les Actes des Apôtres* (Paris: J. Gabalda Éditeur, 1926), 646-647.

[13] Susan J. Wendel, *Scriptural Interpretation and Community Self-Definition in Luke-Acts and the Writings of Justin Martyr* (Leiden: Brill, 2011), 142-143.

conditions for starting an authentic Orthodox mission. The contemplation of the Word of the Gospel and its fulfillment can give direction; it is the correct orientation. Christ's gracious word transfigures the true missionary, who in turn can transfigure the environment in which he comes in contact. But this saving work does not happen because of the missionary. It is the grace of Christ, so that no one should boast (Eph 2:8).

The born-again status from "water and spirit" (John 3:3-5[14]) is a future passive condition without which no one will inherit the Kingdom of Heaven. Unless we receive the Holy Spirit through the baptism of the rebirth, we will not be able to know Christ truly[15], and sin will still be in us. Christ speaks of the Upper Birth in His dialogue with Nicodemus, in order to present the Spirit as above all, because our transformation is not through the water but through the Holy Spirit.[16] Through Him we become new partakers of the divine nature, always making the image of the Archetype[17] in us. Here again, two aspects of God's action in the baptismal rebirth must be deepened: the birth of water (ἐξ ὕδατος) as the living expression of the sacramental element, and

---

14 The adverb ἄνωθεν ("a new birth", "rebirth") is interpreted in the biblical exegesis from two perspectives: the first meaning is the temporal perspective being strengthened by the use of ὕδωρ in 3:5, but also by the use of verb ἀναγεννάω in patristic literature; and the second is the spatial perspective ("from above"). See Răzvan Perşa, "Omul subiect pasiv în renaşterea baptismală. O perspectivă Ioaneică," *Studii Teologice* 66, no. 1 (2011): 221.

15 Ioan Gură De Aur, *Comentariu la Evanghelia de la Ioan* (Satu Mare: Ed. Mănăstirii «Portăriţa», 2005), 121.

16 Origen, *Commentaria in Evangelium Joannis*, PG14, 275B; Richard E. Averbeck, "Spirit, Community, and Mission: A Biblical Theology for Spiritual Formation," *Journal of Spiritual Formation & Soul Care*, no. 1 (2008): 29-30.

17 Cyril of Alexandria, *Expositio sive Commentarius in Joannis Evangelium*, PG73, 147C-147D.

the birth of the Holy Spirit (καὶ πνεύματος), the One who leads the subject to his spiritualisation, under adumbration of grace.[18]

According to the New Testament authors, the born again reality is not only baptismal, but it also occurs through the Word of God (ὁ λόγος[19]), as we see in John 15:3; Romans 1:16[20]; 1 Corinthians 4:15[21]; 15:1-2; Ephesians 1:13; 1 Thessalonians 2:13; 1 Timothy 4:5; James 1:18.21[22] and 1 Peter 1:3.23.[23] Rebirth from above is a

---

18 Francis Martin, "Le baptême dans l'Esprit. Tradition du Nouveau Testament et vie de l'Église," *Nouvelle Revue Théologique* 106, no. 1 (1984): 38; James D.G. Dunn, *Baptism in the Holy Spirit* (Philadelphia: The Westminster Press, 1970), 184; Dirk G. van der Merwe, "Old Testament Spirituality in the gospel of John", *Verbum et Ecclesia* 35, no. 1 (2014): 5-6.

19 The Word must be understood here as the power of God that cleanses us from our passions (John 15:3), it is the power of creation, of reconfiguring our inner man, he communicates not only ideas, but also spiritual transfigurative realities. See in respect Alexander Schmemann, *Din Apă și din Duh* (București: Sofia, 2009), 37-38.

20 Otto Kuss, *Carta a los Romanos*, (Barcelona: Editorial Herder, 1976), 39: St. Paul is not ashamed of the gospe... it is the decisive force by which we are saved by God, He being the only one who can offer help in the misery of this world... After all, the Gospel has a message to the whole world, in which tells us about the salvation from God through Jesus Christ".

21 Saint Chrysostom insists in his commentary on the power of the Word of God in the process of the conversion of the Corinthians, and on this ἐγέννησα (from the *gennāo* root meaning "to be born", "to give birth", "to prove paternity"), clearly showing the efforts of preaching the gospel by St. Paul in the hope of the rebirth of the Corinthians in Christ. See in respect ST. CHRYSOSTOM, *Homilies on First and Second Corinthians* (Edinburgh: T&T Clark, 1889), 74.

22 S. McKnight on the basis of 1:18 speaks of a triple action of God: first is the will of God concerning our regeneration (18a), then we are presented with the means of this rebirth (18b), for ultimately, let us its target is proposed (18c). Concerning the second action, the author is rightly inclined to believe that St. Apostle Jacob by using the genitive *alētheias* regards the message of the Gospel and its role in the icon of the salvation of the community. See Scot McKnight, *The Letter of James* (Grand Rapids: William B.Eerdmans Publishing Company, 2011), 129-132.

23 Father Adrian Murg, in a research centered on the cult of primary Christian life, referring to this text, said: "In 1 Pet. the emphasis falls on the certainty of the inheritance, while in Titus is underlined the actuality of salvation. In Titus, the ideas of the baptism are obvious, while in 1 Pet. they are only implicit, because the *ho anagennēsas* formula

mystery; accomplished both through the Sacrament of Baptism and the Word of the Gospel.[24] Baptism is an epiphanic reality, that is why the Christian unites with Christ by participating in His death and resurrection (by immersing three times in the sanctified water and by lifting it from the water), including for the first time the one who is baptized in his Eucharistic Body.[25] St. Mark the Ascetic first states that Baptism is perfect, the part that targets us is precisely the urge to live "according to Baptism". Being free by Baptism we can choose our perfection, clear evidence of the received grace.[26]

---

does not necessarily indicate the Baptism, but may refer to spiritual renewal through the Word of God". See in respect Adrian Murg, "Cult și viață creștină după Întâia Epistolă sobornicească a Sfântului Apostol Petru," *Teologia* 14, no. 2 (2010): 116; Philip L. Tite, "The Compositional Function of the Petrine Prescript: A Look at 1 Peter 1; 1-3," *Journal of the Evangelical Theological Society* 39, no. 1 (1996): 52. Hammer, based on a linguistic investigation of the term *anagennāo* argues that at the end of the sec. I, he had a cyclical turn: the recurrence of something that existed previously and that volatilized, but now he has returned - and this return is synonymous with his rebirth. See Keir E. Hammer, *Disambiguating Rebirth: A Socio-Rhetorical Exploration of Rebirth Language in 1 Peter*, (Toronto: Centre for the Study of Religion University of Toronto, 2011), 148.

24 Saint John emphasizes the complementary role of the two great events, but recalling that the mystery of Baptism can be accomplished by all who receive the priesthood, for it does not cause too great of a struggle; instead, the annunciation of the Gospel requires a lot of wisdom, and labor, and toil, and hard work, and it is the place of one or of a few. See in respect Ioan Gură de Aur, *Comentariile sau Tâlcuirea Epistolei întâi către Corintheni* (București: Sofia, 2005), 26-27.

25 Oscar Cullmann, *Baptism in the New Testament* (London: SCM Press, 1956), 15; Dumitru Stăniloae, *Teologia Dogmatică Ortodoxă*, vol. 3 (București: Editura Institutului Biblic și de Misiune al Bisericii Ortodoxe Române, 1997), 28: "The Son had to sink into human nature and through it into the water, for that we, sinking in water, to sink in His divine life, or in His Holy Spirit".

26 Marcu Ascetul, *Răspuns acelora care se îndoiesc despre dumnezeiescul botez* (București: Humanitas, 2004), 269-270: "That grace is in us from Baptism, teaching us all the truth according to the word of the Lord (John 16:13), you can know from Scripture and even from the effects we feel...But we don't bring these testimonies to say that all the man who was baptized and received the grace is then unchangeable and has no longer need for repentance. But through them, we show that even from Baptism,

Roumanian priest Iosif Trifa[27], inspired by the writings of St. Athanasius the Great[28] and Reverend Ilarion Felea[29], understand the salvation of man, carried on the three births: the first is the birth from the parents, the next is " from water and from the Spirit " in the mystery of Holy Baptism, and the last is the resurrection (Gal 4:19). The resurrection is birthed within the mystery of repentance through the instigation of the Word of the Gospel. The Word commences the soteriological work commenced at Baptism, renewing and stating the image of Christ in the baptized Christian. St. Symeon The New Theologian refers to this as nothing but "a second baptism."[30] Roumanian New Testament

---

according to the gift of Christ, God's grace was given to fulfill all commandments, but that afterwards all who received it mysteriously, but did not fulfill the commandments, as a result of noncompliance, it is taken in the possession of sin, which is not Adam's, but that of those who disobeyed the commandments, because taking the power of the work does not do the work."

27 Iosif Trifa, *Dumnezeu – Duhul Sfânt* (Sibiu: Editura Oastea Domnului, 2007), 66: "The mystery of Baptism is the spiritual graft of man. Baptism cuts off, kills the old man and graftig the new one. But whoever does not care for the soul and life can lose this grafting. Sins are the old groves that grow underneath the old stalk of the old man. And if these exfoliations are not cleansed, they stifle the new man, the spiritual man. They take his power, they take his life. The old man conquers the new man again. The tree of his life gives yet again wild, worldly fruits (Gal 5:20). Here is the labor of birth again. It cleanses the old offshoots, so that the graft can develop, grow, and produce the fruits of the Holy Spirit".

28 St. Athanasius, *On the Incarnation of the Word* (Edinburgh: T&T Clark, 1891), 43-44: "When He said to the Jews: "If anyone is not born again", He did not refer, as they thought, to the birth of a woman, but to the soul created and born again according to the image of God".

29 Ilarion V. Felea, *Spre Tabor*, vol. 4 (Piatra Neamț: Editura Crigarux, 2010), 43: "In the light of the gospel, man has three births; the first: the birth of the body in the mother's parental breast; the second: the new birth of the soul out of the water and of the Spirit in the mystery of Saint Baptism, and the third: birth or rebirth in the mystery of repentance, which is the continuous renewal of Baptism, the renewal of the image of Christ in the baptized Christian".

30 In the spiritual experience of Saint Symeon, the tears of repentance trickled when the Christian opened his mind's eyes looking around him as he had never again looked, are the sign of the second Baptism - as Christ anticipates it in the dialogue with Nicodemus

scholar, Father Vasile Mihoc, after demonstrating that the baptism is a born-again reality, says that he must also work with birth from above, as a commandment, because the grace received at Baptism also requires our ministry.[31] The very sins committed after Baptism, compels the existence of the Upper Birth[32] event in the life of the Christian.

We are thus justified, St. Gregory of Nyssa's[33] assures, to say that "the birth of the male part, of the strong and tense toward virtue" must be with our inner man, as proof of our free judgment. Because our will is an essential requirement for the work of

---

(John 3:5), saying "from above" to make understood the sense of the birth from the Spirit. See in respect Simeon Noul Teolog, *Cele 225 capete teologice și practice* (București: Editura Institutului Biblic și de Misiune al Bisericii Ortodoxe Române, 1977), 27.

31 Vasile Mihoc, *Nașterea de Sus* (Sibiu: Editura Oastea Domnului, 1996), 16-17, 50: "....but by pressing on an aspect of Orthodox teaching neglected by many in practice, by an accent as necessary as it may be in the context of a world that calls itself Christian but lives in enmity with God, an insistence on an absolutely necessary rebirth to live the Gospel, for the everlasting growth and strengthening in the gift of God, but a gift already received by those to whom the message is addressed".

32 Mihoc, *Nașterea*, 59: "Thus, Baptism is born anew. The baptized man is made a new man. However, after the Baptism sins, a new birth or a rebirth is needed again. This latter term will often be used by Father Iosif Trifa, thus teaching that Baptism is born anew (the first spiritual birth), but that, on the other hand, because of the fall in sins after Baptism, there is yet another birth, that of the man's return to the original status he received through Baptism... The rebirth occurs again when the heart of the sinful man is pierced by the call of the Gospel and by the grace of the Holy Spirit, and he breaks it with the sin by engaging consciously and voluntarily in urging to live according to his call of a baptized man".

33 Grigorie de Nyssa, *Despre viața lui Moise sau despre desăvârșirea prin virtute* (București: Editura Institutului Biblic și de Misiune al Bisericii Ortodoxe Române, 1982), 39: "Therefore the word teaches us that whoever wants to put the beginning of life in virtue, to be born to the tyrant's annoyence, that is to say, in image of this birth, in which our own decision is our midwife... And it is up to our free judgment that this male and virtuous fetus be born". Father Stăniloae, commenting in a footnote on this new dimension of rebirth, makes the analogy between our free will birth (strengthened by the grace of the Holy Spirit in the advancement of virtue and spiritual strength) and the unintentional one (that is, our birth from the flesh subjected to the sin in which it fell).

salvation, without which God does nothing, recalls St. Macarius of Egypt.[34]

The born-again Christian, who renews his life in the Holy Spirit, participates in the mystical body of Christ, which is the Church[35], urged by the living Word to establish this work of salvation (Phil 2:12). In this context, St. Basil the Great speaks of a "new birth after the likeness[36]," according to the pattern of our death and resurrection with Christ, which takes place in Baptism, but which extends throughout our lives. This rebirth is consumed in this space of the necessity of acquiring similarity to Christ.

Our conclusion on this point is resolute: before going to mission and proclaiming salvation through Christ and the love of God the Father, we are first required to be born-again Christians (John 1:12[37]), otherwise our mission can degrade into futile activism.

---

34 Macarius of Egypt, *Homiliae Spirituales*, PG34, 130A: "He commanded as first thing the knowledge (of God). Knowing, the man would be loving, and thus directing himself to the fulfillment of His will. For the mind patiently carries out a work, and this is done by the grace of the Lord, which is given to the one who wants to obey in faith".

35 Panayotis Nellas, *Ortodoxia – divino-umanism în acțiune* (Sibiu: Deisis, 2013), 95, 106.

36 Vasile cel Mare, *Omilii Inedite. Două Cuvinte despre Botez* (Iași: Doxologia, 2012), 177, 191: "We know and are convinced that, as the one born after the flesh of somebody is the same as the one he was born of, so we are necessarily spirit, being born of the Spirit; but not by the glory of the great Spirit, but by the glory of the Holy Spirit, but by the division of each of the harps of God through Christ by the work of all these".

37 The noun in the accusative ἐξουσίαν which is translated by the Synodal Roumanian Bible by "giving them power" also includes another reality; it can also be translated by "freedom of choice" or "the right to act", as we see in 4 Macc 4:5: "... and receiving authority (ἐξουσίαν) upon it, has advanced quickly into our country". See in respect Frederick William Danker, *A Greek-English Lexicon of the New Testament and other Early Christian Literature* (Chicago: The University of Chicago Press, 2000), 339. The authority received or the right to control or rule over someone or something involves, in the alternative, the call to action, as is the case in 2 Thess 3:9 where ἐξουσίαν, in St. Paul's thought, is the authority or power to demand from the listeners maintenance in

Mary and Martha, the example of calling to mission in the name of Christ

This pericope immediately follows the example of the good Samaritan, which denotes a true model of Christian mission, that is why we are entitled to believe that St. Luke understands this episode of Martha and Mary in a spiritual sense, and this truth is noticed clearly when we interpret the text of Luke 10:41-42a: "Martha, Martha, you care and trouble for many, but one thing is necessary." It is also well-known by the scholar I. Marshall that St. Luke does not seek through this pericope to proclaim contemplative life at the expense of ministry and mission, but rather to indicate the most propitious way of serving God: first obey and fulfill His Word and then take care of what is necessary for existence (John 6:27[38]). St. Luke insists on the example of Mary, teaching us the importance of contemplation and prayer, as it does in 11:5-13 or 18:1-8. In both cases, the earnest prayer determines the goodness of God to act.[39] We can say that the Evangelist Luke, through the example of Mary, prepares the ground for us to be able to understand in a spiritual way the wish

---

exchange for the preaching of the Gospel, and its decision to act in this respect. But Paul chooses from free will, to work for maintenance, without receiving food in gift of anyone, precisely in order not to burden his believers with anything. Therefore, in order to fully understand this ἐξουσία of John 1:12, we must bear in mind both the fact that Christ has given us the authority and power necessary to become His children, that is, people reborn to a spiritual life; but has left us also the free choice to cooperate with His grace in reaching the state of God's child. Without our consent, and without our decision to act according to God's call, the prospect of our becoming remains a simple desire.

38 I. Howard Marshall, *The Gospel of Luke. A Commentary on the Greek Text* (Grand Rapids: William B.Eerdmans Publishing Company, 1986), 450-451; Eduard Lohse, *Das Neue Testament als Urkunde des Evangeliums* (Göttingen: Vandenhoeck&Ruprecht, 2000), 210.

39 Mikeal C. Parsons, *Luke. Storyteller, Interpreter, Evangelist* (Peabody: Hendrickson Publishers, 2007), 56.

of the disciple, who asks Jesus in the following scene (11:1) to teach him how to pray to please the Father.[40]

It is first appropriate to look closely at the original text of the proposed pericope, referring to the Greek text of the New Testament following the model of the modern critical editions NA28[28] and UBS5[5]:

Ἐν δὲ τῷ πορεύεσθαι αὐτοὺς αὐτὸς εἰσῆλθεν εἰς κώμην τινά· γυνὴ δέ τις ὀνόματι Μάρθα ὑπεδέξατο αὐτόν.καὶ τῇδε ἦν ἀδελφὴ καλουμένη Μαριάμ, [ἣ, subl. ns.] καὶ παρακαθεσθεῖσα πρὸς τοὺς πόδας τοῦ κυρίου ἤκουεν τὸν λόγον αὐτοῦ.ἡ δὲ Μάρθα περιεσπᾶτο περὶ πολλὴν διακονίαν· ἐπιστᾶσα δὲ εἶπεν, κύριε, οὐ μέλει σοι ὅτι ἡ ἀδελφή μου μόνην με κατέλιπεν διακονεῖν; εἰπὲ οὖν αὐτῇ ἵνα μοι συναντιλάβηται.ἀποκριθεὶς δὲ εἶπεν αὐτῇ ὁ κύριος· Μάρθα Μάρθα, μεριμνᾷς καὶ θορυβάζῃ περὶ πολλά,ἑνὸς δέ ἐστιν χρεία· Μαριὰμ γὰρ τὴν ἀγαθὴν μερίδα ἐξελέξατο ἥτις οὐκ ἀφαιρεθήσεται αὐτῆς. (Luke 10:38-42)

But as they walked, He [Jesus] entered a village, and a certain woman named Martha received Him as a guest [in her house]. (10:39) And she had a sister called Mary[41], and she sat[42] at the feet

---

40 William Hendriksen, *New Testament Commentary. Exposition of the Gospel According to Luke* (Grand Rapids: Baker Book House, 1988), 608.

41 Unlike the noun ὄνομα of (10:38) that has a strictly nominal dimension, and which I translated "by name", the verb καλουμένη, this time referring to Mary, can no longer be translated also "by name." This verb *kaléo* expresses a call, an appointment, with the nuances of the various contexts, and it may also mean an addressing, according to the model in (Luke 6:46) or an invitation (Matt 22:3). This is the reason for which, in the same context, for the names of the two sisters, I use different expressions: "by name Martha" or "who was named Mary."

42 As far as the aorist participle παρακαθεσθεῖσα, the perspectives are not exactly complementary to the Romanian biblical area. The translation of the Orthodox environment (Anania 2009; Synodal 2005) along with the Catholic (Pascal 1992) neglects the meaning of the verb by using the "is sitting" respectively "was sitting" alternatives. The translation (Cornilescu 1994) is a bit better in this respect, by using the expression "sat down"; the grammatical mistake is given by the escape of this pleonasm: *he sat down*. We have a correct translation in the case of the New Testament

of the Lord and listened[43] to His Word. (10:40) But Martha was distracted[44] with much service, [and] rising up said: "Lord, don't you care that my sister left me alone to serve? So[45], tell her to help me". (10:41) And answering, the Lord said to her: "Martha, Martha, you take care and trouble for many, (10:42), but one thing is necessary; Mary chose the good part that won't be taken from her." (Luke 10:38-42[46])

This text is presented only in the Gospel of Luke, although the two sisters are also mentioned in (John 11:1-12:8), being part of the so-called special Lucan material[47]. It is immediately inserted into the parable of the good Samaritan (Luke 10:29-37) probably in order to elucidate the imperative of Christ[48]: εἶπεν δὲ αὐτῷ ὁ Ἰησοῦς·πορεύου καὶ σὺ ποίει ὁμοίως ("Jesus told him: Go as well, and do likewise"). Because the true *Samaritan* is the one who, before acting for the good of his neighbor, feeds with the Word of God, contemplating His beauty. It seems that this one wants to pass on the paradigm Mary and Martha, the two servant sisters.

Edition (SBIR 2014), which proposes the formula "sat" with the classic participle ending in Romanian language in -t or in -s because the participle aorist describes an action that took place before unfolding the action of the regent verb, regardless of the time he represents. See in respect Daniel B.Wallace, *Greek Grammar Beyond the Basics* (Grand Rapids: Zondervan Publishing House, 1996), 614-615; Curtis Vaughan, Virtus E.Gideon, *A Greek Grammar of the New Testament* (Nashville: Broadman Press, 1979), 154.

43 The verb ἤκουεν being in the indicative, imperfect time, translates properly through "listen". See Erich Happ, Friedrich Maier, and Alfred Zeller, *Grammatik. Lautlehre – Formenlehre – Satzlehre* (München: Bayerischer Schulbuch Verlag, 1981), 153-154.

44 In a literal translation, "busy, drawn in all directions," an expression that certifies Martha's endless agitation for some less important details. See in respect MacArthur, *Comentariul Biblic*, 221-222.

45 The conjunction οὖν ("consequently") introduces a logical result that interferes with the previous action. Therefore, a correct translation cannot neglect this part of speech. See in respect Friberg, *Lexicon of the Greek New Testament*, 264.

46 The English translation is mine.

47 Joseph Fitzmyer, *The Gospel according to Luke x-xxiv* (New York: Doubleday, 1985), 891.

48 Walter Grundmann, *Das Evangelium nach Lukas*, (Berlin: Evangelische Verlagsanstalt, 1966), 225.

The Lord does not propose the contemplative life dissociated by the practical missionary model, but it shows us the most effective way of serving Him: it is more desirable to fulfill His Word than to scatter yourself in all sorts of practical actions that do not build on any soul.[49]

Because of its uniqueness, some biblical scholars (R. Bultmann, W. Grundmann) doubt the historicity of the event, denying its authenticity. They consider the entire Lucan narrative content imagined by an evangelist, who produces these words only to harmonize his narrative.[50] The lack of parallel places seems to be the main reason, and scholar J. Brutscheck[51] opts for a pre-Lucan creation, considering that the Evangelist Luke is not its author. However, sustained arguments for the theory of an imaginary composition are not very much at stake; everything remains hypothetical, therefore, these theories cannot be validated from a scientific point of view. The fact that St. Luke does not specify the name of the village (Βηθανίας) as does St. John (John 11:1), is likely because St. Luke chooses to give more attention to what has happened in their essence. And this detail cannot be an argument to show the alleged pseudoepigraphy of the text. The fact that it differs so much from the tradition of the Apostle John proves that this text is also based on an old tradition, but which simply does not ensure its historicity, because it did not propose to do so. The present history is a unitary composition, since the words of Jesus could not circulate independently, or outside an immediate context, I.H. Marshall[52] argues. In spite of all these modern

---

49 Marshall, *Gospel*, 450-451.
50 Darrell L. Bock, *Luke 9:51 – 24, 53* (Grand Rapids: Baker Academic, 1996), 1038.
51 Jutta Brutscheck, *Die Maria-Marta – Erzählung: Eine redaktionskritische Untersuchungen zu Lk 10, 38-42* (Frankfurt am Main: Hanstein Verlag, 1986), 133-143.
52 Marshall, *Gospel*, 451.

theories, some thematic parallels of the pericope[53] can be identified: Jesus hesitates in some other places as well, to enter into a possible dispute (Luke 12:13-15; Mark 10:13-16); Jesus attributes an importance and value to His teaching and His call (Luke 6:47-49; 8:19-21); the images of this text recall other obvious contrasts (Luke 4:3; 8:14).

At the level of the text's integrity, the opening of this text keeps a set of textual differences, but almost all are of secondary interest. Instead of the simple formula Ἐν δὲ τῷ ("But while") that is used by the manuscripts (p$^{45.75}$ BL Ξ 33.579.892.1241.2542) as well as the translations into the Syriac and Coptic languages[54], we come across another variant Ἐγένετο δὲ ἐν τῷ in the manuscripts (A C D K P W Γ Δ Θ Ψ f ^{13} 565.700.1424), as well as in the Latin translation of the Gospel, where the verb Ἐγένετο is meant to indicate a narrative progression, an expression which is often left untranslated and always near an infinitive.[55] In our case, we have the infinitive πορεύεσθαι ("But while were going"). Given that St. Luke uses this narrative progression quite often- Ἐγένετο (1:5; 2:1; 3:2; 4:25; 5:17; 6:13; 8:24 etc.)- and that in our case, preserves a more significant occurrence than the simple formula Ἐν δὲ τῷ, we think the more complex variant is the original one. The expression Ἐν δὲ τῷ appears definitely as a result of the scribes's interventions on the text from the desire to simplify and harmonize the narrative, eliminating this specific narrative progression of St. Luke.

The other problem is the construction αὐτοὺς αὐτὸς εἰσῆλθεν ("they entered"), which has become *textus receptus* of the New Testament modern critical editions (NA[28]; UBS[5]). The Byzantine

---

53 Bock, *Luke, 53,* 1038.
54 Barbara and Kurt Aland, Johannes Karavidopoulos et alii, *The Greek-English New Testament* (Stuttgart: Deutsche Bibelgesellschaft, [28]2012), 456.
55 Hubert Pernot, *Études sur la langue des Évangiles* (Paris, 1927), 189-199.

tradition of the New Testament⁵⁶, along with many other manuscripts (A C K P W Γ Δ Θ Ψ ƒ³ 565.579.700.892.1424.2542 along with the Latin and Syrian translations), instead offers the variant αὐτούς, καὶ αὐτὸς εἰσῆλθεν where the conjunction καὶ together with the singular pronoun αὐτὸς (and He) is meant to indicate that Jesus also entered this village (Bethany) with His disciples. This is a rather important aspect, because the way in which some modern Bible editions (*English Standard Version*; *The New American Bible*; *Holman Christian Standard Bible*; *New Revised Standard Version*; *Traduction Oecuménique de la Bible*; *Zürcher Bibel*; *Reina-Valera Actualizada*) translate this verse by the phrase "He entered a village" or "Jesus entered a village", shows that Jesus alone entered the house of the sisters Martha and Mary, which is prohibited by Jewish law. A rabbi was not allowed to stand alone with a woman to dialogue; all the more so as the Jewish rabbis did not have female disciples⁵⁷. Another textual problem is encountered at the end of the verse, besides Μάρθα ὑπεδέξατο⁵⁸ αὐτόν ("Marta received Him as guest"), other manuscripts (A D K P W Γ Δ Θ Ψ 070 ƒ¹·¹³ 565. 700. 892. 1241. 1424. 2542.) together with Latin, Syrian and Coptic translations, along with some Church Fathers and Writers (Basil the Great, Cyril of

---

56 Maurice A. Robinson, William G. Pierpont, *The New Testament in the Original Greek: Byzantine Textform* (Southborough: Chilton Book Publishing Company, 2005), 151.

57 Maier, *Evanghelia după Luca*, 480-481.

58 The indicative of the aorist verb ὑπεδέξατο, in addition to its basic meaning, "to meet someone," may also mean "to receive someone as a guest" (Luke 19:6; Acts 17, 7; Jas 2:25) which is a better match for our context. See Horst Balz, Gerhard Schneider, *Exegetical Dictionary of the New Testament*, vol. 3 (Edinburgh: T&T Clark International, 1980), 402; Frederick William Danker, Walter Bauer, *A Greek-English Lexicon of the New Testament and Other Early Christian Literature* (Chicago: The University of Chicago Press, 2000), 1037.

Jerusalem and Augustine[59]), add the formula εἰς τὸν οἶκον αὐτῆς ("in her house"). Scholar B. Metzger[60] argues that the shortest version is the original one, and that the addition "in her house" does not belong to St. Apostle Luke.

Another aspect of the structure of the text concerns the meals in Luke's Gospel. The meal narrative specific to the Evangelist Luke is lacking, perhaps because the author wishes to emphasize the condition of the true disciple, leaving all other aspects on a second level. The classic vocabulary of the meal in this gospel contains specific references to the act of nourishment: *esthíō* or *pínō;* these occur in almost every scene of this type (5:30; 7:36; 9:13; 10:7; 12:45; 13:26; 14:1; 15:2; 22:30; 24:43). Also, the pericopes which regard taking the meal include automatically the invitation from the host, underlined by the verb *kaléō* (7:39; 14:8-13); but also an earnest prayer to supper together (7:36; 11:37 emphasized by the verb *erōtáō*).

Similarly, the terminology of the meal is absent not only here, but also in the two previous pericopes that speak of the ministry of women[61] (4:38-39; 8:1-3). These, as I said earlier, because St. Luke wants to highlight the spiritual side of the ministry (the word in the Greek text is διακονίαν which in the apostolic times defines the stage of ministry of deacons, therefore we have a sacramental dimension as well), not just the side related to nutrition. From this reasoning, we believe that the narrative of the ministry of these two sisters, conceals a deeper dimension than is apparent.

---

59 Barbara and Kurt Aland, Johannes Karavidopoulos et alii, *The Greek New Testament*, (Münster/Westphalia: United Bible Societies, 2014), 241.

60 Bruce M. Metzger, *A Textual Commentary on the Greek New Testament*, (Stuttgart: Deutsche Bibelgesellschaft, 1994), 129.

61 Allie M. Ernst, *Martha from the Margins. The Authority of Martha in Early Christian Tradition*, (Leiden: Brill, 2009), 186-187.

The traditional interpretations of this episode, according to J. Kim, make out of Mary and Martha two symbols of some gradual lives: the service of the Word above the service of the neighbor, the contemplative life above the practical life, the love for God and then the love of the neighbor[62]. However, things are not exactly the way this scholar presents them to be, because on the official line of patristic thinking we will never encounter such a vision in which Martha's action will be disqualified. For example, St. Augustine admires Martha saying that she is the example of hospitality, and St. Ambrose of Milano says that the Church of Christ needs listeners of the Word, but also those who do the deeds, precisely as in the model of the deacons in Acts 6. St. Ephrem the Syrian proposes to see Martha's love as being superior to that of Mary because she was ready to serve Him even before Jesus entered her house. Also, in the episode of Lazarus's resurrection (John 11:1-37), she was the first to meet Him.[63] And St. Cyril of Alexandria says that Martha has proven through her ministry that she is precisely like the good Samaritan of the parable, proving a deep love[64]. Martha is painted in a less favorable light because she also wanted to listen to the Word of God, but her somewhat exaggerated hospitality prevented her. The classic word describing the ministry in the New Testament is διακονία, but Martha's action is depicted through the verb περιεσπᾶτο, which goes beyond the boundaries of a natural ministry. It expresses the useless waste of energy that is done in the preparation of a thing. St. Paul the Apostle uses the adverb ἀπερισπάστως ("without distraction") in 1 Cor. 7:35 precisely to reinforce the

---

62 Jungh Yung-Kim, "Three Different Readings of Luke 10: 38-42: Gadamer, Habermas and Ricoeur in Dialogue," *The Expository Times* 123, no. 5 (2012): 220.
63 Arthur A. Just jr., *Luke* (Downers Grove: InterVarsity Press, 2003), 181.
64 St. CYRIL, *A Commentary upon the Gospel According to S.Luke* (Oxford: Oxford University Press, 1859), 315-316.

same idea: not distracting the attention of the Christians in Corinth from the fulfillment of the will of God.[65]

According to the narrator, Jesus Christ is the Son of God, which makes this reality not fit into the categories of human reason, therefore at the invitation of Martha 10:40c: εἰπὲ οὖν αὐτῇ ἵνα μοι συναντιλάβηται, Jesus answers: Μαριὰμ γὰρ τὴν ἀγαθὴν μερίδα ἐξελέξατο ἥτις οὐκ ἀφαιρεθήσεται αὐτῆς (10:42b). He always corrects man's misguided intentions, and thus presents his own opinion on the two sisters: Martha is engaged in all sorts of tumultuous practices - Μάρθα Μάρθα, μεριμνᾷς καὶ θορυβάζῃ περὶ πολλά (10:41b) and Mary proves the true behavior of the beloved disciple. Martha is concerned about many things, Mary has chosen the good part[66] (τὴν ἀγαθὴν μερίδα) that is, the preparation for the mission. The phrase "good part" is a little enigmatic.

The adjective ἀγαθός has as a first sense the idea of moral supremacy, virtue, it is also used to express a high standard of quality (1 Pet 3:10). St. Paul in Romans 2:10 uses this term to describe those who do good in general. In Galatians 6:10 and Ephesians 4:28 he uses it in the sense of the opportunity to do good in social terms[67]. The noun μερίς occurs five times in the New Testament: Luke 10:42; Acts 8:21; 16:12; 2 Cor 6:15; Col 1:12. It translates as "part" or "division." This term has been developed in Greek literature in many ways, but in the New Testament, it expresses a concrete and quantitative part, a specific segment of a possession or inheritance (Luke 15:12). As an adverb, it has a quantitative meaning (1 Cor 11:18), or an individual one

---

65 Marshall, *Gospel*, 452.
66 Joel B.Green, *The Gospel of Luke*, (Grand Rapids: William B.Eerdmans Publishing Company, 1997), 437.
67 James Swanson, *A Dictionary of Biblical Languages: Greek New Testament* (Ouk Harbor: Logos Research Systems, 2001); Frederick William Danker, Walter Bauer, *A Greek-English Lexicon*, 3-4.

(1 Cor 12:27). It can be understood gradually, either in part or as an extension (Rom 15:24; 2 Cor 2:5), but also numerically, either in turn or in detail[68] (1 Cor 14:27; Heb 9:5). So the good and high-quality part or segment that Mary chose is precisely the disposition to stand at the feet of the Lord and listen to His teachings about the inheritance of the Kingdom of Heaven.[69] Christ insists on the obedience of His Word, as the only necessary thing. All of Martha's agitation was useless and that is why Mary is presented as the only one who knew how to act properly.[70] This "good part" of Mary brings to mind the good and fertile land in which the sower sows its seed[71] (Luke 8:8).

The expression ἑνὸς δέ ἐστιν χρεία ("but one thing is necessary" – 10:42a) is the most accepted by the scholars[72], this is the reading of papyruses (p^{45}, p^{75}) and codices (A, C, K, P, Δ, Ψ etc.) even though in the *Codex Sinaiticus*[73] the adjective is ὀλιγων ("few [things are needed]"). The translation in this case, says J. Fitzmyer[74], should be like this: "few things are needed" or "few things are necessary". Several other manuscripts (p^3, a^c, B, C^2, L, 33 etc.) simply combine the two readings: *oligōn de estin chreia hē henos* ("few things are necessary, including one alone").

---

68 Horst Balz, Gerhard Schneider, *Exegetical Dictionary of the New Testament*, vol. 2 (Edinburgh: T.&T. Clark, 1990), 409.

69 Thomas W. Manson, *The Sayings of Jesus: As Recorded in the Gospels according to St. Matthew and St. Luke* (London: SCM Press, 1949), 264.

70 Alois Stöger, *El Evangelio Según San Lucas* (Barcelona: Editorial Herder, 1979), 314-315.

71 François Bovon, *Das Evangelium nach Lukas Lk 9,51-14,35* (Zürich und Düsseldorf: Neukirchener Verlag, 1996), 108.

72 Kurt Aland, Matthew Black et alii, *The Greek New Testament* (Stuttgart: United Bible Societies, 1966), 254-255.

73 Frederick H. Scrivener, *A Full Collation of the Codex Sinaiticus with the Received Text of the New Testament* (Cambridge: Deighton, Bell and Co., 1864), 50.

74 Joseph A. Fitzmyer, *El Evangelio Segun Lucas: Traduccion y Comentario Capítulos 8,22-18,14* (Madrid: Ediciones Cristiandad, 1987), 298-299.

Finally, we can summarize Jesus's counsel to Martha: "few things" as an urge to simplicity and temperance in the social sphere. Christians need to be content with what they have on this earth. "One thing" suggests the theme of faith, obedience and fulfillment of the Word. This must be the main goal of Christians. "Few things, including one alone," is a dual construction, where few things refer to material goods, and "one alone" refers to giving our life entirely to God.[75]

The Mary and Martha paradigm, according to St. Apostle Luke, calls for both the practical, social mission, and especially for the contemplation and fulfillment of the Word of God. The mission of today's Church must be guided by this messianic imperative: Before engaging in philanthropic campaigns, Church missionaries must first choose the "good part," that is, the contemplation and fulfillment of the Word of the Gospel, or the formation according to the authentic Christian missionary model. Because a Christian mission without its liturgical and logos-centered dimension will get lost in all sorts of charitable actions in which the clergy or laity missionaries will always be distracted (περιεσπᾶτο) from true ministry. The social dimension of the Luke Gospel is well known, where believers are mandated to share their material goods with the poor according to the will of God.[76] But this social concern must not go beyond the need to contemplate the Word of God and its fulfillment. Our main action, says St. John Casian[77], must be the translation of the will of God into deeds. This must be the path our heart will immediately follow. Any other concern needs to be regarded as secondary, and even dangerous. The sisters Martha and Mary offer us a plenary scriptural model of this mode

---

75 Bovon, *Das Evangelium nach Lukas*, 110.
76 John Gillman, *Possessions and the Life of Faith: A Reading of Luke-Acts* (Collegeville: Liturgical Press, 1991), 11-12.
77 St. John Cassian, *Conference* 1.8 (New Jersey: Paulist Press, 1985), 42-43.

of activity, in which Christ does not criticize Martha for anything, but cannot praise at all her entire activity.

This is why I decided to dedicate this research in honor of Father Nadim Tarazi's 75th birthday. Because he is a spiritual person that encompasses in his ministry the Mary and Martha paradigm with such an *infectious* enthusiasm. Have a long and fruitful ministry, our beloved father Nadim, for many years to come!

Conclusions

The pericope Mary and Martha, provides us with the true pattern of Christian ministry, Mary being thus portrayed as *typos* of the authentic Christian missionary, the one who is embarked on the full mission. The Martha model only raises a basic level of our faith. For that reason, we are called to practice the pattern of Mary; to transcend immediate demands, to the perfect contemplation of the Kingdom. The obedience and fulfillment of the Word of God produces within us a spiritual rebirth. According to the New Testament texts, the rebirth of the highest being is accomplished both through the sacrament of Baptism and the Word of the Gospel. That is why Christ the Lord insists on this reality, emphasizing that Mary's option to contemplate the Word corresponds to the wise man that has chosen the good part, that is, his christification (Theosis).

The example of Martha is not to be rejected, but is an insufficient one because of the concerns for the secondary things. Her action is characterized by St. Luke through the verb περιεσπᾶτο, which suggests a useless effort, a waste of energy for passing things, and misses the encounter with the essence, with the Logos of life. The love with which Martha welcomes her guests should be appreciated. Some Holy Fathers even praise her intentions, but nothing can be more important than preaching the Gospel (Acts 6:2).

This pericope, as we have seen, presents some slight textual differences, but without affecting in any way its integrity or its strong message. Regardless of the manuscripts compared and contrasted, the corollary remains the same: the good part chosen by Mary is the Christian imperative to examine the Scriptures in order to fulfill the will of God. There can be no concern in our missionary agenda more important than the contemplation of the Word of the Gospel and the preaching to all men. The Mary and Martha model calls for both mission and contemplation, but always takes first the contemplation and fulfillment of the Scriptures. The authentic missionary Christian listens and interprets the Word according to his humility; always struggling through fasting and exercising mercy, to understand; and through this means, offer correct direction so that others might choose the right path that will not be taken from him forever.

Introduction to
Philippians: A Commentary

V. Rev. Dr. Paul Nadim Tarazi

Editor's Note: *Insofar as the senior honors the junior, it seemed fitting to conclude this volume with an excerpt from Fr. Paul's own work. By including the Introduction to his Philippians: A Commentary, it is our hope that the reader will gain some sense of how his work has impacted the papers of his former students, now colleagues. To us, this Festschrift volume, together with the publication of his monumental* The Rise of Scripture, *unites our voices with his in the proclamation of God's written teaching.*

This Introduction is unconventional. Instead of approaching the text as a document for personal study in order to figure out its meaning and then elaborate on it, I shall concentrate on using it according to its own literary fabric. One might ask, "What is the difference? Is not any text literature after all?" Yes, indeed it is, in the sense that it is made out of letters (*literae* in Latin) and words. However, not every text functions in the same way. One basic difference between texts lies in their audience. Some texts are intended for a specific audience and are usually to be "studied" and "debated" by those who are both interested and capable to pursue such tasks. Other texts are "public" and thus "open" in the sense that they are written essentially to be immediately heard. The assumption then must be that they are readily understandable and, consequently, non debatable. They are either to be *readily* accepted or refused but, at any rate, not analyzed. If so, then they must be at the lowest possible common denominator of understanding. On the other hand, if such texts were merely informational, they would not make sense since the hearer would not be getting anything practically or theoretically, especially if the recipient is not allowed any analysis or debate. They would make sense only if they are instructional in a double sense: an instruction to be understood *and* to be followed, that is, a commandment. If so, then such texts are meant to be heard in the double sense of that verb: to be received and to be hearkened to.[1]

This is precisely how the biblical texts present themselves. Let us hear, for instance, the impressive divine injunction to the prophet Ezekiel:

> And he [the Lord] said to me: "Son of man, I send you to the people of Israel, to a nation of rebels, who have rebelled against me; they and their fathers have transgressed against me to this very day. The people also are impudent and stubborn: I send you to them; and you shall say to them, "Thus says the Lord God." And whether they hear or refuse to hear (for they are a rebellious house) they will know that there has been a prophet among them. And you, son of man, be not afraid of them, nor be afraid of their words, though briers and thorns are with you and you sit upon scorpions; be not afraid of their words, nor be dismayed at their looks, for they are a rebellious house." (Ezek 2:3-6 RSV)

> And he said to me: "Son of man, go, get you to the house of Israel, and speak with my words to them. For you are not sent to a people of foreign speech and a hard language, but to the house of Israel—not to many peoples of foreign speech and a hard language, whose words you cannot understand. Surely, if I sent you to such, they would listen to you. But the house of Israel will not listen to you; for they are not willing to listen to me; because all the house of Israel are of a hard forehead and of a stubborn heart." (Ezek 3:4-7)

> Moreover he said to me, "Son of man, all my words that I shall speak to you receive in your heart, and hear with your ears. And go,

---

[1] The Hebrew verb *šama'* and its Greek counterpart *akouō* bear this double connotation just as often as the English "hear." The Greek also uses the cognate *hypakouō* which has the specific meaning of "obey." The understanding is assumed since the intention is that the instructions be obeyed; hence, the necessity of the lowest possible common denominator in their phraseology and presentation.

get you to the exiles, to your people, and say to them, "Thus says the Lord God"; whether they hear or refuse to hear." (Ezek 3:10-11)

Two things are very clear: (1) the message is readily understandable; (2) it is a message that is intended to be heeded. There is no room for analysis and debate as though the text were a thesis to be proven or defended. Still the question that remains is, "What is the basis for such an absolute authoritative stand?"[2] To answer by referring to a philosophical Almighty God who can do whatever he wills is begging the question, since one would first need to prove his existence, which is repeatedly shown to be a futile endeavor; and even if one were able to do so, what is the proof that this is precisely what he wills? Moreover, to try to find a premise outside the text would open the door for debate regarding the premise itself and its validity. Besides, such an approach would rob the text of its authority, since it would need a prop from outside. This, in turn, would mean that we would be not hearing the text itself, but reading into it.

The only way out of this dilemma is to inquire from the text itself. The answer is actually readily available when one realizes that the text is *not* a compendium of formulas and statements about a "subject matter" that is "out there," existing before and independently of the text and that was incorporated into the text in diverse manners ranging from childish stories to more sophisticated utterances.[3] The text itself is a narrative *through time* since it spans generations: notice Ezekiel's "they *and their fathers* have transgressed against me to this very day," and the rebellious

---

2 This is not the same as saying the commandments are autocratically imposed through the medium of physical power and oppression; if such were the case, then they cannot be "refused."

3 If it were so, then one wonders if the text is necessary at all. In actuality, the wide range of "theologies" does show that the biblical text is manipulated rather than heard, let alone hearkened to. Every theologian reads into the text his premise, which then becomes a magical hermeneutical key to unlocking and understanding the entire Bible.

addressees are not the "fathers" whose city was destroyed, but the younger generation living in the land of exile as a consequence of God's punishing their fathers' city. That this is not a passing remark in Ezekiel is borne out by the three extensive and repetitious "narratives" (in chs. 16, 20 and 23) which are central to the message of the prophet and which extend the lineage of the fathers to the times of the oppression in Egypt (Ezek 20:6-10). Consequently, for the text to be a narrative, it has (1) to have a beginning and an end, and (2) to follow a thread that holds it together and thus makes it "credible," that is to say, makes sense of the movement between *that* beginning and *that* end. The choice of these three Ezekelian chapters is actually very much *à propos* since they form, in a nutshell, the narrative line of the expanded biblical "story" stretching from Genesis or Exodus until 2 Kings. In both cases, the beginning is an act of unexplainable magnanimity on the part of a God toward a people that kept proving itself unworthy of such generosity and kept repaying that God with unimaginable ungratefulness, not found even among nations whose deities did much less for them (Jer 2:9-13). At the end, after having multiplied his gracious visitations, God had no choice except to visit his people with the punishment of destruction and exile.

It is worth digressing here in order to explain the statement "God had no choice except to act in a given way." Such may sound hard to accept for people who have been indoctrinated into viewing and thus defining God as an Almighty Being who is not bound by anything and can do whatever he wills. This was not the view of deities in the Ancient Near East. The basic function, and thus definition, of a deity was that of a judge. If a deity ceased to be a judge, and assumedly an equitable one, then it lost all its divine attributes and prerogatives. This reality is summed up in Psalm 82:

> A Psalm of Asaph. God has taken his place in the divine council; in the midst of the gods he holds judgment: "How long will you judge unjustly and show partiality to the wicked? Selah Give justice to the weak and the fatherless; maintain the right of the afflicted and the destitute. Rescue the weak and the needy; deliver them from the hand of the wicked." They have neither knowledge nor understanding, they walk about in darkness; all the foundations of the earth are shaken. I say, "You are gods, sons of the Most High, all of you; nevertheless, you shall die like men, and fall like any prince." Arise, O God, judge the earth; for to thee belong all the nations!

It is clear then that the biblical God is not the only God, in a philosophical, ontological sense, but rather the only *true* God in a real, functional sense. He *alone* among the gods acts as he is supposed to act: as an equitable judge.[4] Judging is his duty without which he would not be *truly* (that is, de facto)[5] what he is (supposed or expected to be). This explains his reasoning in the following passage of Ezekiel:

> Have I any pleasure in the death of the wicked, says the Lord God, and not rather that he should turn from his way and live? But when a righteous man turns away from his righteousness and commits iniquity and does the same abominable things that the wicked man does, shall he live? None of the righteous deeds which he has done shall be remembered; for the treachery of which he is guilty and the sin he has committed, he shall die. Yet you say, "The way of the Lord is not just." Hear now, O house of Israel: Is my way not just? Is it not your ways that are not just? When a righteous man turns away from his righteousness and commits iniquity, he shall die for it; for the iniquity which he has committed he shall die. Again, when a wicked man turns away from the wickedness he has committed and does what is lawful and right, he shall save his life. Because he considered and turned away from all the transgressions which he had committed, he shall surely live, he shall not die. Yet the house

---

4 See further Ps 96:13; 97:2, 6; 98:9; 99:4.
5 This is actually the meaning of the Hebrew *'emet*.

of Israel says, "The way of the Lord is not just." O house of Israel, are my ways not just? Is it not your ways that are not just? Therefore I will judge you, O house of Israel, every one according to his ways, says the Lord God. Repent and turn from all your transgressions, lest iniquity be your ruin. Cast away from you all the transgressions which you have committed against me, and get yourselves a new heart and a new spirit! Why will you die, O house of Israel? For I have no pleasure in the death of any one, says the Lord God; so turn, and live. (Ezek 18:23-32)

And the crux of the matter lies in that were he not a judge, and again assumedly an equitable one, then there would be no hope for all of us, as Paul reasons, along the same premise as Ezekiel:

Then what advantage has the Jew? Or what is the value of circumcision? Much in every way. To begin with, the Jews are entrusted with the oracles of God. What if some were unfaithful? Does their faithlessness nullify the faithfulness of God? By no means! Let God be *true* though every man be false, as it is written, "That thou mayest be justified in thy words, and prevail when thou art judged." But if our wickedness serves to show the justice of God, what shall we say? *That God is unjust to inflict wrath on us?* (I speak in a human way.) By no means! *For then how could God judge the world?* (Rom 3:1-6)

But then, why does the biblical story not end with the divine punishment? Again, to answer from a philosophical premise grounded in a given understanding of God as being almighty at will or ethically good, or being the expression of ultimate goodness, is to fall into *eisegesis*: reading the text in the light of a foreign premise. A judge is not to act willfully or, for that matter, be "good" as opposed to being "evil," character wise. A judge is by definition neither willful, nor good or evil. He is bound to be just; otherwise he would not be a judge. For him to act willfully, or to try to be "good," may affect his verdict and ultimately his being a judge. And, if so, to plagiarize Paul, "how could he judge" and maintain the world he has established? For indeed:

> Say among the nations, "The Lord reigns! Yea, the world is established, it shall never be moved; he will judge the peoples with equity.⁶" Let the heavens be glad, and let the earth rejoice; let the sea roar, and all that fills it; let the field exult, and everything in it! Then shall all the trees of the wood sing for joy before the Lord, for he comes, for he comes to judge the earth. He will judge the world with righteousness, and the peoples with his truth. (Ps 96:10-13)

Even more, a judge, as judge, is actually above ethics. He produces the good and the evil in the sense that his just verdict will be good for the one found innocent and bad for the one found guilty. Were the judge not capable of producing either good or evil, his judgment would not be effective since he would not be in control of the situation and his world. This is precisely how God presents himself in the Bible: "I form light and create darkness, I make weal and create woe, I am the Lord, who do all these things." (Isa 45:7)⁷ Again, the clue to finding the meaning of this statement has to lie in the immediate background of the text, the Ancient Near East. Besides being the judge of his people, a god was also the father of that people, the one who reared them and took care of their needs. Notice God's opening statement in Isaiah as preamble to his harsh verdict:

> Hear, O heavens, and give ear, O earth; for the Lord has spoken: "Sons have I reared and brought up, but they have rebelled against me. The ox knows its owner, and the ass its master's crib; but Israel does not know, my people does not understand." (Isa 1:2-3)

Notice also the confession of the repentant people in the same book: "For thou art our Father, though Abraham does not know us and Israel does not acknowledge us; thou, O Lord, art our Father, our Redeemer from of old is thy name." (Isa 63:16) Still,

---

6 From the root *yašar* (upright).

7 One can imagine how this text would create havoc, as it actually did over the centuries, if it were handled on Gnostic philosophical terms. It would a basis for God being (ontologically) good and evil at will!

by itself the deity's "fatherhood" does not explain why God, who is also and essentially a judge, had a way out in not allowing the story to end with his verdict of condemnation, without jeopardizing his justice. In order to find the valid and appropriate explanation one must look into another basic aspect of Ancient Near Eastern reality, which plays a paramount role in the biblical narrative, namely that deities ruled through the intermediacy of their appointed monarchs.

By the mere fact that the king was seated on the divine throne, he himself was functionally divine in the sense that he represented his god and thus had to act on the latter's behalf. Anything less than divine behavior on the part of the king, while seated on the throne of righteousness and justice, would be jeopardizing his god's status and thus tantamount to committing the ultimate blasphemy: allowing the name of the deity to be mocked. The king is referred to as "god" in Psalm 45:

> Your throne, O God, endures for ever and ever. Your royal scepter is a scepter of equity; you love righteousness and hate wickedness. Therefore God, your God, has anointed you with the oil of gladness above your fellows. (Ps 45:6-7)

Also the divine titles of "god" and "father" appear in the royal protocol:

> For to us a child is born, to us a son is given; and the government will be upon his shoulder, and his name will be called "Wonderful Counselor, Mighty God, Everlasting Father, Prince of Peace." Of the increase of his government and of peace there will be no end, upon the throne of David, and over his kingdom, to establish it, and to uphold it with justice and with righteousness from this time forth and for evermore. (Isa 9:6-7)

On the other hand, given his divine status, the king had full responsibility as well as full power; consequently, he would get all the glory if his realm was prosperous or victorious against the enemies and, conversely, he would be accountable for any mismanagement and its aftermath. Such is made very clear in the Prophets as well as in the Books of Samuel and Kings, where the kings and the entire leadership are singled out for the blame. To be sure, all the people are also punished for the sin of their leader in the same way as an army or a city suffers loss for the mistake of its general or its monarch, respectively. The king can be fully cut off from the ruling office either literally, through death, or through the demise of his dynasty. The people, however, are usually never totally obliterated: the survivors either are exiled or remain where they are under foreign rule, no longer in control of their destiny as an entity. Put otherwise, the king ceases to be a ruler and suffers a change in his functionality, whereas the individual basically remains what he was before, under the rule of someone else.[8]

Putting the burden on the king and the leaders of the people allowed the Prophets to extend the end beyond the end of a kingship and a city. However, in order to keep matters in perspective and not surmise that God was bound by the Prophets' hope but rather solely by what makes him God, his justice, they expressed their hope in the language of divine promise. Such language fits perfectly within the realm of the judge's authority. He can at any time decide to lessen the penalty imposed upon the guilty; usually this is done either because the condemned has shown remorse and started behaving in a becoming manner, or because the judge considers that the elapsed time of penalty is enough and he decides to give another chance to the condemned.[9]

---

8 That is why, from the perspective of the Bible, the citizens of Judah or Israel under Solomon and the following kings were in a situation similar in kind to that in which their fathers fared under Pharaoh.

9 See, e.g., Is 40:1-2 (Comfort, comfort my people, says your God. Speak tenderly to Jerusalem, and cry to her that her warfare is ended, that her iniquity is pardoned, that she has received from the Lord's hand double for all her sins.)

The latter would be an act of sheer mercy, and it is the path followed by the biblical prophetic teaching. However, in this case, the mercy is conditional in the sense that the one who was given another chance is to show fruits of one's repentance according to the conditions and rules of behavior imposed by the merciful judge. A classic text for the above is found in Ezekiel:

> Thus says the Lord God: I will gather you from the peoples, and assemble you out of the countries where you have been scattered, and I will give you the land of Israel. And when they come there, they will remove from it all its detestable things and all its abominations. And I will give them one heart, and put a new spirit within them; I will take the stony heart out of their flesh and give them a heart of flesh, that they may walk in my statutes and keep my ordinances and obey them; and they shall be my people, and I will be their God. But as for those whose heart goes after their detestable things and their abominations, I will requite their deeds upon their own heads, says the Lord God. (Ezek 11:17-21)

The new spirit and new heart are none other than those God has been requiring from the people all along so that they would not fall under his condemnation (Ezek 18:23-32 quoted above). The forgiven people, then, are not free to do their own will, but rather to abide by the same statutes and ordinances they had broken thereby losing their life and liberty. Lest they forget this matter and fall in the sin of arrogance, which was the reason for their demise, the third and final Ezekelian passage referring to the new spirit and the new heart makes it clear that the new state of affairs will have as a result concomitantly the glorification of the merciful judge and the constant reminder to the people of their past shameful actions that had forced the judge's hand in punishing them:

> A new heart I will give you, and a new spirit I will put within you; and I will take out of your flesh the heart of stone and give you a

heart of flesh. And I will put my spirit within you, and cause you to walk in my statutes and be careful to observe my ordinances. You shall dwell in the land which I gave to your fathers; and you shall be my people, and I will be your God … Then you will remember your evil ways, and your deeds that were not good; and you will loathe yourselves for your iniquities and your abominable deeds. It is not for your sake that I will act, says the Lord God; let that be known to you. Be ashamed and confounded for your ways, O house of Israel. Thus says the Lord God: On the day that I cleanse you from all your iniquities, I will cause the cities to be inhabited, and the waste places shall be rebuilt. And the land that was desolate shall be tilled, instead of being the desolation that it was in the sight of all who passed by. And they will say, "This land that was desolate has become like the garden of Eden; and the waste and desolate and ruined cities are now inhabited and fortified." Then the nations that are left round about you shall know that I, the Lord, have rebuilt the ruined places, and replanted that which was desolate; I, the Lord, have spoken, and I will do it. (Ezek 36:26-28, 31-36)

It is precisely this chronological story "line" that forms the thread of the biblical narrative consigned in the Law and the Prophets. The ultimate beginning starts with God, who for no apparent reason from our perspective, established the world on a sane (viable, as it is supposed to be)[10] basis and settled the human being in a garden with all the necessary ingredients for that being to conduct a sane (healthy, viable, as it is supposed to be)[11] life until his demise, since after all "the Lord God formed man of dust from the ground" (Gen 2:7) and "you are dust, and to dust you shall return" (Gen 3:19). This original state of viability is not to be taken for granted since it is ensured solely by God's will and action. The Hebrew verb *bara'* with which the biblical narrative opens (Gen 1:1) means "render healthy, sane, viable." This

---

10 This is the meaning of the Hebrew *šalem*, consequently the peace (sanity, *šalom*) is the original status of things.

11 See previous note. This view expressed in the story of the forming of man in Gen 2 is in conformity with that found in the story of the creation of the world in Gen 1.

explains why this divine action takes place against the odds of destruction (represented by the threatening darkness and the raging waters)[12] and desolation (*tohu wabohu*).[13] The same applies to the human being who has to acknowledge that his life in the setting where everything is provided for him to live, a garden watered and yet never threatened by the four mighty rivers that flow through it (Gen 2:10-14), was conditional and depended on his abiding by God's will, i.e., according to his command:

> And the Lord God *commanded* the man, saying, "You may freely eat of every tree of the garden; but of the tree of the knowledge of good and evil you shall not eat, for in the day that you eat of it you shall die." (Gen 2:16-17)

When man contravened God's commandment, it is God who, as a judge, implemented the verdict:

> And to Adam he said, "Because you have listened to the voice of your wife, and have eaten of the tree of which I commanded you, "You shall not eat of it, "…you are dust, and to dust you shall return." (Gen 3:14, 19)

However, instead of the total death of Adam, which would have eradicated humanity, God gives the latter a chance by exiling Adam. Still, the Adamic progeny did not fare better:

> The Lord saw that the wickedness of man was great in the earth, and that every imagination of the thoughts of his heart was only evil continually. And the Lord was sorry that he had made man on the earth, and it grieved him to his heart. So the Lord said, "I will blot out man whom I have created from the face of the ground, man and

---

12 Notice how, in the narrative, both these elements are not God's work. His work, actually, consists in wrenching out of them the light and dry land, which are the actual "world" of the earthly flora and fauna as well as of the human being, an earthly mammal.

13 This expression is found in scripture to describe the situation of rubble in which a destroyed city and country find themselves (Isa 24:10-12; 34:11; Jer 4:23-26).

beast and creeping things and birds of the air, for I am sorry that I have made them." (Gen 6:5-7)

But again, God was gracious and contained the destructive powers of the flood as a passing episode within the life span of Noah instead of allowing it to put an end to all life on earth:

> These are the generations of Noah ... And Noah had three sons, Shem, Ham, and Japheth ... Noah was six hundred years old when the flood of waters came upon the earth ... After the flood Noah lived three hundred and fifty years. All the days of Noah were nine hundred and fifty years; and he died. These are the generations of the sons of Noah, Shem, Ham, and Japheth; sons were born to them after the flood. (Gen 6:9-10; 7:6; 9:28-10:1)

However, this time, in order to ensure that the sins of the human beings would not affect his decision, God binds the latter to a unilateral covenantal commitment on his part:

> This is the sign of the covenant which I make between me and you and every living creature that is with you, for all future generations: I set my bow in the cloud, and it shall be a sign of the covenant between me and the earth. When I bring clouds over the earth and the bow is seen in the clouds, I will remember my covenant which is between me and you and every living creature of all flesh; and the waters shall never again become a flood to destroy all flesh. When the bow is in the clouds, I will look upon it and remember the everlasting covenant between God and every living creature of all flesh that is upon the earth. (Gen 9:12-16)

Yet again, humanity falls prey of its condemnable hubris (Gen 11:1-9). Thus, the introductory story consigned in the first ten and a half chapters of Genesis ends on a very sour note. So God, we are told, decides to go a different route. This time round he picks up where he had ended the first time, with a promise (Gen 12:1-3) linked to a covenant (Gen 17:1-22), just as he did with

Noah,[14] inaugurating a lengthy and much more complex overarching narrative defining the entire scripture of the Law and the Prophets. This narrative, which is the story of how God finally gains control of the situation in spite of the human being, starts with a covenant based on a promise and ends with a promise of an everlasting covenant. Between this beginning and that end lies, at the heart of the entire story, a third covenant which is bound to a set of instructions. Just as was the case with Adam, these instructions are meant to sustain life granted by God. By the same token, should man contravene them, death ensues as punishment. This conditional covenant, though apparently harsh when it is compared to the non-conditionality of the others, is actually the ultimate expression of God's gracefulness. It was the only way God could maintain his caring fatherhood toward us without jeopardizing what defines him as deity, his being judge.

Let us analyze in more detail how this set of instructions, the *torah*, actually controls the entire narrative of the Law and the Prophets and, by the same token, functions as the expression of God's fatherly care and love for us. The stories of Abraham (Abram) the forefather and of Jacob-Israel, representing the hearers of the message, underscore the recurrence of the same sin throughout the generations: instead of awaiting the necessary bread from the divine father, each of them runs down to Egypt to secure that bread from strangers. This phraseology is clearly in view of what will be the main point of the *torah*:

> All the commandment which I command you this day you shall be careful to do, that you may live and multiply, and go in and possess

---

[14] Notice the intended parallelism between Noah and Abraham: "Noah was a righteous man, *blameless in his generation; Noah walked with God* … And God said to Noah … "*I will establish my covenant with you*" (Gen 6:9, 13, 18); "When Abram was ninety-nine years old the Lord appeared to Abram, and said to him, "I am God Almighty; *walk before me, and be blameless. And I will make my covenant between me and you*, and will multiply you exceedingly."" (Gen 17:1-2)

the land which the Lord swore to give to your fathers. And you shall remember all the way which the Lord your God has led you these forty years in the wilderness, that he might humble you, testing you to know what was in your heart, whether you would keep his commandments, or not. And he humbled you and let you hunger and fed you with manna, which you did not know, nor did your fathers know; that he might make you know that man does not live by bread alone, but that man lives by everything that proceeds out of the mouth of the Lord. (Deut 8:1-3)

Although Abram's mistake could have cost the life of Sarai (Sarah) and thus the existence of Jacob-Israel, God comes to the rescue immediately in order to show that he is capable of subduing his people's enemies at will. Abram's descent to Egypt, including his short stay there, is glossed over as an interlude during his sojourn at Bethel.[15] On the other hand, Jacob, who should have known better from the experience of his forefather, was punished for the same mistake with an exile of four hundred thirty years (Exod 12:40-41). Here, for the first time, we have the pattern, which I introduced earlier on the basis of Ezekiel's teaching, of splitting between the demise of the leader as the main culprit (Jacob dies in Egypt) and the preservation of the people in exile for an eventual restoration. Furthermore and more importantly, again following Ezekiel's lead, this second chance is not only bound to, but actually in view of "walking in God's statutes and observing his commandments." It is, indeed, very clear in the Book of Exodus that the exodus out of Egypt is not the main

---

15 "Thence he removed to the mountain on the east of Bethel, and pitched his tent, with Bethel on the west and Ai on the east; and there he built an altar to the Lord and called on the name of the Lord. And Abram journeyed on, still going toward the Negeb. Now there was a famine in the land. So Abram went down to Egypt to sojourn there, for the famine was severe in the land … So Abram went up from Egypt, he and his wife, and all that he had, and Lot with him, into the Negeb. Now Abram was very rich in cattle, in silver, and in gold. And he journeyed on from the Negeb as far as Bethel, to the place where his tent had been at the beginning, between Bethel and Ai, to the place where he had made an altar at the first; and there Abram called on the name of the Lord." (Gen 12:6-8; 13:1-4)

action of God, but rather it is done *with the aim* of getting the people to the divine mountain where God appears to Moses and commissions him to bring the people out of Egypt so that he, God, could inform them of his statutes and ordinances that would secure their preservation in the future. Put otherwise, were it not for the handing down of the *torah* there would have been no exodus or, at least, such exodus would have been meaningless since it would be oxymoronic that people would leave a place where bread abounds in order to end up condemned to death in a wilderness where nothing grows.

But the statutes and commandments found in Exodus, Leviticus, and Numbers, especially those linked to offerings of grains and livestock, are meant to be implemented in Canaan and not in the wilderness. When one hears the Pentateuch narrative, one gets the distinct impression that, while God was providing bread and water as the need arose in the wilderness, his main concern was to hand down to the people the "rules" for them to *keep* when in Canaan, the land of plenty, so that God would *keep* them and not shorten their days there by exiling them to another "Egypt."[16] Thus, in scripture, God's law is given with the following generations—and not the actual one—in mind when it comes to divine protection. The first generation, in whose times

---

16 There is definitely in scripture a recurring play on the use of the verb *šamar* (keep) in both directions: the people are to keep God's law for him to be indeed their God and thus keep them. Actually, as we heard earlier in Ezekiel, it is only then that they are his people and he is their God: "I will take the stony heart out of their flesh and give them a heart of flesh, that they may walk in my statutes and keep my ordinances and obey them; and they shall be my people, and I will be their God. But as for those whose heart goes after their detestable things and their abominations, I will requite their deeds upon their own heads, says the Lord God" (Ezek 11:19-21); "A new heart I will give you, and a new spirit I will put within you; and I will take out of your flesh the heart of stone and give you a heart of flesh. And I will put my spirit within you, and cause you to walk in my statutes and be careful to observe my ordinances. You shall dwell in the land which I gave to your fathers; and you shall be my people, and I will be your God." (Ezek 36:26-28)

God's prophets spoke or his Law was given, is already doomed. This is at its clearest in the Pentateuchal narrative: the entire generation that left Egypt, including Moses, died before entering Canaan. In view of that, the Law was issued a second time in a *book*, Deuteronomy, to be preserved for the ages:

> These are the words of the covenant which the Lord commanded Moses to make with the people of Israel in the land of Moab, besides the covenant which he had made with them at Horeb … And the Lord would single him out from all the tribes of Israel for calamity, in accordance with all the curses of the covenant written in this book of the law … And Moses wrote this law, and gave it to the priests the sons of Levi, who carried the ark of the covenant of the Lord, and to all the elders of Israel … When Moses had finished writing the words of this law in a book, to the very end, Moses commanded the Levites who carried the ark of the covenant of the Lord, "Take this book of the law, and put it by the side of the ark of the covenant of the Lord your God, that it may be there for a witness against you" … And when he [the king] sits on the throne of his kingdom, he shall write for himself in a book a copy of this law (mišneh hattorah, deuteronomion) from that which is in the charge of the Levitical priests; and it shall be with him, and he shall read in it all the days of his life, that he may learn to fear the Lord his God, by keeping all the words of this law and these statutes, and doing them; that his heart may not be lifted up above his brethren, and that he may not turn aside from the commandment, either to the right hand or to the left; so that he may continue long in his kingdom, he and his children, in Israel (Deut 29:1, 21; 31:9, 24-26; 17:18-20).

Joshua, Moses's minister, whose name means "the Lord saves," will lead God's people into Canaan not as a general—this role will be incumbent on the commander of the army of the Lord (Josh 5:13-15)—but as someone who was commissioned in these words:

> No man shall be able to stand before you all the days of your life; as I was with Moses, so I will be with you; I will not fail you or forsake you. Be strong and of good courage; for you shall cause this people to inherit the land which I swore to their fathers to give them. Only

be strong and very courageous, being careful to do according to all the law which Moses my servant commanded you; turn not from it to the right hand or to the left, that you may have good success wherever you go. This book of the law shall not depart out of your mouth, but you shall meditate on it day and night, that you may be careful to do according to all that is written in it; for then you shall make your way prosperous, and then you shall have good success. Have I not commanded you? Be strong and of good courage; be not frightened, neither be dismayed; for the Lord your God is with you wherever you go. (Josh 1:5-9)

What Joshua and his elders abided by all the days of their lives was soon forgotten: at their death, the people forsook the Lord's commandments (Josh 24:31; Judg 2:7-13). Yet, the Lord refrained from implementing his just and justified wrath announced in the Law. The reason is, as Ezekiel clearly stated, that the Lord be ultimately shown a just judge when he ultimately condemns. This is precisely what Paul underscored:

> Do you suppose, O man, that when you judge those who do such things and yet do them yourself, you will escape the judgment of God? Or do you presume upon the riches of his kindness and forbearance and patience? Do you not know that God's kindness is meant to lead you to repentance? But by your hard and impenitent heart you are storing up wrath for yourself on the day of wrath when God's righteous judgment will be revealed…Then what advantage has the Jew? Or what is the value of circumcision? Much in every way. To begin with, the Jews are entrusted with the oracles of God. What if some were unfaithful? Does their faithlessness nullify the faithfulness of God? By no means! Let God be true though every man be false, as it is written, "That thou mayest be justified in thy words, and prevail when thou art judged." But if our wickedness serves to show the justice of God, what shall we say? That God is unjust to inflict wrath on us? (I speak in a human way.) By no means! For then how could God judge the world? (Rom 2:3-5; 3:1-6)

This divine forbearance is actually reflected in the biblical narrative itself. The period of the Judges amounts to four hundred twenty years, the same as the sojourn in Egypt. Again, according to the narrative, a similar time period elapses under the kings of Israel and Judah until the fall of Jerusalem and its temple in 587 B.C. This means that, before God released his wrath, he waited double the amount of time Israel sojourned in Egypt due to Jacob's sin. The message cannot be clearer: God, who delivered as a father would, is now rightfully intervening as the just judge. Thus, all the following generations ended up not being better than the first one who received the Law: they, each in turn, had the Law and yet did not abide by it. Now that the message is clear, God, in his mercy, intervenes for the third and final time, biblically speaking, and gives his people the last chance, which is also the last chance for all nations (see especially Isa 40-66). However, since this last chance is offered by the same God, it is again, and this time very clearly, tied to his law and the people's abiding by it. What Ezekiel taught, is underscored in Isaiah 40-55 where this message, being the last chance, is made universal: God's law will be taught not only to Israel but also to all nations, who will have to abide by it and walk in its light, lest it consumes them as fire (Isa 2). That this chance is indeed the last can be seen in that the end of the line is not a restored Jerusalem, but the heavenly one (Isa 56-66) where Gentiles as well as Israel will be serving the Lord on an equal footing and always reminded of God's wrath spoken of in his law:

> Rejoice with Jerusalem, and be glad for her, all you who love her; rejoice with her in joy, all you who mourn over her; that you may suck and be satisfied with her consoling breasts; that you may drink deeply with delight from the abundance of her glory. For thus says the Lord: Behold, I will extend prosperity to her like a river, and the wealth of the nations like an overflowing stream; and you shall suck, you shall be carried upon her hip, and dandled upon her knees. As one whom his mother comforts, so I will comfort you; you shall be

comforted in Jerusalem. You shall see, and your heart shall rejoice; your bones shall flourish like the grass; and it shall be known that the hand of the Lord is with his servants, and his indignation is against his enemies. For behold, the Lord will come in fire, and his chariots like the stormwind, to render his anger in fury, and his rebuke with flames of fire. For by fire will the Lord execute judgment, and by his sword, upon all flesh; and those slain by the Lord shall be many. Those who sanctify and purify themselves to go into the gardens, following one in the midst, eating swine's flesh and the abomination and mice, shall come to an end together, says the Lord. For I know their works and their thoughts, and I am coming to gather all nations and tongues; and they shall come and shall see my glory, and I will set a sign among them. And from them I will send survivors to the nations, to Tarshish, Put, and Lud, who draw the bow, to Tubal and Javan, to the coastlands afar off, that have not heard my fame or seen my glory; and they shall declare my glory among the nations. And they shall bring all your brethren from all the nations as an offering to the Lord, upon horses, and in chariots, and in litters, and upon mules, and upon dromedaries, to my holy mountain Jerusalem, says the Lord, just as the Israelites bring their cereal offering in a clean vessel to the house of the Lord. And some of them also I will take for priests and for Levites, says the Lord. For as the new heavens and the new earth which I will make shall remain before me, says the Lord; so shall your descendants and your name remain. From new moon to new moon, and from sabbath to sabbath, all flesh shall come to worship before me, says the Lord. And they shall go forth and look on the dead bodies of the men that have rebelled against me; for their worm shall not die, their fire shall not be quenched, and they shall be an abhorrence to all flesh. (Isa 66:10-24)

The significance of this last point lies in that it is not peculiar to Isaiah. It is actually shared by the Scroll of the Twelve Prophets, which is a counterpart to Isaiah. They both have a parallel structure: both span the entire "story" of the kingdoms of Samaria and Jerusalem, their destruction, the exile, and the post-exilic period.[17] At the end of Malachi we have a passage where the hearer is actually thrown into a situation similar to that extant at the end of Deuteronomy—the last book of the Law—with an invitation to listen to Moses's followers:

> For behold, the day comes, burning like an oven, when all the arrogant and all evildoers will be stubble; the day that comes shall burn them up, says the Lord of hosts, so that it will leave them neither root nor branch. But for you who fear my name the sun of righteousness shall rise, with healing in its wings. You shall go forth leaping like calves from the stall. And you shall tread down the wicked, for they will be ashes under the soles of your feet, on the day when I act, says the Lord of hosts. Remember the law of my servant Moses, the statutes and ordinances that I commanded him at Horeb for all Israel. Behold, I will send you Elijah the prophet before the great and terrible day of the Lord comes. And he will turn the hearts of fathers to their children and the hearts of children to their fathers, lest I come and smite the land with a curse (Mal 4:1-6).

Both these aspects, God's unconditional mercy, expressed in his everlasting covenant,[18] and the way to keep oneself within it, by abiding in his will embedded in a written Law,[19] are clearly reflected in two features of the teaching of Ezekiel and Second-Isaiah (Isa 40-55). The centrality of the Law in that period of the last chance can be seen in the prominence of the sabbath in Ezekiel, which speaks to the exiles in view of the post-exilic period, and Third-Isaiah (Isa 56-66) whose setting and concern is the post-exilic situation. With the exception of Hosea 2:11, Amos 8:5, Isaiah 1:13, and Jeremiah 17:21-27, the occurrences of "sabbath"

---

17 Actually the Latter Prophets (Isaiah, Jeremiah, Ezekiel, and the Twelve Prophets) form an *inclusio*: the two comprehensive stories sandwich Jeremiah and Ezekiel who deal specifically with the fall of Jerusalem, the former from within its walls and the latter from the land of its exile.

18 See, e.g., Isa 55:3; 61:8; Ezek 16:60; 37:26.

19 Notice how the new Law of the new everlasting covenant (Jer 32:40) will be "written" on their hearts (Jer 31:33).

are confined in the Prophetic Books to Ezekiel (Ezek 20:12, 13, 16, 20, 21, 24: 22:8, 26; 23:38; 44:24; 45:17; 46:1, 3, 4, 12) and Third-Isaiah (Isa 56:2, 4, 6; 58:13; 66:23). The whole purpose of the institution of the sabbath is to secure in the mind of the people an everlasting remembrance that it is God's everlasting word embedded in the words of the Law, which makes them who they are—God's people—and sustains them in the same way as bread sustains human life. In other words, the people gather on the sabbath day in order to recall that the divine commandments, which are inscribed once and for all ages in the Law and which each of the previous generations disobeyed, are still valid "this day," as Deuteronomy repeatedly underscores, and are delivered to the hearers in order to be obeyed. However, to make it clear to the hearers that this is indeed the last chance after which comes God's final judgment, Second-Isaiah likens this last covenant to the Abrahamic, and beyond it the Noachic, covenants where it is God's mercy and unilateral commitment that are brought out (Isa 51:1-2 and Isa 54:1-10). Since both of these covenants are inclusive (Noah is the father of the post-diluvial humanity and Abraham's covenantal tent encompasses any and every one "born in your house, or bought with your money from any foreigner who is not of your offspring"), the final horizon is the Adamic garden of Eden (Isa 51:3; Ezek 35:36). Yet again, each one is to live by the righteousness required by the everlasting Law; the righteousness of others will not help as was the case in Abraham's times (Gen 18:20-33):

> Son of man, when a land sins against me by acting faithlessly, and I stretch out my hand against it, and break its staff of bread and send famine upon it, and cut off from it man and beast, even if these three men, Noah, Daniel, and Job, were in it, they would deliver but their own lives by their righteousness, says the Lord God. If I cause wild beasts to pass through the land, and they ravage it, and it be made desolate, so that no man may pass through because of the beasts; even if these three men were in it, as I live, says the Lord

God, they would deliver neither sons nor daughters; they alone would be delivered, but the land would be desolate. Or if I bring a sword upon that land, and say, Let a sword go through the land; and I cut off from it man and beast; though these three men were in it, as I live, says the Lord God, they would deliver neither sons nor daughters, but they alone would be delivered. Or if I send a pestilence into that land, and pour out my wrath upon it with blood, to cut off from it man and beast; even if Noah, Daniel, and Job were in it, as I live, says the Lord God, they would deliver neither son nor daughter; they would deliver but their own lives by their righteousness. (Ezek 14:13-20)

The questions that remains are, "If God's mercy expressed in his everlasting covenant is granted now to both Israel and the nations, does this mean that there is injustice or, at least, unfairness with God?" "Why was Israel given more than one chance whereas the nations are offered only the last one?" First and foremost, the message of the everlasting covenant is to the actual generation of its hearers in Israel who would thus be themselves receiving it for the first time. By the same token, when the nations hear the same message, they also hear of the stubborn disobedience of the previous generations of addressees. Therefore, for all intents and purposes, recipients of the message, both Jews and Gentiles, are on the same footing and there are de facto absolutely no privileges. Secondly, since the biblical narrative does not start with Jacob, but goes back to Abraham, Noah and Adam, and repeatedly includes the "sins" of the nations, then these nations are part of the narrative. Thirdly, and most importantly, the sinful experiences of the generations of the "forefathers" are an integral part of the heritage of the nations. Indeed, "you are a people holy to the Lord your God; the Lord your God has chosen you to be a people for his own possession, *out of all the peoples that are on the face of the earth*" (Deut 7:6; 14:2), which means that Israel was one people or nation among the rest of the peoples or nations. In Ezekiel, when it comes to sinning, this close connection is expressed in a way that levels any and all differences between Israel and the nations:

> Thus says the Lord God to Jerusalem: "Your origin and your birth are of the land of the Canaanites; your father was an Amorite, and your mother a Hittite...You are the daughter of your mother, who loathed her husband and her children; and you are the sister of your sisters, who loathed their husbands and their children. Your mother was a Hittite and your father an Amorite. And your elder sister is Samaria, who lived with her daughters to the north of you; and your younger sister, who lived to the south of you, is Sodom with her daughters." (Ezek 16:1-3, 45-46)

This is precisely what allowed Paul to write authoritatively:

> I want you to know, brethren, that *our fathers* were all under the cloud, and all passed through the sea, and all were baptized into Moses in the cloud and in the sea, and all ate the same supernatural food and all drank the same supernatural drink. For they drank from the supernatural Rock which followed them, and the Rock was Christ. Nevertheless with most of them God was not pleased; for they were overthrown in the wilderness. *Now these things are warnings for us, not to desire evil as they did ... Now these things happened to them as a warning, but they were written down for our instruction, upon whom the end of the ages has come.* (1 Cor 10:1-6, 11)

The same Paul unequivocally stresses that God's final salvation wrought through his Messiah indeed brought about a freedom from exile and bondage, yet a freedom *under God's aegis* (Rom 6). Consequently, this freedom is secured for us so long as we remain within the confines of God's will by abiding by "the law of [his] Christ" (Gal 6:2), which is "the law of the Spirit of life" (Rom 8:2) heralded by Ezekiel. In Galatians the Apostle requires the fulfillment of the entire Law under the leadership of God's spirit:

> For you were called to freedom, brethren; only do not use your freedom as an opportunity for the flesh, but through love be servants of one another. For the whole law is fulfilled (*peplērōtai*) in one word, "You shall love your neighbor as yourself" … But I say, walk (*peripateite*) by the Spirit, and do not fulfill (*telesēte*) the desire (*epithymian*) of the flesh. For the flesh desires (*epithymei*) against the Spirit, and the Spirit [is][20] against the flesh; for these are opposed to each other, to prevent you from *doing* what you would. But if you are led (*agesthe*) by the Spirit you are not under a law. Now the works of the flesh are plain … I warn you, as I warned you before, that those who do (*prassontes*) such things *shall not inherit the kingdom of God* … If we live by the Spirit, let us also walk (*stoikhōmen*) by the Spirit. (Gal 5:13-25)[21]

I kept close to the original text on purpose, in order to show how Paul was putting pressure on the Galatians not to do their own will, which is nothing other than the desire of the flesh (the human being). God granted them his spirit (3:2-5) in order for them to implement *his* will imbedded in his commandments. Should we not *do* so, then we shall have proven that we did not trust (have faith) indeed in his promise and consequently will not inherit his kingdom contained in this promise. The assuredness, then, is not a guarantee that we shall end up there, but stems from the guarantee that we have been turned back (returned)[22] to the right "way," which we shall have to "walk." The "way" in which we "stand (firm)" is still a "way" that we have to "walk":

> Therefore, since we are justified by trust (faith), we have (the eschatological) peace with God through our Lord Jesus Christ.

---

20 RSV has "the desires of the Spirit," which is quite against what Paul is saying. The spirit has a "will," not a "desire;" actually, under his guidance, "those who belong to Christ Jesus have crucified the flesh with its passions and desires." (Gal 5:24)

21 I kept on purpose close to the original in order to underline the centrality of doing God's will. The verb *peripateō* (Greek), *halak* (halak), used in Gal 5:16, appears in the Old Testament in conjunction with the commands of the Law. The verb *stoikheō* is more forceful since it has the connotation of walking in line as in an army.

22 See 1Thess 1:9; Gal 4:9.

> Through him we have obtained *access* (*prosagōgēn*)[23] to this grace in which we *stand*, and we rejoice in our hope of sharing the glory of God. More than that, we rejoice in our sufferings, knowing that suffering produces endurance, and endurance produces character, and character produces hope, and *hope does not disappoint us*, because God's love has been poured into our hearts through the Holy Spirit which has been given to us. (Rom 5:1-5)

Thus a "believer" is someone who puts one's trust (*pistevōn*) in the *promise* of the Kingdom for which one has to hope *because* one has trusted, i.e., to hope *in that which* one has trusted. In the meantime, one is to express one's trust in God's (word of) promise by abiding by his (word of) commandments which are subsumed in the love for the others: "For through the Spirit, by faith, we wait for *the hope of righteousness*. For in Christ Jesus neither circumcision nor uncircumcision is of any avail, but faith working through love." (Gal 5:5-6) Hence, one is not *already* righteous in Christ; no issuance of any verdict is possible before God's final judgment. Rather, "righteousness by faith" means simply that one puts one's trust in God who has shown us and even put us on the "way" leading to his kingdom. This Point A, whereby we were returned from our wayward paths onto the right(eous) way, has been done through sheer gracefulness on God's part; we ourselves had no part in this action. Yet, although it is the way of life eternal, it is still a "way" that we have to walk in order to reach Point Z, life eternal. In order to reach that point we are to follow God's instruction given to us in the Law. Put otherwise, in order to walk that way, we have to walk in God's ways, which are not ours (Isa; Ezek; Gal; Rom).

Consequently, faith is not, as it has unfortunately developed into, a formulaic expression of one's understanding of God's will

---

[23] From the same root *ag—* as the verb *agesthe* (are led; Gal 5:18) with the preposition *pros* (toward).

or being, which one would pin down against the "faith" of others.[24] The original meaning of both the Hebrew *'aman* and the Greek *pistevō* is to put one's trust in a statement *made by someone else and not by oneself.* This trust is expressed in an attitude. It is not a mental acquiescence to our own views. Otherwise, faithfulness is to ourselves and not to another. Now, when the required trust is in a word of promise, then we are to stay the course until the promise is realized. However, when that word of promise is linked to a covenant requiring that we follow certain rules, then our trust is expressed exclusively in our following those rules, and the only one who will judge if we are indeed doing so is the one who issued the covenant, and he will do so at the appointed time of judgment. This understanding is found at its clearest in Romans 1-2 and Matthew 25: it is those who do God's will, *albeit unaware,* who will be found righteous, and not those who have a *mental* knowledge of it. Actually, the mental knowledge will play against those who "know":

> And the Lord said: "Because this people draw near with their mouth and honor me with their lips, while their hearts are far from me, and their fear of me is a commandment of men learned by rote; therefore, behold, I will again do marvelous things with this people, wonderful and marvelous; and the wisdom of their wise men shall perish, and the discernment of their discerning men shall be hid." (Isa 29:13-14)

> As for you, son of man, your people who talk together about you by the walls and at the doors of the houses, say to one another, each to his brother, "Come, and hear what the word is that comes forth from the Lord." And they come to you as people come, and they sit before you as my people, and they hear what you say but they will not do it; for with their lips they show much love, but their heart is set on their gain. And, lo, you are to them like one who sings love

---

24 As, e.g., the "Orthodox faith" in contradistinction to the "Non-Chalcedonian," "Catholic," "Anglican," or "other like faiths."

songs with a beautiful voice and plays well on an instrument, for they hear what you say, but they will not do it. (Ezek 31:30-32)

The Pauline epistles, then, are not so much "learning material" or even "teaching material" as a textbook would be, as they are "instructional" in the same sense as the *torah*. They assume Point A, which is that God, for no apparent reason, gave us access to the "way" leading unto salvation and life in his city, the Jerusalem above (Rom 5:1-11). That it is so for no apparent reason accounts for the central term "grace," an expression of God's inexplicable "delight": the Semitic phrase "to find grace in someone's eyes" means no more and no less than "to be liked by that someone," or "that someone likes us." This is the (humanly speaking) inexplicable premise with which the Pauline epistles start and end: "divine grace be with (to) you."[25] It is grace because the one who is delivering it is Paul the Apostle. A circumcised and Benjaminite son of Abraham, free in regards to any Jewish authority, and a Roman citizen, free in regards to the Gentiles he preached to, most of whom were slaves, he was commissioned as an headmaster (*oikonomos*) in the house of his master to be subservient to all (1 Cor 9:16-22). He actually is the tangible face of divine grace: his addressees can count their blessings that Paul was forcibly enlisted to carry the news of his message of salvation to the Gentiles by God who so has willed both to decide to save the Gentiles and to find a messenger to spread that news. And the way in which as well as the reason both actions were carried out are, as Second-Isaiah taught, not due to the worth or readiness of the recipients, but simply because it was God's sheer "delight, pleasurable will" (*ḥaphes*; Isaiah *passim*).[26] The following stop on the "way" after this initial Point A is the "peace" of the Kingdom, which is Point

---

25 Paul's best explanation in Rom 5:1-11 is that it cannot be explained!
26 See Gen 34:19 where this verb means "to like." See also Num 14:8 where God delights in us on the condition that we follow his will.

Z. Between these two there are no other points, there is just the "way" to be *followed and not chosen*, let alone mentally debated, by the recipients. This means that there is no upward progress on this road, as though one would "improve"—if so, then one would "earn" and not "inherit" the Kingdom!—but rather a forward movement not until the end of the road, but until the end "comes." The only "effort" on our part is to make sure that we be "on the road, on the way" (*en hodō*) when the end that is coming toward us arrives. Since we do not know "the time and the hour," this means that we are to stay (on) the course *at all times*. Any slight deviation is catastrophic. This, in turn, explains why Ezekiel and Second-Isaiah (Isa 40-66), the prophets to Israel, relentlessly remind Israel of its forefathers' as well as its own sins: old habits may pop up again at any moment, and this time round there will be nothing other than ultimate (just) judgment, since ultimate mercy has been granted. This also explains why Paul, the Apostle to the nations, virtually never has words of praise, but rather expresses harshly his displeasure with his addressees.

Since Point A is already behind us all and Point Z is ahead of us all, Paul's letters cannot then be but exhortations to stay the course, paternal exhortations that are instructions to follow, in the same way as is the Torah (and the Prophets). Hence, the epistles are scripture inasmuch as they are written according to the scriptural fabric. They *are* scripture and do not need an outside authority to declare them so. Actually, Galatians, the first of and blueprint for any New Testament scripture, was written *against* any such authority. Yet, more importantly, since they are scripture, they are to be heard as such: straightforward instructions that need no explanation to be obeyed, and not as treatises or informational material about "theological" topics for the mental *passe-temps* of the believers. If they are not meant to bring us on a higher level of "knowledge"—"Knowledge puffs up, but love builds up" (1 Cor 8:1)—much less are they intended to bring us to an advanced level of self-righteous assuredness or a little further on our trek toward the Kingdom. There is actually no movement at all, and the hearers are thrown at the end of the letter back to the point at which they were at its beginning, a little beyond Point A which is behind them. Point Z, the eschatological peace, which is lumped "in hope" with Point A, God's graceful act of mercy, at the beginning of the letters (grace and peace be to you...), disappears at the end of the same letters leaving the hearers with only "grace be with you." This is precisely what Deuteronomy does, and I have shown that Galatians was actually conceived and written *à la* Deuteronomy.[27]

Most of us, who have been trained in theological discourse, often assume, without realizing it, that the biblical books are themselves theological discourses for us to use, to further develop, or even to improve upon the thoughts imbedded in childish narratives for the commoner. But theological discourse is the product of the *human* mind. Scripture, on the other hand, repeatedly, if not relentlessly, presents itself as *divine* words coming from God's mind, which are inscribed *verbatim* by the sole recipient of these *words*. They are even delivered as such in a scroll whether the recipients hear them or not (Ezek 2-3); actually they are consigned in writing in a scroll *because* the recipients refused to hear them (Isa 8:11-22 and Jer 36). And, if the scriptural assumption is that we, the hearers, refused, and keep refusing, to listen to the message, it does not make any sense for us to entertain the thought of analyzing that message to try to get information regarding our concerns, which may not even be the message's concerns. Accepting the message means to accept *its* concerns that are revealed within the message itself, and not brought into the message from outside. To plagiarize scripture itself, "the Lord's concerns are not (necessarily) our concerns, and his ways to go about them are not (necessarily) our ways" (Isa

---

27 *NTI₁* 35-6.

55:8). The real discrepancy actually lies in the "ways" to go about realities. Unfortunately, under the influence of philosophy and human discourse pervading the upper echelon of ecclesiastical leaders in the early centuries and their concern to dialogue philosophically with their non-Christian counterparts, theology developed into a discussion about God, man, salvation, life, death, eternal life, and the like, trying to give these ideas their "true definition or understanding." With time, such gave the false impression that scripture had a different, new, view of the meaning of words compared to their extant meaning. There ensued a differentiation between a physical realm and a spiritual one, a natural truth opposed to a theological-revelational one, a mystical reality beyond or deeper than a mere reality, and the like. One even began to speak of a Christian or theological versus a non-Christian or non-theological understanding of everyday realities such as man, life, death. Whereas, in reality, all the biblical terms were such common currency that everyone readily understood their meaning, and there was no need for further comments; otherwise, how would the hearers have been accountable for all the repeated indictments against them in the scriptural texts?

The proposed reading of Philippians in this commentary is actually a presentation of how the addressed hearers understood *immediately* the message of the Apostle that was read to them while gathered to hear it, without the luxury of being allowed to "take it home and study it," let alone discuss it. Instead of reading the epistle as though it were a philosophico-theological treatise to be dissected in order to "figure out" its deep(er) meaning in the "light" of a "theology" that developed later,[28] I shall endeavor to transpose my readers in time and space so that they become part of the Philippian gathering addressed by Paul. Once this is done,

---

[28] If anything, it is rather this later understanding that has to be not only explained but also *assessed* against the scriptural teaching.

they will be able to *immediately* perceive Paul's message. Such an endeavor will simply entail an explanation of the terminology that was common currency for the Philippians but is not for us today. Nevertheless, this task is not as simple as it looks for the following reasons:

1. The Roman "world" is in many ways no more ours. The gods and the emperor, who were integral and essential parts of that world to the extent that it "rested" on them and their cult, are for us, for all practical purposes, non-entities. For us, their gods are simply not; they do not exist. At best, they are "demons," whereas for the Roman Philippians they were "realities" of everyday life. For us, the cult of the emperor is a mere curiosity of the past and is even non-understandable, whereas for them it was the basis that held the empire together and thus all life within it.

2. If our worldview is not theirs, then the meaning of the same words is not necessarily the same. And this is precisely our Achilles' heel when we deal with basic terms, such as power, salvation, gospel, faith, righteousness, peace, life, death, resurrection, heavens, earth. We assume that their meaning is obvious when, in fact, they reflect realities we are unfamiliar with. One can only begin to imagine the resulting mayhem when theologians start quoting scripture in support of their views. The worst aspect of this mayhem is that those who misuse scripture are often not even aware they are doing so.

Still the effort will prove to be worthwhile since it will allow my readers to engage firsthand with the text and make their own educated decisions regarding the meaning and intention of the scriptural book. In turn, such will broaden the constructive dialogue among those truly interested in submitting to the authority of scripture rather than using it as a tool for "guru-ism" in order to subjugate others and "glory in their flesh" (Gal 6:13), as the Apostle's opponents tried to do in Galatia. The Apostle was not interested in training the Galatians in "theological discourse" but in having them "inherit the kingdom of God" (Gal 5:21); similarly he was not interested in introducing the Philippians to "theology," but rather in having them "behave as citizens of the heavenly Jerusalem" (Phil 1:27; 3:20; see also Gal 4:26). Hopefully this present work will help my readers to join the community of the Apostle's Philippians while listening to his letter to them and thus be challenged not to "fathom" God's kingdom, but to inherit it.

In this commentary series, I have included both Greek and English texts for each verse. The English is the RSV translation, which I have been using in my writings. In my comments, however, I often defer to the Greek with my own translation in order to render the meaning as close as possible to the original text.

www.ingramcontent.com/pod-product-compliance
Lightning Source LLC
Chambersburg PA
CBHW051040160426
43193CB00010B/1012